CW00764938

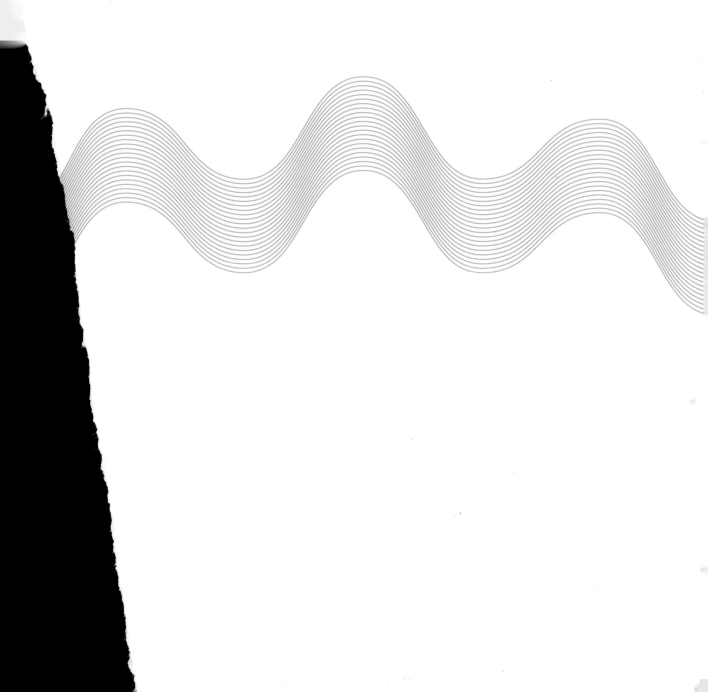

EMI PROTOTYP[E]
MIXER (1979)

A pioneering [
this minicomp
track mixing
time digital
perform mixi
and auxiliar
racks of cor
required to
The first e
sessions t

THE ART OF
SOUND

A VISUAL HISTORY
FOR AUDIOPHILES

TERRY BURROWS

in collaboration with
EMI ARCHIVE TRUST

850+ illustrations

Thames & Hudson

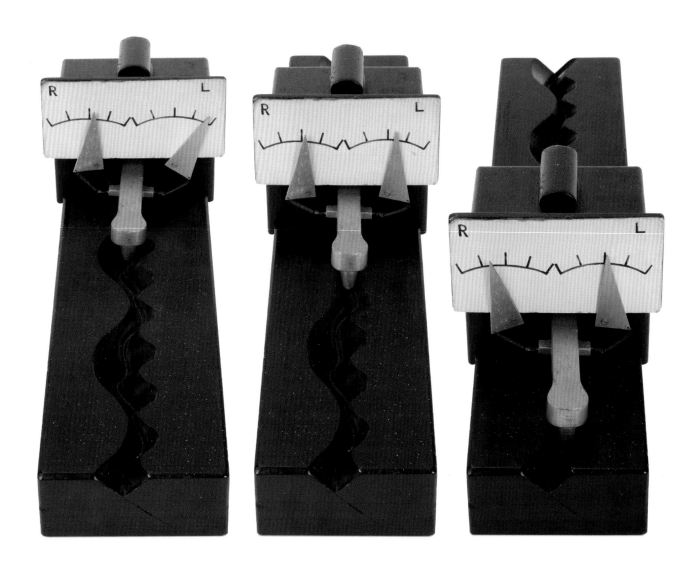

STEREO GROOVE (1933)

Alan Blumlein demonstrated
the idea of a stereophonic
gramophone record using this
model in the early 1930s. It
shows how a specially cut groove
can store two separate channels
of sound that can be played back
simultaneously using a single
gramophone needle.

CONTENTS

1875   1895   1905   1915   1925   1935   1945   1955   1965   1975   1985   1995   2005   2015

During the 19th century, three remarkable technologies emerged that would fundamentally alter humanity's relationship both with the world and with itself. In around 1826, Frenchman Nicéphore Niépce produced the earliest surviving photolithograph – the precursor to the modern photograph – which depicted the faint image of the inventor's estate in Burgundy. More than thirty years later, in Paris, Edouard-Léon Scott de Martinville used his own invention, the 'phonautograph', to capture the first ever recordings of the human voice. Finally, in 1888, Louis Le Prince shot what is today regarded as the first example of a motion-picture film – albeit one just 2.11 seconds in length.

These astonishing audio and visual breakthroughs offered something previously impossible: a means of, in a manner of speaking, storing time. Notable figures in history may have been cast in bronze or painted by the great artists of their day, but never before had humanity come so close to seeing, or hearing, such an exact likeness of an historic event. We can read accounts of the rhetoric of Socrates – as rendered by Plato – but we can never know exactly how they sounded.

On a more prosaic level, when we watch the moving pictures that the Mitchell & Kenyon company produced in Lancashire from the end of the 19th century onwards, we make a direct connection with a long-past generation. Viewing filmed scenes of mundane everyday life, we are not only given a unique glimpse of what it was like to be an 'ordinary person' almost 120 years ago, but we are also offered the most profound memento mori, the realization that even the youngest child captured playing in the park in those grainy black-and-white scenes is no longer alive.

It's of no small significance that these new technologies were sometimes viewed as a practical means of maintaining a kind

1

SPORTING FIRST
On 6 December 1902, Mitchell & Kenyon filmed what is regarded as the earliest footage of the football team Manchester United under that name, in a match against Burnley. The film was not shown at the time and did not re-surface for another century.

of relationship with the dead. As macabre as it might seem to modern sensibilities, the early Victorian photographer would sometimes have been called upon to engage in post-mortem portraiture, wherein recently deceased family members were formally dressed, posed and photographed alongside their living relatives.

Interestingly enough, Thomas Alva Edison – a pivotal figure in the early development of recorded sound – and early wireless-sound pioneer Nikola Tesla both considered the possibility that their work could be used to communicate with the dead. Edison's fascination with the subject led him to make a pact with one of his engineers, William Dinwiddie, that whichever one of them died first should try to communicate with the survivor. Edison speculated about ideas for recording the voices of the dead using a 'spirit phone', an extension of his phonograph invention. Yet although widely discussed, no design for such a device has ever been discovered, nor was any such patent filed.

<u>2</u>

Tesla produced what has subsequently been called a 'spirit radio'. Later, in 1901, he recalled listening to the device: 'My first observations positively terrified me as there was present in them something mysterious, not to say supernatural, and I was alone in my laboratory at night.' Twenty years later, he came to an alternative view: that he was 'actually hearing real voices from people not of this planet'. There are those who believe Tesla's signals may have represented what are now known as 'Electronic Voice Phenomena' (EVP). Generally, however, these flirtations with the paranormal are viewed today as the eccentricities of otherwise brilliant men.

NOTATION AND AUTOMATIC MUSIC
Of course, this book is principally concerned with the media used across time for the storage of music. And it could

<u>2</u>
SCIENCE AND THE SPIRIT WORLD
In the 30 October 1920 issue of *Scientific American*, Edison stated: 'I don't claim that our personalities pass on to another existence or sphere. I don't claim anything because… no human being knows. But I do claim that it is possible to construct an apparatus which will be so delicate that if there are personalities in another existence…who wish to get in touch with us…this apparatus will at least give them better opportunity….'

reasonably be argued that the earliest form of 'recording' came with the birth of musical notation. Until the development of recorded sound, most music was disseminated via the oral tradition, but notation provides one form of instruction as to the way a piece of music should be played, and so leaves behind a permanent record of its existence.

Although most widely used as part of the Western classical tradition, musical notation in its various forms has a far grander history. In 1952, archaeologists unearthed clay tablets among the ruins of the ancient Syrian city of Ugarit. Dating back 3,400 years, these contained engraved cuneiform symbols denoting the world's oldest notated song. In 1972, Professor Anne Draffkorn Kilmer of the University of California ³ produced a detailed study of the tablets, culminating in her own interpretation of the material using contemporary music notation. The resulting music was subsequently performed on the lyre – the instrument on which it was most likely originally played. It is another example of a system enabling a direct link to a long-forgotten past.

Musical notation has now evolved to a sophisticated level. We may never be able to hear near-mythical virtuoso performers such as Paganini or Liszt, but stylistic fashion and interpretation aside, we are able to listen to large-scale pre-20th-century orchestral works being performed by musicians using the same 'instructions' as those who played the piece for the first time centuries earlier.

Put simply, notation is a method of recording musical content – in much the same way that plays from ancient Greece by Aeschylus and Euripides are still performed using the original texts. A different mode of pre-recording storage exists, however, in the form of mechanical devices capable of reproducing the performances of identical sounds. Examples of what we might call

3
INTERPRETING THE TABLET
The upper part of the
tablet contained words; the
instructions for the music
appeared on the lower part.

automatic music can be traced back to 9th-century Baghdad: in *The Book of Knowledge of Ingenious Devices*, the three Banū Mūsā brothers described and illustrated designs for a series of water-powered clocks that could repeat patterns of whistles and drums in what could be seen as the first music sequencer.

4 The earliest music boxes appeared during the 18th century. Comprising a series of tuned pronged 'teeth' plucked by a set of pins on a rotating cylinder or disc, these were first built into ornate snuffboxes so that when the lid was opened a simple melody would play. By the 1850s, music boxes had evolved into large pieces of room furniture capable of playing back complex and sophisticated musical arrangements at the same sort of volume as a piano. Owners could also buy additional discs containing different pieces of music. Often found in coffee houses and other public places, these were the original jukeboxes of their day.

But the closest experience we can have of a genuine pre-recording-era musical performance is perhaps provided by 5 the player piano. First demonstrated in Philadelphia in 1876 – not long before the birth of Edison's phonograph – this musical instrument had the appearance of an ordinary piano (and could be used as such) but was fitted inside with a mechanism that enabled it to play notes automatically. By pedalling up and down in time on a pair of foot pedals, the operator caused a roll of paper to wind horizontally across a playback mechanism; tiny holes cut into the paper activated the hammers, causing individual notes to sound. Player pianos later became so sophisticated that the rolls could 'cut' from actual performances by noted musicians. So, although there are no audio recordings of Claude Debussy playing his own compositions, we do have a series of Welte-Mignon piano rolls that accurately captured some of his performances, and these can still be listened to today.

4
MUSICAL FIRSTS
It is widely accepted that the earliest recognizable 'comb' music box was created by the Swiss watchmaker Antoine Favre-Salomon in 1796. The earliest dedicated music box factory opened in Switzerland in 1815.

5
KEY PERFORMANCES
Other great composers of the period who recorded rolls for player pianos included Gabriel Fauré, Manuel de Falla, George Gershwin, Edvard Grieg, Gustav Mahler, Sergei Rachmaninoff, Maurice Ravel, Camille Saint-Saëns, Alexander Scriabin and Richard Strauss.

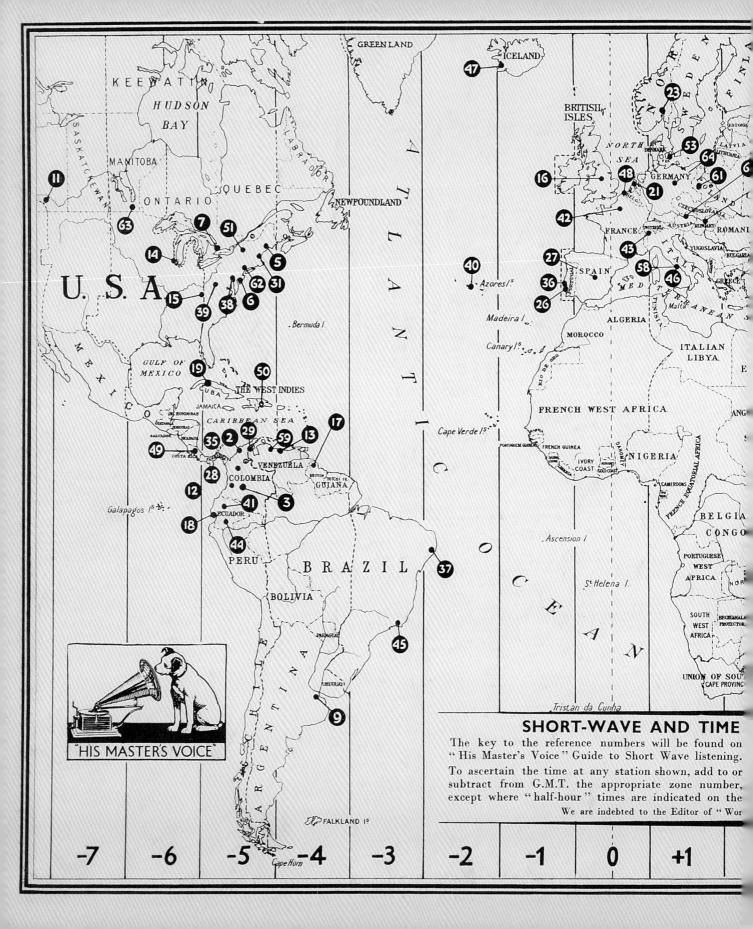

SHORT-WAVE AND TIME

The key to the reference numbers will be found on "His Master's Voice" Guide to Short Wave listening.

To ascertain the time at any station shown, add to or subtract from G.M.T. the appropriate zone number, except where "half-hour" times are indicated on the

We are indebted to the Editor of "Wor

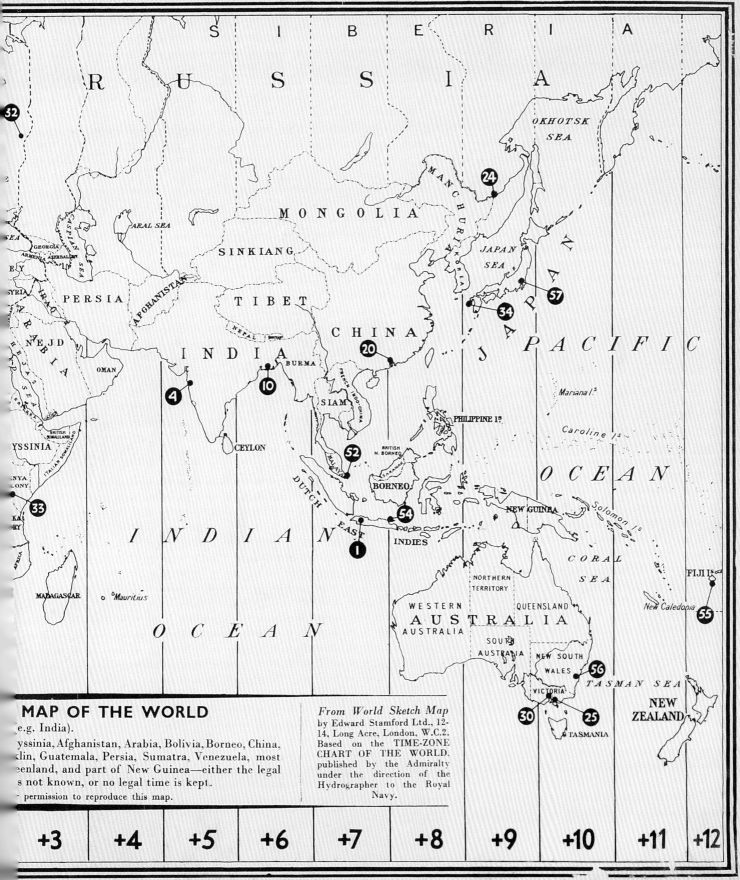

MAP OF THE WORLD

(e.g. India).

...yssinia, Afghanistan, Arabia, Bolivia, Borneo, China,
...lin, Guatemala, Persia, Sumatra, Venezuela, most
...eenland, and part of New Guinea—either the legal
...s not known, or no legal time is kept.

...permission to reproduce this map.

From World Sketch Map
by Edward Stamford Ltd., 12-
14, Long Acre, London, W.C.2.
Based on the TIME-ZONE
CHART OF THE WORLD,
published by the Admiralty
under the direction of the
Hydrographer to the Royal
Navy.

| +3 | +4 | +5 | +6 | +7 | +8 | +9 | +10 | +11 | +12 |

Part No.   Issue 2

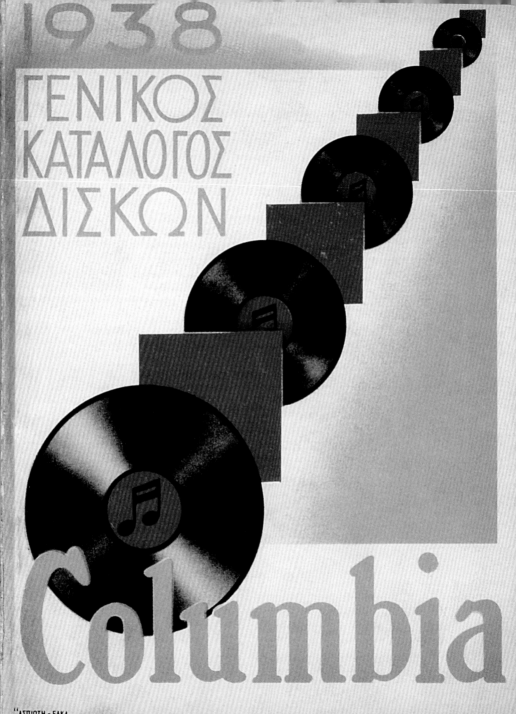

pages 10-11

SHORTWAVE RADIO MAP (1920s)

His Master's Voice produced this
time-zone map of the world with
shortwave radio stations plotted
on it. A separate key provided
frequencies for each station.
The map was based on the *World
Sketch Map* by Edward Stanford
Ltd, which was itself based
on the *Time Zone Chart of the
World* published by the Admiralty
under the direction of the
hydrographer to the Royal Navy.

pages 12-13

INTERNATIONAL CATALOGUES

Monthly catalogues containing
details of new releases were
produced by record companies
across the world. Shown here
is a Columbia label catalogue
from Greece, issued in 1938,
and an Art Deco-style German
Odeon Records listing from 1929.

pages 14-15

ABBEY ROAD STUDIOS

A view from the control room of
Studio 1 at Abbey Road in north
London, arguably the most famous
recording facility in the world.

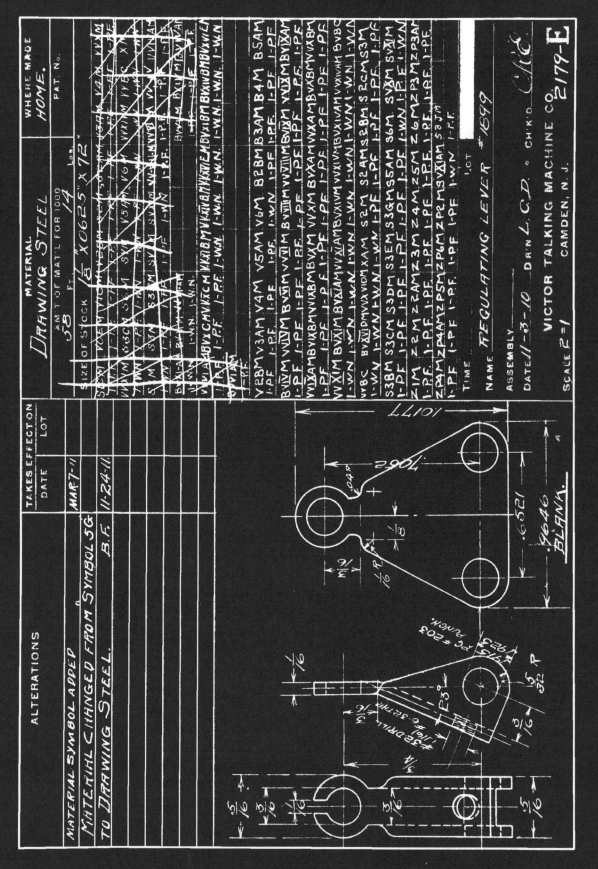

1910: REGULATING LEVER NO.1899

16.17

blueprints : 1

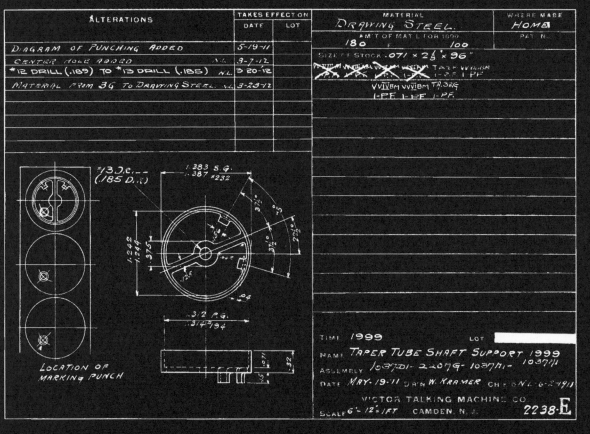

| ALTERATIONS | TAKES EFFECT ON | | MATERIAL | WHERE MADE |
| | DATE | LOT | See Note | HOME |

Material Changed from Drawing Brass to See Note — 1-3-1911
MATL SYMBOL 3G ADDED — 3-14-11

AM'T OF MAT'L FOR 1000: 260 — 228
SIZE OF STOCK .08 X 2 15/16 X 96
TA33C TA33D
1-PF. 1-PF.

NOTE:- Soft cold rolled steel, good surface, suitable for deep drawing (Symbol-3G)

TIME 1800   LOT
NAME TAPER TUBE SHAFT UPPER BEARING #1800
ASSEMBLY 1807C-
DATE 8-17-10 DR'N WBH CH'K'D JRS.
VICTOR TALKING MACHINE CO.
SCALE 12-1 CAMDEN, N.J.   2078-E

| ALTERATIONS | TAKES EFFECT ON | | MATERIAL | WHERE MADE |
| | DATE | LOT | DRAWING STEEL. | HOME |

DIAGRAM OF PUNCHING ADDED — 5-19-11
CENTER HOLE ADDED — N.L. 9-7-12
#12 DRILL (.189) TO #13 DRILL (.185) — N.L. 3-20-12
MATERIAL FROM 3G TO DRAWING STEEL — N.L. 3-23-12

AM'T OF MAT'L FOR 1000: 180 — 100
SIZE OF STOCK .071 X 2 5/8 X 96"
TA33 VVV18M
1-PF 1-PF
VVV18M VVV18M TA.32G
1-PF 1-PF 1-PF.

LOCATION OF MARKING PUNCH

TIME 1999   LOT
NAME TAPER TUBE SHAFT SUPPORT 1999
ASSEMBLY 1037D1- 2207G- 1037M1- 1037H
DATE MAY-19-11 DR'N W. KRAMER CH'K'D NL 6-2-1911
VICTOR TALKING MACHINE CO.
SCALE 6-12=1 FT CAMDEN, N.J.   2238-E

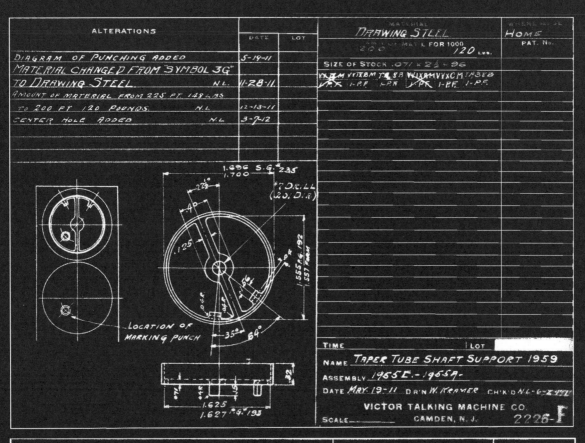

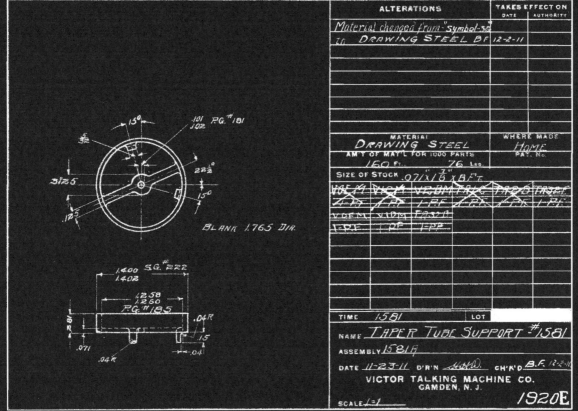

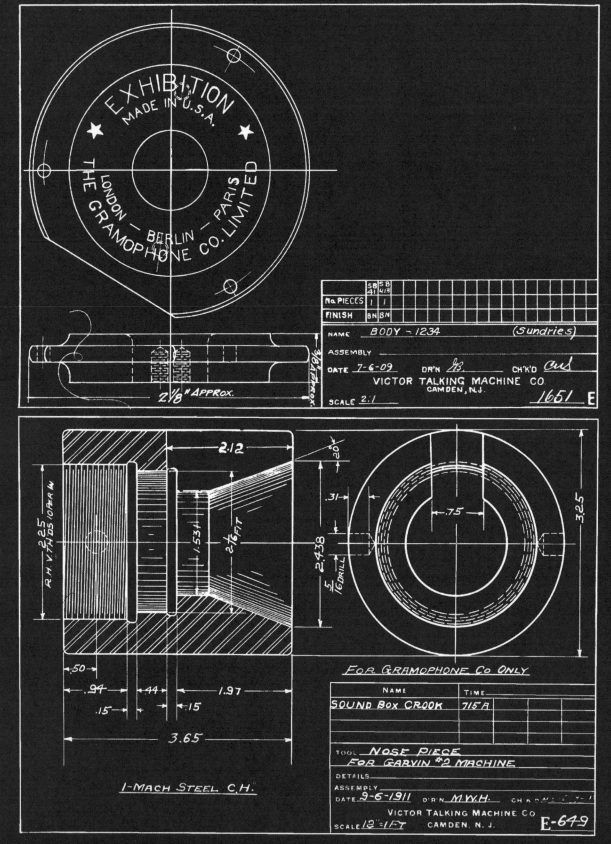

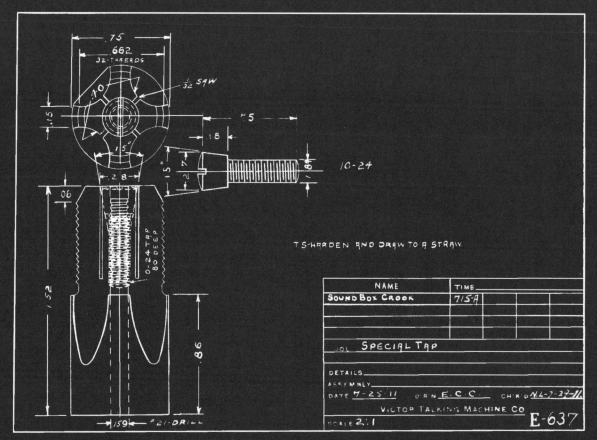

T.S-HARDEN AND DRAW TO A STRAW.

10-24

NAME	TIME		
SOUND BOX CROOK	715-A		

TOOL   SPECIAL TAP

DETAILS

ASSEMBLY

DATE 7-25-11   D'R'N E.C.C.   CH'K'D N.L-7-27-11

VICTOR TALKING MACHINE CO

SCALE 2:1   E-637

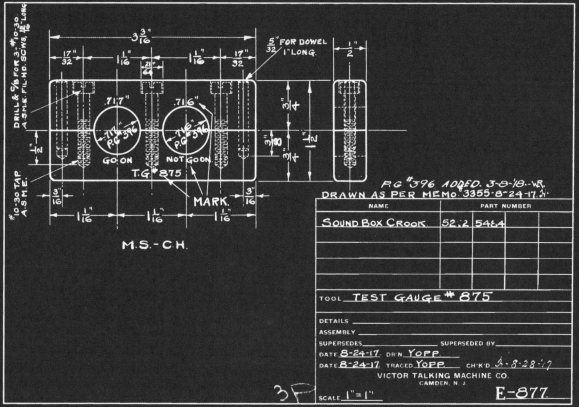

M.S.-C.H.

P.G #396 ADDED. 3-8-18.-WR.
DRAWN AS PER MEMO #3355-8-24-17.R.

NAME	PART NUMBER		
SOUND BOX CROOK.	52.2	5484	

TOOL   TEST GAUGE #875

DETAILS

ASSEMBLY

SUPERSEDES _____ SUPERSEDED BY

DATE 8-24-17. DR'N YOPP.

DATE 8-24-17 TRACED YOPP.   CH'K'D 3-8-28-'17

VICTOR TALKING MACHINE CO.
CAMDEN, N. J.

SCALE 1"=1"   E-877

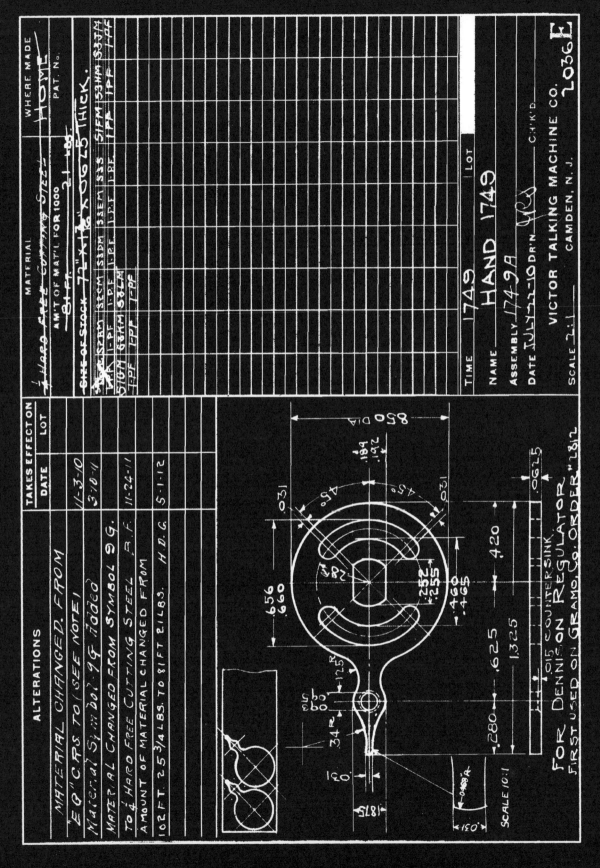

1910: HAND NO. 1749

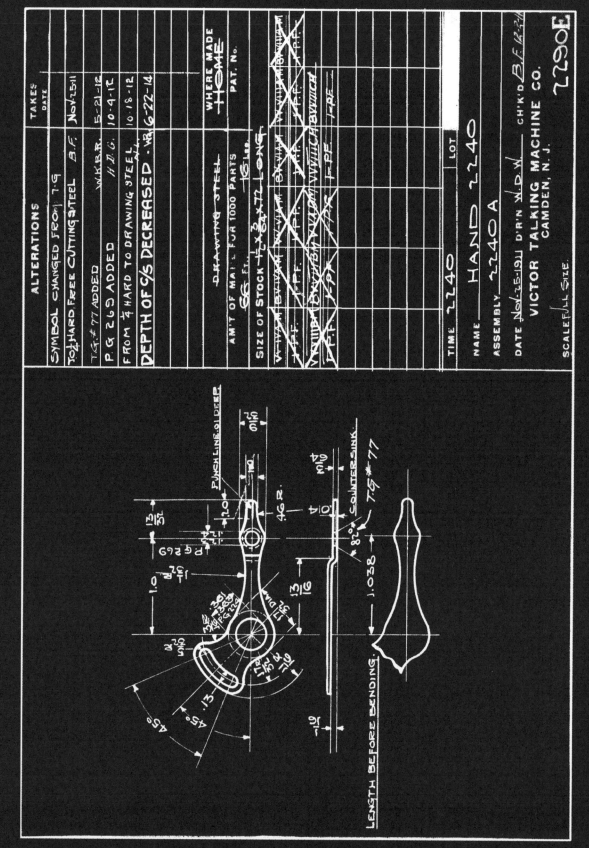

1911: HAND NO. 2240

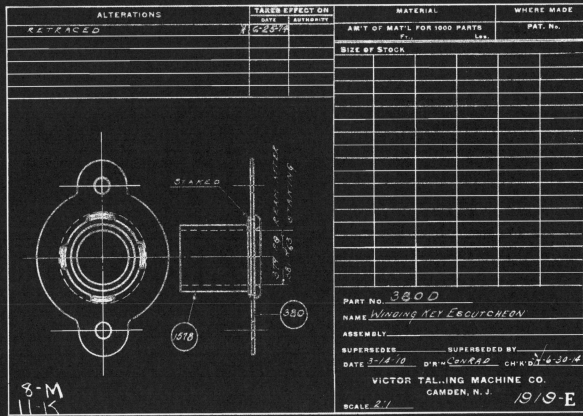

ALTERATIONS	TAKES EFFECT ON		MATERIAL		WHERE MADE
	DATE	AUTHORITY			PAT. No.
RETRACED	6-28-14		AM'T OF MAT'L FOR 1000 PARTS		
			FT.	LBS.	
			SIZE OF STOCK		

PART No. 380D

NAME WINDING KEY ESCUTCHEON

ASSEMBLY

SUPERSEDES   SUPERSEDED BY

DATE 3-14-'10   D'R'N CONRAD   CH'K'D 6-30-14

VICTOR TALKING MACHINE CO.
CAMDEN, N.J.

SCALE 2:1   1919-E

8-M
11-15

STAKED
1518
380

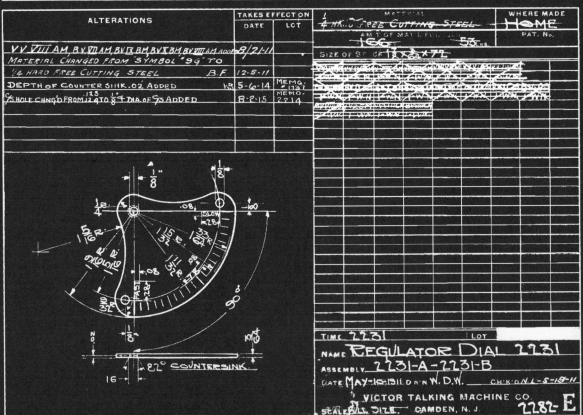

ALTERATIONS	TAKES EFFECT ON		MATERIAL	WHERE MADE
	DATE	LOT	¼ HARD FREE CUTTING STEEL	HOME
VV VIII AM. B.V VII AM. B.V IX BM. B.V X BM. B.V VIII AM. ADDED	8/21/11		AM'T OF MAT'L FOR 1000	PAT. No.
MATERIAL CHANGED FROM "SYMBOL '9G' TO	12-5-11		166 53 LBS.	
¼ HARD FREE CUTTING STEEL B.F.			SIZE OF STOCK 1⅛ x 2⅛ x 72	
DEPTH OF COUNTER SINK .02 ADDED WR	5-6-14	MEMO. 1737		
C/S HOLE CHNG'D FROM .12 TO .123 ⅛ DIA. OF C/S ADDED	8-2-15	MEMO. 2214		

TIME 2231   LOT

NAME REGULATOR DIAL 2231

ASSEMBLY 2231-A-2231-B

DATE MAY-10-1911   D'R'N W.D.W.   CH'K'D N.L-5-18-11

VICTOR TALKING MACHINE CO.

SCALE FULL SIZE   CAMDEN, N.J.   2282-E

⅛"
⅛
1½
4
15/16 R
.08
SLOW 28
15 E 3½
33 4 R
11 3½ R
.08
FAST 28
½ R
3/32
90°
82° COUNTERSINK
16

first wave
ACOUSTIC ERA

1857

Edouard-Léon Scott de Martinville patents his phonautograph, the first-known device for recording sound.

1877

Thomas Edison invents the phonograph. He quickly loses interest in the device, however, anticipating little immediate commercial use for it.

1883

The Krakatoa volcano, in present-day Indonesia, erupts, resulting in the loudest sound in modern times. Registering some 172 decibels at a distance of 100 miles (161 km), the sound travels around the world four times and is heard 3,000 miles (4,828 km) away in Australia. It ruptured the eardrums of people 40 miles (64.37 km) from the source.

1887

Debut of the gramophone, created by Emile Berliner. Sound is preserved within the grooves of a flat disc, establishing a new format that will dominate recording during the 20th century.

1901

Emile Berliner and Eldridge Johnson form the Victory Talking Machine Company.

1906

Reginald Aubrey Fessenden transmits the first voice message by radio on 23 December. He transmits his voice between two 50-foot- (15.25 m) tall towers about a mile apart on the Potomac River in Washington, DC. Six years later, he performs the first audio radio broadcast, a 'Christmas concert' to ships in the Caribbean and Atlantic.

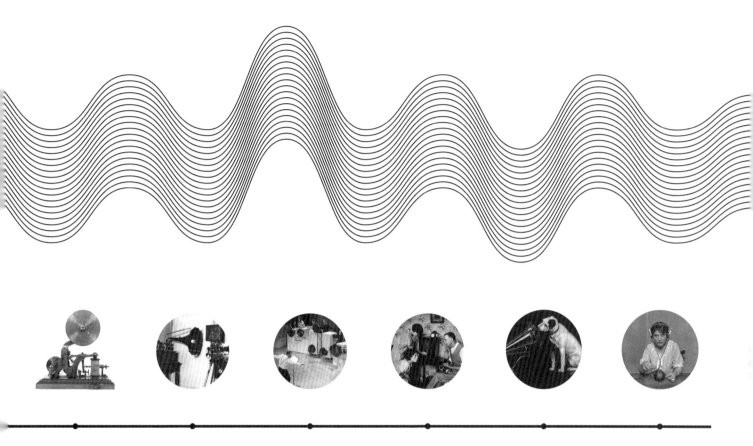

1910

On 22 July, the captain of the SS *Montrose* – en route from London to New York – telegraphs the ship's owners to relate his suspicions about two passengers. Dr Hawley Harvey Crippen and his lover Ethel Le Neve are subsequently arrested when the ship reaches Montreal – the first time wireless telegraphy has been used to capture a suspect. Crippen is later hanged for murdering his wife.

1913

Thomas Edison demonstrates a 'talking movie' using his Kinetophone, synchronizing his phonograph with a film projector. The results are flawed, however, and Edison abandons movie-making within five years.

1914

Two works by Italian Futurist Luigi Russolo, entitled 'Awakening of a City' and 'The Meeting of Aeroplanes and Automobiles', are performed by a 'noise orchestra' playing his self-invented *intonarumori* (noise-generating devices).

1918

The sounds of war are recorded for the first time using a phonograph: a gas shell bombardment by the Royal Garrison Artillery prior to British troops entering Lille on 9 October.

1919

The Radio Corporation of America (RCA) is founded.

1921

Record sales begin to decline in the USA, as listening to live music on radio becomes increasingly popular.

The basic principles of sound have been known for centuries. One of Leonardo da Vinci's key discoveries was the fact that sound travels in waves. In 1637, French theologian and scientist Marin Mersenne described the frequency of oscillation of a stretched string. Sound is the energy that an object produces when it vibrates; a plucked string vibrates at a very high speed causing the air around it also to vibrate. As the air moves, it carries the energy from the string until the air inside the human ear also begins to vibrate – the ear (and brain) then perceives the vibrating as the sound of the plucked string.

Perhaps unsurprisingly, the earliest known device for capturing sound was inspired by studying the anatomy of the human ear. The 'phonautograph' was patented in 1857 [1] by Edouard-Léon Scott de Martinville. He reasoned that by constructing a mechanical device that simulated the functions within the ear – the canal and eardrum – it would be possible to capture in some form the vibratory motions of the sound wave. For a recording device, an open-ended barrel-shaped horn was constructed; a flexible membrane was stretched over one end of the barrel to create a diaphragm, attached to which was a fine pig-bristle stylus. The storage medium was a card or glass slide covered in lampblack – a carbon deposit created by holding it over the smoke from an oil lamp. By bringing the stylus into contact with the carbon and moving it laterally at the same time, the vibrations of any sound picked up via the open end of the horn would alter the air pressure moving the diaphragm, which would then be reflected in the line cut by the stylus into the carbon.

In 2008, David Giovannoni and his team at the Lawrence Berkeley National Laboratory in California discovered some original phonautograph recordings filed in Paris with the original

[1]
NO PLAYBACK
An undervalued figure in the history of audio recording, Scott de Martinville was not a scientist. He was a publisher by trade and had conceived his system only as a means of recording sound. De Martinville did not concern himself with how those sounds would be played back afterwards.

patent and were able to convert them into playable digital audio files. One of them was a 20-second recording of a man – most likely the inventor himself – singing the French folk song 'Au clair de la lune'. Recorded in 1860, it is now recognized as the earliest-captured musical performance.

French inventor Charles Cros devised a way of hearing the sound of a phonautograph recording. Using what he termed a 'paleophone', Cros would create a similar stylus and diaphragm to that of Scott de Martinville, but his design would cut the vibrations into a metal groove. A 'mirror' device would then play this information back – so that when the stylus moved across the groove the vibrations could be converted back into sound through the diaphragm and horn, in effect reversing the process. On 30 April 1877 Cros submitted a notice to the Academy of Sciences in Paris with a detailed description of his paleophone design. Unfortunately, before he had the opportunity to build a prototype, Thomas Alva Edison demonstrated the cylinder phonograph at his Menlo Park laboratory in New Jersey. All evidence would suggest that neither man knew of the other's work.

Thomas Alva Edison was arguably the greatest and most prolific inventor of the modern age. It was his early groundbreaking work with the telegraph and the telephone that led him to invent the cylinder phonograph. While working on a device that could transcribe telegraphic messages through indentations on paper tape, Edison began to speculate that a telephone message could also be recorded in a similar manner. He would use the same sort of diaphragm and stylus arrangement pioneered by De Martinville, but with the point held against fast-moving paraffin paper; the speaking vibrations from the telephone would make indentations in the paper. Edison adapted this idea further, substituting a metal cylinder wrapped with tin foil for the paper. His machine comprised a pair of diaphragm/stylus

2

<u>2</u>
THE INVENTOR SPEAKS
Snippets of Scott de Martinville talking were also discovered; dating back to 1853, these are the earliest examples of recorded human speech, although they are largely unintelligible.

units, one to record the sound and one to play it back. Edison gave the plans to his engineer, John Kruesi, telling him to build the first phonograph.

Edison recalled the event in 1927: 'Kruesi, when he had nearly finished it, asked what it was for. I told him I was going to record talking, and then have the machine talk back. He thought it absurd. However, it was finished, the foil was put on; I then shouted "Mary had a little lamb," etc. I adjusted the reproducer, and the machine reproduced it perfectly. I was never so taken aback in my life. Everybody was astonished.'

A demonstration of his invention at the offices of *Scientific American* in New York City was widely reported in the national press, generating considerable interest in the device. To exploit the invention, the Edison Speaking Phonograph Company was established on 24 January 1878. Ever the innovative thinker, in the May/June edition of *North American Review* that year, Edison suggested ten potential uses for his phonograph. It could be utilized for dictation, as an alternative to using a stenographer. It allowed for the creation of audiobooks, read out by a professional reader – now commonplace, this is the first ever mention of such an idea. The invention could be employed to teach elocution. It allowed for reproduction of music. Family records could be produced with it ('...preserving the sayings, the voices, and the last words of the dying members of the family...'). The phonograph could be used to produce music boxes and toys. It could act as a speaking clock that reads out the time every hour – another idea for which no record exists before the publication of this article. It offered a means of preserving languages. Advertising could utilize it. Finally, the phonograph could be used to record speech ('...to preserve for future generations the voices as well as the words of our Washingtons, our Lincolns, our Gladstones, etc.'). Edison ended by noting that his invention might interface

3
HISTORIC PIONEERS
Until the discovery of Scott de Martinville's phonautograph recordings in 2008, Edison's recitation of this children's nursery rhyme was thought to be the oldest audio recording of any kind.

with the telephone ('The phonograph will perfect the telephone and revolutionize present systems of telegraphy').

It required a degree of expertise to use the phonograph properly. Moreover, the tin foil covering the cylinders into which the vibrations were etched was easily damaged and produced very low-quality audio. Although the invention generated a great deal of interest initially, the public quickly tired of what was widely seen as a novelty item. Edison himself turned his back on the phonograph and concentrated on perfecting and commercializing perhaps his most celebrated work – an incandescent light bulb.

Others saw greater potential in the phonograph, however. Working in the Volta Laboratory established by Alexander Graham Bell, scientist Charles Sumner Tainter and Bell's cousin Chichester greatly improved Edison's design. Their 'graphophone' differed most notably in that it used a wax cylinder instead of tin foil, as well as introducing the first floating stylus. The device was still difficult to use, but the quality of sound was now much improved. Bell and Tainter were awarded a patent for their device in 1886. The American Graphophone Company was founded in 1887 to exploit the invention, eventually becoming part of the Columbia Gramophone Company.

Aware of Bell and Tainter's activities, in 1888 the Edison Phonograph Company was founded and a year later the 'perfected' phonograph was introduced. Edison found it difficult, though, to exploit the invention in the ways he'd expected, notably for professional business uses, including as an office dictation machine. Soon he came to realize that the field of entertainment might offer the greatest prospects for commercial success.

Both music-cylinder systems ran concurrently well into the 1920s. And many of the most popular artists of the day were captured on 'brown wax' cylinder. Standard-sized cylinders were

4
AN EYE TO POSTERITY
Scott de Martinville also clearly had archival possibilities in mind, when he wondered: 'Will one be able to preserve for the future generation some features of the diction of one of those eminent actors, those grand artists who die without leaving behind them the faintest trace of their genius?'

4¼ inches (11 cm) long, with a diameter of 2³⁄₁₆ inches (5.5 cm) and played at 120 revolutions per minute (rpm). There were two very significant problems with the cylinders, however. Firstly, they were restricted to a maximum of two minutes in length; this was improved in 1899 by more than doubling the diameter to 5 inches (13 cm). But far more seriously, there was no satisfactory way of mass-duplicating the cylinders, each one of which had to be engraved by a recording stylus in 'real time', making the process costly and cylinders expensive to buy. By 1905, a moulding process had been invented that enabled a single machine to produce up to 150 cylinders per day, but by this time the days of the music cylinder were numbered: in 1887, another of Alexander Graham Bell's former researchers, Emile Berliner, filed a patent for what he called the 'gramophone'. His storage system – a flat disc – was to prove much more popular with consumers.

Berliner's design was based on what was now the established principle of vibrations etched into a groove that could be played back by a stylus/diaphragm/amplifying horn arrangement. The sound, however, was stored in a spiral groove etched into a disc that began at the edge of the 'record' and worked its way towards the centre. For playback, the record was placed on a rotating platter; a needle attached to a pivot arm slotted into the groove, reading vibrations and transmitting the sound acoustically through the loudspeaker horn.

A major advantage of Berliner's system was that gramophone discs could be more easily bulk-manufactured – stamped using an inverse master disc that would imprint the groove pattern onto the final record. From 1889, Berliner produced gramophone discs with a diameter of 5 inches (13 cm), cut from vulcanized rubber. They were very low in audio quality. The first major improvement came in 1896, when shellac was used to press the records. This

5

CHILD'S PLAY
US patent 372,786 for
the gramophone was filed by
Berliner on 4 May 1887 and
granted on 8 November that
year. Initially, the invention
was taken up by toy makers.
German toy manufacturers Kammer
and Reinhardt began selling a
small gramophone, which was hand-
driven and had a cardboard horn.

remained standard until the 1930s, when RCA Victor introduced a less brittle and superior-sounding vinyl-based compound – variations of which are still used in record manufacture to the present day.

Acoustic-era recordings were all extremely low in fidelity, capturing only a narrow band of the audible spectrum – from around 250 Hz up to about 2,500 Hz. As a result, both music and musicians were chosen to match the limitations of the format. Singers with loud, clear voices were favoured; brass instruments such as trumpet, cornet and trombone were effective; the quiet volume of the guitar meant that the banjo was more widely heard on early recordings. Instruments at the extremes of the frequency range were often substituted. The bass drum, for example, with its fundamental frequency of between 40 Hz and 100 Hz, was barely audible, so it was sometimes replaced by a wood block played loudly. Of course, there were no microphones or mixing desks. Instead, the performers would gather around a large recording horn that funnelled sound waves towards the cutting stylus; changes to the sound mix were made either by playing specific instruments at different volumes or by changing the position of the musician relative to the horn.

Emile Berliner's gramophone system differed from those of Edison and Bell and Tainter in that the device sold to the consumer could only play discs that had already been recorded. As the gramophone became dominant, Edison placed greater emphasis on the benefits of using his devices to make records. By 1912, technology's first major format war was effectively over. Cylinders were still produced for several more decades, but by this time they merely contained reproductions of recordings already made for release on gramophone. The record would continue as the dominant medium for music consumption throughout most of the 20th century.

6

6
EARLY RECORDS
Prior to 1925, all 78-rpm discs were produced acoustically using a recording horn. Music was limited to between three and five minutes per side, depending on whether the disc had a 10-inch (25-cm) or 12-inch (30-cm) diameter.

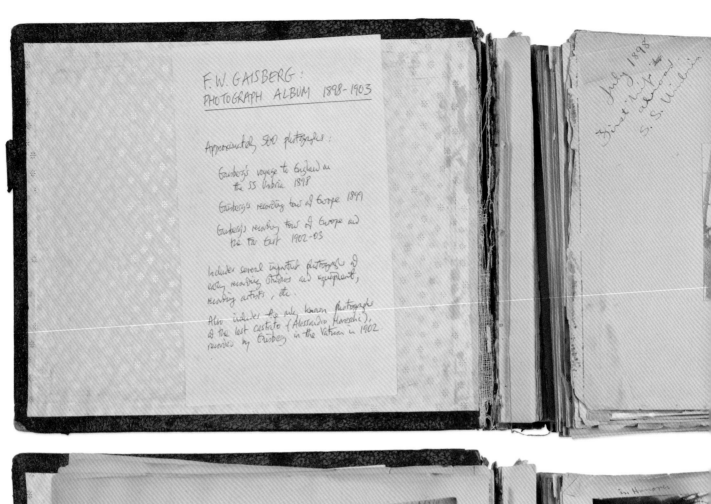

F.W. GAISBERG:
PHOTOGRAPH ALBUM 1898-1903

Approximately 500 photographs:

Gaisberg's voyage to England on the SS Umbria 1898

Gaisberg's recording tour of Europe 1899

Gaisberg's recording tour of Europe and the Far East 1902-03

Includes several important photographs of early recording studios and equipment, recording artists, etc.

Also includes the only known photograph of the last castrato (Alessandro Moreschi), recorded by Gaisberg in the Vatican in 1902

FRED GAISBERG — THE FIRST
VOYAGE TO LONDON (1898)
Photographs taken by American
sound engineer Fred Gaisberg, who
had been hired by The Gramophone
Company (later EMI) to create
Europe's first recording studio.
Gaisberg was one of the first
people to capture the voice of
celebrated tenor Enrico Caruso
on a gramophone record.

RECORDING STUDIO (c. 1900)
At this time, most recordings
were made in simple surroundings.
The 'mouth' of a recording horn
faced the musicians or singers.
At its other end, a stylus cut
the master gramophone disc.

THOMAS ALVA EDISON

INVENTOR OF
THE PHONOGRAPH

Thomas Alva Edison was perhaps the most widely celebrated American of his generation, and with 1,093 patents to his name certainly the most prolific inventor. Although he lacked much in the way of formal education, Edison's innovations, such as the phonograph, the electric light bulb, the Kinetograph motion-picture camera and alkaline storage batteries, can truly be said to have changed the world. An astute businessman, his approach to his work was simple: 'I find out what the world needs. Then I go ahead and try to invent it.'

Thomas Alva Edison was born in Milan, Ohio, USA, the youngest of seven siblings. Suffering poor health from birth, he didn't begin school until he was eight years old. He failed to settle and struggled with lessons, so his mother, a former schoolmistress, began educating him at home, teaching him reading, writing and arithmetic. By the age of ten, he was an avid reader, being especially inspired by the science textbook *School of Natural Philosophy* by Richard Green Parker.

At the age of twelve, Edison began work as a 'candy butcher', selling confectionery to passengers on the Grand Trunk Railroad. His first entrepreneurial venture came after he was given the exclusive right to sell magazines on the train. In 1862, aged fourteen, he assembled a printing press in a corner of a baggage car where he wrote, typeset, printed and marketed his own daily newspaper, the *Grand Trunk Herald*, which he sold on the train.

Finding work as a telegraph operator, during his spare time Edison continued his self-taught science education, looking for ways to realize and exploit his own inventions. Unsurprisingly, most of Edison's early ideas were based around telegraphy. His first major success came when he moved to New York City, where he invented a universal stock printer for synchronizing stock tickers so that share prices were transmitted and printed at the same time. He sold his invention to Western Union for $40,000,

1

1
EARLIEST PATENT
In 1869, Edison filed the first of his patents, for an electrographic vote recorder, intended to help speed up the voting process in the US Congress.

which was enough money to set up his own factory. Next came the quadruplex telegraph machine, which could send and receive four messages at once; this was also sold to Western Union.

By the time Edison had reached the age of thirty, he was already a wealthy man. Ever expanding his business, in 1876 he set up an industrial research facility at Menlo Park, New Jersey. By 1880, he was employing a staff of around sixty workers, many of whom were talented scientists, engineers and inventors in their own right.

On 21 November 1877, Edison announced the invention of the first device for recording and replaying sound. A landmark technology, it meant that for the first time in history the sound of a specific moment could be captured permanently and replayed at will. Edison's 'phonograph' worked by engraving a visual representation of a sound wave on a foil-covered cylinder: the sound was captured as a series of indentations in the foil using a cutting stylus, which responded to the vibrations of the sound being recorded. When a playback stylus passed over the cylinder, a low-fidelity representation of the original recording could be heard. The inventor's first recorded words were the nursery rhyme 'Mary Had a Little Lamb'. A decade later, Charles Sumner Tainter and Chichester Bell built on Edison's work and produced a higher-quality cylinder using wax-coated cardboard. The basic principles that governed the invention of the phonograph were later brought into play by Emile Berliner, who instead of a cylinder used a spiral groove cut into a 'record' as a means of storing sound.

Thomas Alva Edison died from complications relating to diabetes, aged eighty-four years. He was still working shortly before his death. Of the many inspirational quotes attributed to him, underlying his peerless achievements there was one simple personal philosophy: 'There is no substitute for hard work.'

THOMAS ALVA EDISON
BORN: 11 February 1847,
Milan, Ohio, USA
DIED: 18 October 1931,
West Orange, New Jersey, USA

2
PIONEERING THINK TANK
The Menlo Park research facility was the first institution created with the specific purpose of hothousing technological innovation.

3
PRESIDENTIAL AUDIENCE
Edison presented his invention to the National Academy of Sciences, at a gathering that included President Rutherford B. Hayes. The *Washington Post* described the occasion as 'a scene…that will live in history'.

COLUMBIA TYPE AB GRAPHOPHONE (1901)

Charles Sumner Tainter and Chichester Bell made improvements to Edison's phonograph to create their graphophone. One of the most popular models of its time, the Columbia Type AB is an 'open works' graphophone: the playing mechanism (made of aluminium) is exposed. Operated by a key, it includes a detachable horn, making the unit portable. It has interchangeable mandrels - the spindles on which the cylinders are fitted - allowing it to play standard 2-inch (5-cm) cylinders as well as the superior 5-inch (13-cm) concert cylinders. The Type AB was sold in Europe as the Double Eagle and is also known as the 'Macdonald', after its Scottish designer, Thomas Macdonald - Columbia's chief engineer.

PHONOGRAPH CYLINDERS (c. 1905)

Recorded music quickly became globally popular, embracing everything from English military bands (left) to French chansonniers (right). 'Hector Grant' (centre) was actually the noted Australian opera tenor Peter Dawson, who adopted the pseudonym when recording his humorous parodies of Scottish music-hall singers.

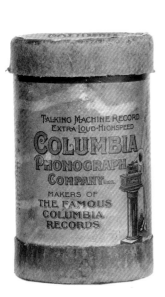

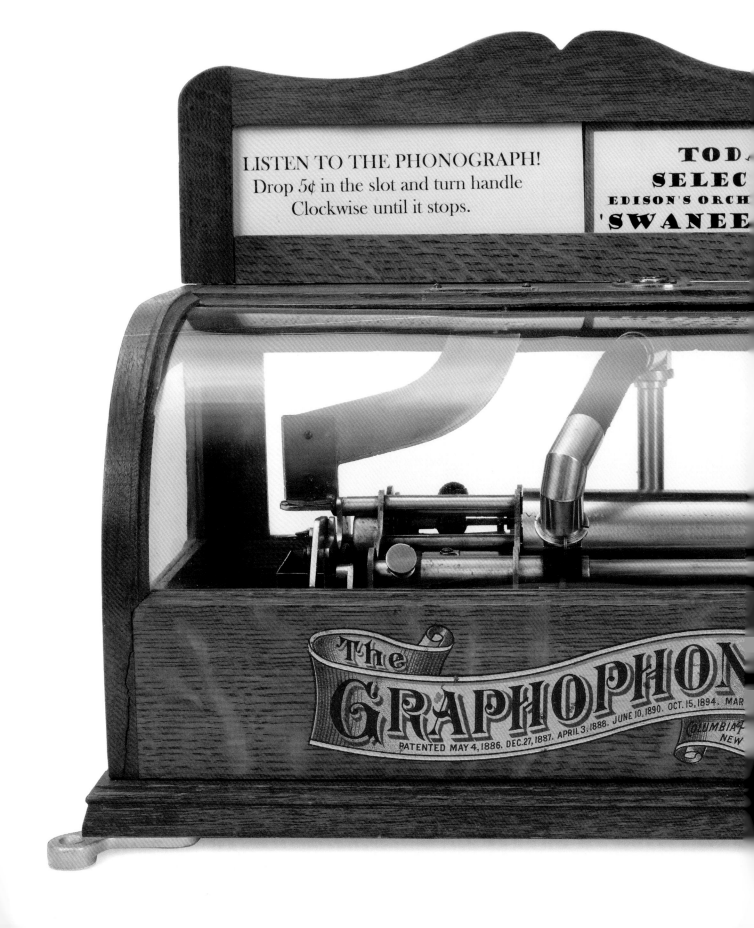

COLUMBIA TYPE BS COIN-
OPERATED GRAPHOPHONE,
AKA THE 'EAGLE' (1898)
The Columbia Type BS is a
coin-operated graphophone.
It was too expensive for most
households (it launched with
a price of $20 - almost $1,000
in today's money), but local
distributors found an ingenious
way of demonstrating models
and simultaneously making money,
by fitting a BS Eagle in public
places such as bars, diners and
amusement arcades. For a penny
(or a nickel in the USA) it was
possible to listen to a complete
two-minute cylinder played back,
using listening 'tubes' - a
crude, early form of headphones.
The Columbia Eagle could also
be fitted with a horn so that it
could be heard at greater volume
- although by its very nature,
an acoustic graphophone would
struggle to be heard over loud
conversation in a café. The metal
feet were intended to be screwed
down to a counter, to prevent
the machine from being stolen.

EDISON GEM MODEL A
PHONOGRAPH (1899)

Edison introduced the Gem -
which was small and very basic
- in 1899, to compete with other
low-cost cylinder players.
Unlike most phonographs and
graphophones, which were built
on oak plinths, the body of the
Gem is made from cast iron. It
is powered by a single spring,
key-wound motor; a metal tray
beneath prevents oil dripping
from the mechanism from marking
furniture. The reproducer stylus
that comes into contact with the
surface of the cylinder is built
into the carrier arm. The Gem
was produced until 1913.

EDISON STANDARD MODEL D PHONOGRAPH (1908)

After the commercial launch of
the graphophone, Thomas Edison
improved his own phonograph, and
both systems - incompatible with
one another without modification
- sold concurrently. Edison's
National Phonograph Company
built the Standard Model D
phonograph between 1908 and
1911. Edison envisaged his
invention being used as a
dictation machine rather than
as a means of replaying music.
The Model D also came with
a 14-inch (35.5-cm) recording
tube - a crude type of acoustic
microphone. The speaker talks
into the mouthpiece and the
vibrations are cut into the brown
wax cylinder. The recording can
then be replayed.

PATHÉ LE MÉNESTREL (c. 1905)
Beautifully ornate, with a cast-
iron base and cover decorated in
the Louis XV style, the Ménestrel
was licensed for exclusive sale
in France by J. Girard & Cie.,
a Parisian mail-order company
well known for the sale of early
cameras. The phonograph had an
adjustable carriage assembly
and a mandrel adapter that
allowed it to play both concert
and standard cylinders. It has
a simple key wind motor and
a simple screw speed regulator.
The Ménestrel came in three
parts: the base, the cover
and the horn. When not in use,
the horn was detached and the
playing mechanism on the base
hidden by the cover, leaving
an attractive, decorative piece
of furniture. Available in
blue and green, its design was
clearly intended to fit in with
the surroundings of wealthier
Parisian homes. The name of the
machine is an Old French term
from which the word 'minstrel'
is derived.

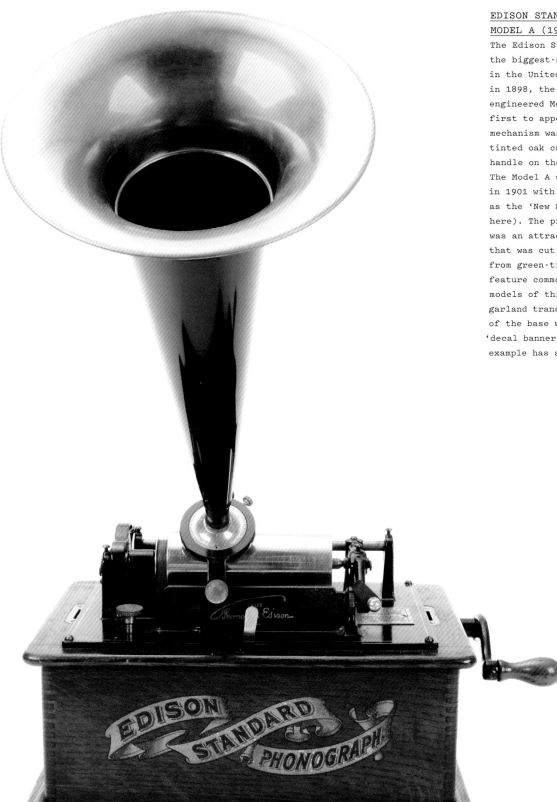

EDISON STANDARD PHONOGRAPH
MODEL A (1903-06)

The Edison Standard models were the biggest-selling phonographs in the United States. Launched in 1898, the rugged and well-engineered Model A was the first to appear. The phonograph mechanism was fitted into a tinted oak case with the crank handle on the right of the box. The Model A underwent a redesign in 1901 with what became known as the 'New Style' cabinet (seen here). The principle difference was an attractively domed lid that was cut, as was the base, from green-tinted oak - a feature common to all domestic models of this period. The full garland transfer at the front of the base was known as the 'decal banner'. This particular example has a Model C reproducer.

LE GRAN

Chante, Parle e
de tou

La plus Merveilleuse
Invention du si cle

FRENCH ADVERTISEMENT (c. 1905)
A Parisian store poster invites
customers to try out 'the most
wonderful invention of the century'.

IOPHONE

Joue ——

les Instruments

AUDITION ICI

EMILE BERLINER

INVENTOR OF THE GRAMOPHONE

A key figure in the history of both audio recording and playback systems, Emile Berliner not only modified Alexander Graham Bell's telephone transmitter to create one of the earliest microphones, but also invented the gramophone, a mechanical apparatus that could play sounds stored on engraved discs – or records, as they would come to be known. Yet there was little in his background or early education to suggest such a future.

Berliner hailed from a large Jewish merchant family in Hanover, Germany. Leaving school at the age of fourteen, he was apprenticed in the family business, but emigrated to the United States at the outbreak of the Franco-Prussian War in 1870, to avoid being drafted into the army. Berliner had a burgeoning interest in science, and supported himself as a manual labourer while studying physics at the Cooper Union Institute in New York. In 1876, he attended a demonstration of Alexander Graham Bell's telephone, which was taking place as part of America's centennial celebrations. Studying the apparatus, he noted that its most significant weakness lay in its sound transmitter – the mouthpiece. Working in isolation, from his boarding house, in 1877 Berliner created a new 'loose contact' transmitter, by adding a layer of carbon particles between the two contacts, one of which would then act as a diaphragm; movement of this diaphragm altered the pressure on the particles, allowing differing amounts of electricity to pass through. This principle was used for all microphones built during the next fifty years.

Having patented his carbon microphone, Berliner sold the rights to Bell for $50,000, and was also hired by him as a full-time researcher. After seven years with Bell, Berliner set up his own company and began experiments with sound recording and storage. Thomas Alva Edison had already developed the cylinder recording system, but it was the graphophone, unveiled in 1886 by Charles Sumner Tainter and Chichester Bell, that inspired

1

RIVALRY WITH EDISON
To Berliner's chagrin, in 1892 the US Supreme Court ruled that the patent was void, and that Thomas Alva Edison - who had also filed a similar patent earlier in 1877 - was the true inventor. Berliner went to his grave in 1929 still convinced that Edison had stolen his idea.

Berliner's own design. In 1887, he filed a patent for what he called the 'gramophone' – a sound recording system using flat discs etched with a spiral groove that stored the sound. The disc rotated on a platter on the gramophone; a pivot arm supported a needle that slotted into the groove, reading vibrations and transmitting the sound via a speaker horn.

For record manufacture, tests were carried out with different materials, including copper, wax-coated zinc and celluloid. By 1889, Berliner had settled for using hard, vulcanized-rubber 5-inch (13-cm) discs, 'stamped' from etched zinc masters. The first records to be produced contained speech, mostly Berliner's own voice. By 1895, the size of the discs had been standardized to 7 inches (18 cm), and more than 1,000 gramophones had been sold, along with 25,000 records.

Using and storing Berliner's discs may have been more convenient than Edison's cumbersome cylinders. But the mechanism was unreliable and the sound from the vulcanized-rubber discs was inferior. In 1896, Berliner contracted Eldridge Johnson to produce an improved spring motor, and that same year shellac was introduced as the material for manufacturing records. In 1901, Berliner and Johnson merged to form the Victor Talking Machine Company, and at this point the 10-inch (25-cm), 78-rpm 'single' became the norm. By the early 1910s, the gramophone had won the media war and Edison's cylinders gradually fell from use; by the end of the 1920s, the format was dead.

A philanthropist and active advocate for improving public health, in 1929 Berliner died from a heart attack. He was seventy-eight years old. With continual refinements long after the death of its inventor, the gramophone record would continue as the dominant medium for music consumption throughout most of the 20th century, until the ascendency of the digital compact disc in the 1980s.

EMILE BERLINER
Born: 20 May 1851,
Hanover, Germany
DIED: 3 August 1929,
Washington, DC, USA

2
GOING ON RECORD
The earliest recording artists, such as noted Irish baritone George J. Gaskin, were chosen not only for their celebrity but for their loud voices and clear enunciation.

3
THE POLYMATH
Emile Berliner did not restrict himself to working in the field of audio recording. He also developed the first acoustic tiles, created a loom for the mass-production of cloth, and devoted the final two decades of his life to developing technologies for vertical flight - including the first radial aircraft engine.

THE BERLINER
GRAMOPHONE (1895)

The first 'record player'
was produced by the Berliner
Gramophone Co. of Philadelphia.
The turntable was mounted on an
oak plinth and rotated manually
by a hand crank, requiring
the operator not only to find
the correct speed but also to
maintain that speed. The arm,
which was also made from oak,
housed the needle and diaphragm
together with the conical brass
horn. This meant that the angle
of the horn altered as the arm
moved across the record.

THE GRAMOPHONE COMPANY
STYLE NO.5, AKA THE
'TRADEMARK MODEL' (1898)
The first Gramophone Company
models were produced in the
United States and exported
to Great Britain, and featured
some of the innovations of Emile
Berliner's Improved Gramophone
of 1897. The most significant
was Eldridge Johnson's invention
of a spring-loaded motor that
regulated the speed of the
turntable. Johnson and his
collaborator Alfred C. Clark
also devised a new soundbox,
the unit containing the
diaphragm in which the needle
is housed, and which connects
to the horn. This gramophone
is known as the 'Trademark Model'
because it features in the
painting of Nipper, the famed
His Master's Voice dog.

EARLY GRAMOPHONE RECORDS

The first records were of various
sizes, materials and rotational
speeds. By the start of the
20th century, a diameter of
10 inches (25 cm) running at
78 rpm had become standard.
Sometimes the discs were etched
on one side with early company
branding (below).

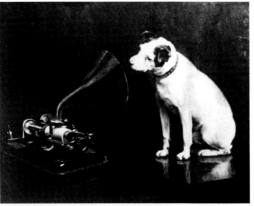

left
NIPPER AND THE GRAMOPHONE
The His Master's Voice brand
(above right) began as an 1898
painting of a dog named Nipper
(above left) by his owner, the
artist Francis Barraud (left).
Originally, Nipper was seen
staring down the horn of an
Edison-Bell phonograph. The
manager of The Gramophone Company
in London agreed to buy the
painting if the phonograph was
replaced by one of his company's
own gramophones (left).

opposite
NIPPER THE ICON
The image of Nipper and the
gramophone became a trademark of
Victor, HMV and other associated
record labels across the globe.
By the 1930s, Nipper was already
established as one of the music
industry's most famous logos,
spawning countless dolls, toys
and other likenesses. Seen here
are models made from plastic and
plaster, among them a very rare
model by the famous Steiff toy
company (see far right).

THE SOUNDBOX

The gramophone soundbox featured
a diaphragm with a metal needle
bar, into which the needle was
inserted. It fitted at the end
of the tonearm and converted
vibrations from the needle into
audible sound that was amplified
acoustically by the horn.

EARLY SINGING STAR (1911)

Gertrude 'Gertie' Millar was
one of the most popular English
singers and stage actresses
of the time. An early star
of the gramophone, she was
well known for the hit
'Moonstruck' from the 1903
musical *Our Miss Gibbs*.

Miss GERTIE MILLAR

PHOTO. RITA MARTIN.

HAS SUNG
HER LATEST SUCCESSES
"A QUAKER GIRL"
"MOONSTRUCK"
and other songs for
The Gramophone Co., Ltd.
You know it by this

"His Master's Voice"

THE BANNED OPERA
"THE MIKADO"
MAY BE HEARD WITHIN

♪ GRAMOPHONE RECORDS BY
MELBA
COME IN AND HEAR THEM

"HIS MASTER'S VOICE"
CAN BE HEARD WITHIN.

You know it by this.

NO INSTRUMENT OR RECORD IS MANUFACTURED AND SOLD BY THE GRAMOPHONE CO LTD THAT DOES NOT BEAR THIS TRADE MARK

FAREWELL TOUR OF SOUSA'S BAND

previous pages

EARLY MUSIC ADVERTS (1905-10)

Gramophones and records were
initially sold in music stores,
where the main activity was
the sale of sheet music, pianos
and other musical instruments.

Artists such as pianist Ignacy
Jan Paderewski, soprano Dame
Nellie Melba, and the tenor
Enrico Caruso all enhanced their
concert reputations by making
gramophone recordings.

above and opposite

RECORD BAGS

Dedicated sleeve artwork didn't
exist before 1938. Gramophone
records came in simple paper or
card sleeves with a hole in the
centre for the label.

R

overleaf, left

NEEDLES

A needle became blunt after
playing only one or two sides.
His Master's Voice sold three
styles (loud tone, half tone and
soft tone) for different music.

overleaf, right

OPERA IN THE HOME

The gramophone offered the only
means of hearing singers such as
Louise Kirkby Lunn without going
to London's Royal Opera House
or the New York Metropolitan.

LIORET LE MERVEILLEUX
(c. 1895)

Le Merveilleux was the work of highly respected French clockmaker Henri Lioret. It was the first machine made entirely by him and sold for 20 francs. Taking an interest in 'talking machines' in 1893, he collaborated with dollmaker Emile Jumeau to create Bébé Jumeau, a doll that could talk. Lioret used his skills as a clockmaker to create a tiny phonograph that fitted inside the doll. Technically more advanced than the Edison phonograph, it featured a clockwork motor and used removable cylinders made from a durable moulded celluloid. Lioret took this mechanism from the doll and fitted it into a small pasteboard box with a simulated leather covering. Le Merveilleux houses a side flap, giving access to the three-quarter-inch (2-cm) cylinder that plays back around 30 seconds of sound; a top flap opens to reveal the integral horn. Despite its size and fragility - few undamaged examples have survived - it produces quite a loud sound.

THE CHOCOLATE RECORD PLAYER (1902)

The Stollwerck gramophone was a novelty toy designed to play chocolate discs! Stollwerck had been founded in Germany in 1839, and by the end of the century was one of the world's biggest confectionary companies. Stollwerck aimed their gramophone squarely at the festive market, newspaper advertisements describing it as 'ein Spielzeug für den Weinachtstisch' ('a toy for the Christmas table'). The particularly novel idea was that the tiny ($3\frac{1}{16}$-inch; 7.6-cm), vertically cut chocolate records could be eaten after use! This was nonetheless a working gramophone, the ornate green tin model (below) being powered by a Junghans clock motor. The platter itself doubles as a storage compartment - when lifted it can hold six schokoladedisken ('chocolate discs'). Stollwerck also produced a simpler wooden version (left).

GRAMOPHONE FACTORY

Manufacturing a gramophone in the early 20th century called for more than the detailed engineering skills required to construct the turntable mechanism, spring motor, soundbox diaphragm and horn. As gramophones became more commonplace in homes, demand grew for models that could be concealed when not in use. Skilled cabinetmakers were employed to create attractive pieces of living-room furniture that could be opened up to reveal the gramophone inside.

below and opposite

THE GRAMOPHONE
IN RUSSIA (1900-06)

In spring 1900, Fred Gaisberg and William Sinkler Darby of The Gramophone Company travelled to St Petersburg to demonstrate the gramophone and make recordings at the opera. They returned a year later to record local music in Russia and Eastern Europe, many styles of which had never been heard in the West. The gramophone quickly became popular across Russia. By 1904, almost half of the company's profits came from the country.

overleaf

ROYAL APPOINTMENT (1902)

The Gramophone and Typewriter Company (one of The Gramophone Company's pre-EMI names) issued a Berliner-style 7-inch (18-cm) commemorative plate and gramophone record to mark the coronation of King Edward VII and Queen Alexandra in 1902. The disc has no centre spindle hole, but was issued with a separate base enabling it to be played. A similar plate had been produced a year earlier after the death of Queen Victoria.

АКЦІОНЕРНОЕ ОБЩЕСТВО ГРАММОФОНЪ

МОСКОВСКОЕ ОТДѢЛЕНІЕ.

МОСКВА: Тверская улица.

Телефонъ № 74.40.

На Нижегородской Ярмаркѣ, Главный домъ, № 62.

•

РУПОРЪ „ЛОТОСЪ"

ДЛЯ ТОНАРМНАГО ПРИСПОСОБЛЕНІЯ.

Подъ этимъ наименованіемъ мы выпускаемъ въ продажу новый рупоръ, изготовленный въ формѣ цвѣтка лотоса. Рупоръ этотъ, благодаря своей оригинальной формѣ, дѣйствуетъ весьма артистически и употребляется съ извѣстнымъ тонармнымъ приспособленіемъ. Длина его 60 сантим., діаметръ отверстія 57 сантим.; окраска его черная, красная или зеленая. Онъ съ успѣхомъ можетъ замѣнить наши мѣдные рупора Т. А. для извѣстныхъ аппаратовъ „Тонармъ" B, № 15, № 15a и № 15b, также какъ и для автоматическихъ аппаратовъ № 3a и № 3b.

Не говоря о звуковыхъ совершенствахъ, сопряженныхъ съ новымъ нашимъ рупоромъ „ЛОТОСЪ", разнообразіе его окраски даетъ возможность художественнаго приспособленія граммофона къ стилю и убранству любой гостиной.

Цѣна 10 рублей.

ПАРОВАЯ ТИПО-ЛИТ. И. РОЗЕНОЕРА, ЛИТЕЙН. 48.

Оптовая цѣна 7 рублей.

above

MONTHLY CATALOGUES (1909)

With limited scope for
advertising, record companies
such as Grammophon issued monthly
catalogues of new releases. The
covers above are from Austro-
Hungary and were published
in German and Hungarian.

opposite

CELEBRITY ENDORSEMENT

Shortly before his knighthood
in 1911, celebrated British
conductor (and former
vocal coach) Henry J. Wood
publicly declared that the
gramophone could be used
in singing tuition.

What Mr. HENRY J. WOOD
says of the
GRAMOPHONE

Mr. HENRY J. WOOD, in the course of a speech at Sheffield last month, addressing 350 members of the Sheffield Festival Chorus, remarked :—

" Have you all got a Gramophone ? If not, get one at once, as it is of the utmost educational value to all musicians. In listening to the records of such great artistes as Patti, Melba, Caruso, Plancon, Battistini, etc., you will hear what true, right vocal tone is. As a vocal teacher of twenty-five years' experience, and as a devotee of the great Garcia method, I can assure you of the tremendous value of this invention, and how grateful we vocal teachers are for the aid it gives us in showing our pupils what right and beautiful tone is ; especially in the Provinces, where it is often impossible to hear the greatest voices.

I firmly believe that if all teachers of singing had a Gramophone in their studios as well as the finest vocal records as published by the City Road Gramophone Company, and could let their pupils hear the brightness and ring of good voice production, it would do more to dispel and eradicate our fluty, hooty, breathy, dull, weak English voices, than hundreds of pounds spent on useless lessons and in fruitless argument and controversy."

His Master's Voice

CAPTAIN SCOTT'S
MONARCH (1905)

Introduced in 1905, The HMV Monarch Senior was a luxury gramophone. It featured a quartered-oak case, brass barrelled triple-spring motor and tonearm. It was one of the first models fitted with the Exhibition soundbox, which was used on most HMV models until 1925. The example seen on these pages was one of a pair donated to Captain Robert Falcon Scott by The Gramophone Company and accompanied his team on their (doomed) South Pole expedition of 1910. According to diaries kept by Scott's men, music played an important role in lifting spirits. Scott himself noted: 'We find we have a splendid selection of records.' The Monarch was later recovered from one of the abandoned camps. In spite of its age and the extremes of temperature it endured, only the felt on the turntable and grease in the motor had to be renewed. It remains in working order today.

گراموفون اینڈ ٹائپ رائٹر لمیٹڈ

کے

ہندوستانی ریکارڈوں

کی

فہرست

مندرجہ بالا "ٹریڈ مارک" (کاروبار کا نشان) ، ہر ایک گراموفون ریکارڈ پر ہوتا ہے
خریداروں کو ریکارڈ خریدنے سے پہلے ہمیشہ یہ نشان ریکارڈ پر دیکھ لینا چاہئے

گراموفون ریکارڈ گراموفون کی ہی سوئیوں سے بجانے چاہئیں سستی نقلی سوئیاں ریکارڈوں کو
بہت جلد خراب کردیتی ہیں ۔ گراموفون کی سوئیاں کاغذ کی پڑیوں میں نہیں بکتیں ۔ بلکہ ٹین کی
ڈبیوں میں ہوتی ہیں ۔ جن پر ہمارا مندرجہ ذیل "ٹریڈ مارک" ہوتا ہے ۔

ہم پرانے اور ٹوٹے ہوئے گراموفون ریکارڈ واپس لے لیتے ہیں ۔ اور نئے ریکارڈوں
کی قیمت میں سے ہر ایک دس انچ ریکارڈ کے لئے ایک روپیہ ایک آنہ اور ہر ایک
سات انچ ریکارڈ کے لئے آنے وضع کردیتے ہیں ۔

گراموفون اینڈ ٹائپ رائٹر لمیٹڈ
اسٹیلینیڈ ۔ کلکتہ

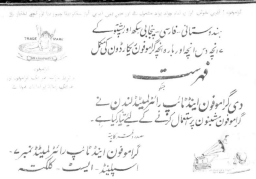

Nagri.   MARCH, 1908.

April 1908   URDU.

URDU.   OCTOBER, 1907.

above and opposite

THE GRAMOPHONE IN INDIA

In 1902 the first gramophone record was released in Calcutta, India. J. W. Hawd had set up a branch of The Gramophone Company a year earlier and sound engineer Fred Gaisberg made 500 recordings of local musicians. Early Indian gramophone records were pressed in Germany. When zinc made way for shellac, India became the principle supplier, providing more than three-quarters of the world's lac production.

overleaf

AN EARLY RECORDING SESSION

Acoustic-era recording was very basic. With no electrical microphones or mixing desks, a balance of sound was achieved by putting the loud instruments (e.g. brass) at the rear of the room.

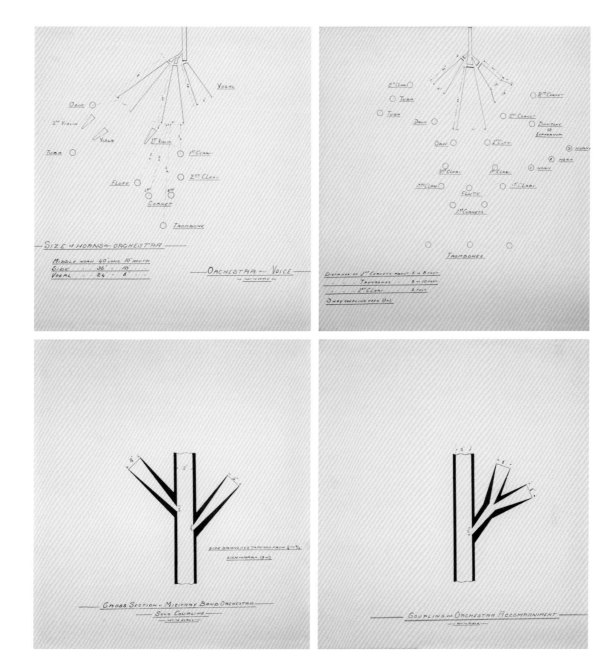

opposite

RECORDING HORNS (1905-20)
Acoustic recording horns used
by The Gramophone Company.
Prior to electrical recording
in 1925, sound was captured using
a recording horn connected to
a cutting stylus that etched the
vibrations into a record groove.

above

RECORDING METHODS (c. 1907)
These drawings are from a report
detailing recording methods used
by the Victor Talking Machine
Company. The top two diagrams
indicate the number, size and
positioning of acoustic horns
necessary to record an orchestra
and voice. The bottom two
illustrate alternative couplings
of acoustic horns to amplify a
military band and an orchestra.

OVERSIZED DISCS (c. 1910)

Several European record labels, including major players such as Pathé in France and Odeon in Germany, engaged in some experiments with disc sizing. These two examples were 19½ inches (50 cm) in diameter, almost double that of a standard gramophone record. Their fragility and unwieldiness made them unpopular, however, and they were only available briefly.

PATHÉ · PLATTEN

DIE TONE LOB, aus "TANNHÄUSER"

G⁵⁵ von Heinrich Hensel - Gross-h. Bad Kammersänger

54985.

BREYETE

S. G. D. G.

DISQUE

PATHÉ

85980. ER 14

"Zur gefälligen Beachtung.—Um die Platten vor dem Einstauben zu schützen, müssen dieselben stets nach dem Spielen in das Futteral zurückgelegt werden.

=== WICHTIGE BEMERKUNG ===

☞ Die PATHÉ-Platten beseitigen das lästige Auswechseln der Nadel.

☞ Die PATHÉ-Platten müssen mit einer PATHÉ-Schalldose gespielt werden.

☞ Die PATHÉ-Platten müssen vom Zentrum der Platte aus gespielt werden. *Man setze die Schalldose auf den inneren erhabenen Rand der Platte.*

☞ Die PATHÉ-Platten müssen mit einer Geschwindigkeit von 90 bis 100 Umdrehungen in der Minute gespielt werden.

☞ Die PATHÉ-Platten können auf allen Sprechmaschinen, welche mit einer PATHÉ-Schalldose versehen sind, gespielt werden.

RECORDING IN CHINA

In around 1906 a young Frenchman named Labansat was said to have set up a stall on Tibet Road in Shanghai. He had a gramophone and a comedy record called 'Laughing Foreigners', which he charged curious crowds 10 cents each to hear - with the guarantee that if they didn't laugh they would be given their money back. By 1908, Labansat had set up China's first record company, a subsidiary of Pathé in France, and made the first recordings of the Peking Opera. The following year the Columbia Phonograph Co. started recording local musicians in China, producing their first catalogues of Chinese records in 1909 (top left and, both front and back, top right). The performance of a Chinese opera lasted for weeks or even months and involved many musicians, each of whom took several different parts. The entire opera was recorded and selections of the recording released on up to twenty discs. In a formal photograph taken by the Columbia Phonograph Co. for an edition of *The Talking Machine News* (below) a group of leading Shanghai musicians are depicted standing or seated either side of the graphophone that recorded their performance.

RECORDING IN NORTH AFRICA

In 1910 the French subsidiary of The Gramophone Company produced this catalogue of songs recorded in Algeria.

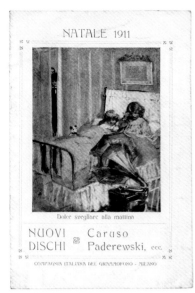

NATALE 1911

Dolce svegliare alla mattina

NUOVI DISCHI — Caruso Paderewski, ecc.

COMPAGNIA ITALIANA DEL GRAMMOFONO - MILANO

MAGGIO 1912
NUOVI DISCHI
ISABEAU

BERNARDO DE MURO
COMPAGNIA ITALIANA DEL GRAMMOFONO
MILANO - VIA S. PROSPERO, 5

"E nella notte echeggeranno i canti"

I grammofoni portatili
AGOSTO 1912
COMPAGNIA ITALIANA DEL GRAMMOFONO — MILANO — Via S. Prospero, 5

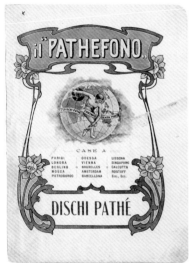

il "PATHEFONO"

CASE A
PARIGI   ODESSA   LISSONA
LONDRA   VIENNA   SINGAPORE
BERLINO   BRUXELLES CALCUTTA
MOSCA   AMSTERDAM ROSTOFF
PIETROBURGO BARCELLONA Ecc. Ecc.

DISCHI PATHÉ

il "PATHEFONO"

CASE A
PARIGI   ODESSA   LISSONA
LONDRA   VIENNA   SINGAPORE
BERLINO   BRUXELLES CALCUTTA
MOSCA   AMSTERDAM ROSTOFF
PIETROBUR O BARCELLONA Ecc. Ecc.

DISCHI PATHÉ

il "PATHEFONO"

CATALOGO DEGLI APPARECCHI
e REPERTORIO DEI DISCHI

PATHÉ-CONCERT

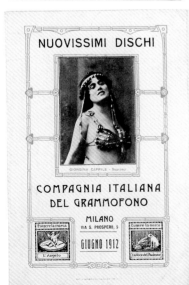

NUOVISSIMI DISCHI

GIORGINA CAPRILE - Soprano

COMPAGNIA ITALIANA
DEL GRAMMOFONO
MILANO
VIA S. PROSPERO, 5
GIUGNO 1912

SOCIETÀ NAZIONALE DEL
"GRAMMOFONO"
MILANO - Piazza del Duomo (Via Orefici 2)

NOVEMBRE 1913.

CARUSO
Nuovi Superbi Dischi

I. DICEMBRE 1913

SOCIETÀ NAZIONALE DEL
"GRAMMOFONO"
MILANO - Piazza Duomo (Via Orefici, 2)

Nuovi   Dischi
BATTISTINI

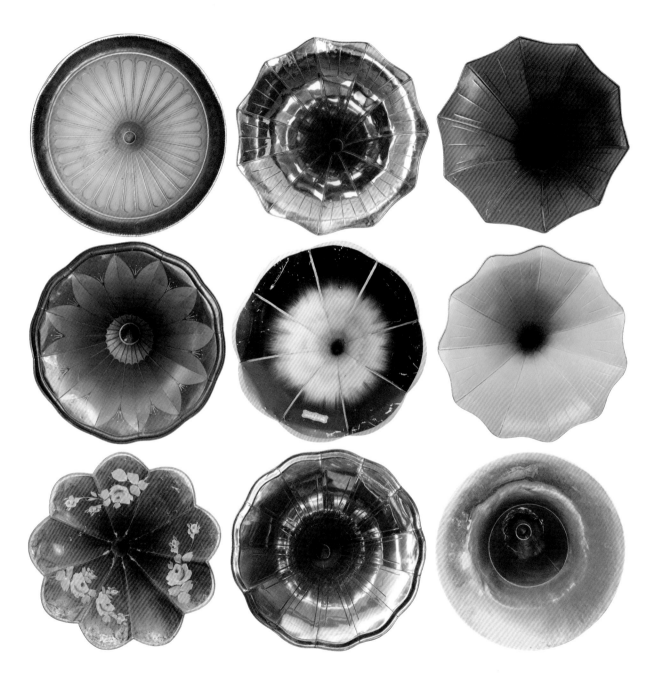

opposite

ITALIAN GRAMOPHONE CATALOGUES
(1909-12)

Opera recordings from Milan were
highly prized, given the fame
of singers such as Enrico
Caruso and Mattia Battistini
('The King of Baritones').

above

GRAMOPHONE HORNS

The first gramophones were
built so that the horns could
be detached and the device packed
away. There were many colourful
and attractive alternatives to
dull, functional brass cones.

PATHÉPHONE

Pathé-Concert

CATALOGUE des APPAREILS
et RÉPERTOIRE des DISQUES

JUILLET 1909

previous pages
FURNITURE PIECES (c. 1909)
Integrated gramophones designed
to fit with the living-room
furniture were sold in the same
catalogues as the records. These
French and Italian models were
forerunners of the 'radiogram'
that began to appear in the 1930s.

below
FRENCH CATALOGUE CARDS
Recordings issued in France by
The Gramophone Company in 1907
and 1908 were labelled 'Disque
Gramophone' and still featured
the 'Nipper' trademark with the
phrase 'La voix de son maître'
('His master's voice').

opposite
**PATHÉ FRÈRES CAFÉ MACHINE,
FRANCE (c. 1909)**
Pay-to-play music reproducers
appeared in the late 1890s. This
coin-operated gramophone uses a
weighted spring mechanism to stop
the turntable when the stylus
reaches the end of the record.

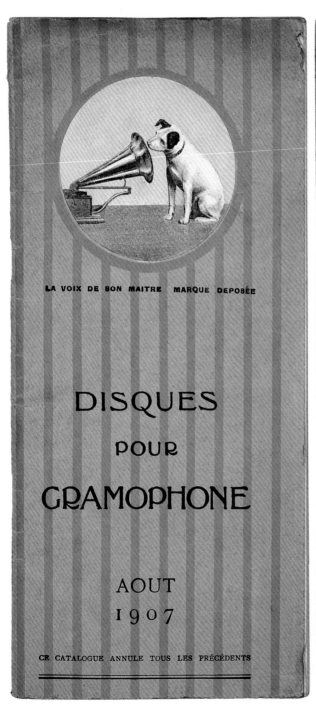

ZUR ERINNERUNG AN DAS FÜNFUNDZWANZIGJÄHRIGE REGIERUNGS-JUBILÄUM SEINER MAJESTÄT DES KAISERS UND KÖNIGS WILHELM II.

* 1888 – 1913 *

Elisabeth Boehm van Endert, Kammersäng.
M 043228 Aveläuten, Text von Ernst Zahn,
Musik von Oscar von Chelius. (Am
Klavier: Der Komponist.)

opposite

TWIN SERPENT HORN
(c. 1905)

Dating back to the first decade
of the 20th century, this highly
unusual double-branched brass
amplifying horn was manufactured
in Germany and could be fitted
to a gramophone in order
to increase the volume.

above

DEUTSCHE GRAMMOPHON
COMMEMORATIVE DISC (1913)

Issued to mark the 25th
anniversary of Kaiser
Wilhelm II's reign, this
single-sided disc features a
performance by soprano Elisabeth
Böhm van Endert. It came in this
ornate 12-inch (30-cm) container.

overleaf

GERMAN CATALOGUES (1911)

Many of these covers are for
Deutsche Grammophon, founded by
Emile Berliner in 1898 and based
in his birth city of Hanover in
Germany. Deutsche Grammophon is
the oldest extant record company
and one of the most successful
classical music labels.

previous pages, left

PETER PAN COLLAPSIBLE GRAMOPHONE (c. 1924)

Produced in London, this Peter Pan
gramophone is an early example of
a 'Cameraphone' - so named because
of its similarity to the folding
cameras of the period. It was
housed in a black, leatherette-
covered box 7 × 6 × 4¼ inches
(18 × 16 × 12 cm) in size. The
sound was amplified by means
of a small telescopic collapsible
horn that was fitted to the centre
of the soundbox. The turntable
was comprised of three spokes
that folded neatly together
in the box when not in use.

previous pages, right

THORENS EXCELDA POCKET GRAMOPHONE (c. 1940)

Hermann Thorens started his
family business in 1883 in
Sainte-Croix, Switzerland.
Produced between 1935 and 1947,
the Excelda 'pocket' gramophone
had a tonearm, soundbox and crank
that could be detached and slotted
into the case. The soundbox
also doubled up as an amplifying
horn. The mechanism could all
be broken down into a slim case
for transportation and could
even play 12-inch (30-cm) records.

right and opposite

OPERA DIVAS (c. 1907)

The gramophone record provided
a vast new audience for many
of the great opera stars of the
early 20th century, among them
the soprano Florence Austral
(far right), shown here as
Brünnhilde in Wagner's *Der
Ring des Nibelungen*.

RECORD LABELS (1905-29)

Dedicated record companies began to form shortly after the launch of the gramophone. Historically significant names such as Parlophone - for whom The Beatles first recorded - Zonophone, Pathé and His Master's Voice were all founded at the end of the 19th century. The selection of labels shown here illustrates the immediate global popularity of the gramophone, with examples from Britain, the United States, France, Germany, Russia, the Ottoman Empire (now Turkey) and India.

above

LE PATHÉGRAPHE MODÈLE NO.1
LANGUAGE MACHINE (1912)
The first audiovisual device
built specifically for teaching
languages, the Pathégraphe
horn played back the audio
from a spoken-language disc
while synchronized text
scrolled from a paper cylinder.

opposite

KLINGSOR GRAMOPHONE (1908)
Built in Germany, the Klingsor
combined two technologies:
the gramophone and the harp.
Set in a large wooden cabinet,
the gramophone horn was hidden
from view, only the mouth being
visible behind a large soundhole.
A wire-strung Art Nouveau-style
harp surrounds the hole. Its
strings resonate according to
the frequencies played on the
gramophone, and for this reason
were known as 'sympathy strings'.
In order for the Klingsor to
operate correctly, the tuning
of the harp strings had to be
checked regularly.

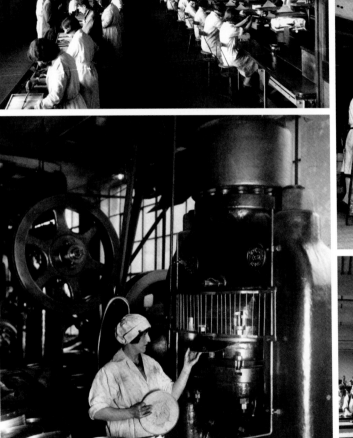

UK FACTORY IN WARTIME
(c. 1914)

At the outbreak of World War I, many of the young men working at The Gramophone Company's Hayes factory volunteered for armed service. To continue production, their jobs were filled temporarily by women. The factory later came under government control and was used to produce munitions for the war on the Western Front.

The Song the Bubble Sang

THE SWING

By Robert Louis Stevenson
Music by Liza Lehmann

How do you like to go up in a swing,
 Up in the air so blue?
Oh, I do think it the pleasantest thing
 Ever a child can do!

Up in the air and over the wall
 Till I can see, so wide,
Rivers and trees and cattle and all
 Over the countryside—

13

NIRONA CHILDREN'S GRAMOPHONES (c.1925)

Miniature gramophones for children began to appear during the 1920s. Some of the most interesting models were built by Nier & Ehmer of Beierfeld in Germany under the brand name of Nirona. These compact devices were designed to play discs that were 5½ inches (14 cm) in diameter - almost half the standard size. Album books that contained sets of stories and gramophone records (opposite) were widely available at this time; the recordings were either 'talking book' narrations or accompanying music. Most of the Nirona models were made from tin and decorated around the edges with nursery scenes (left), although more sober-looking devices were occasionally made (above). Particularly notable were the bell-shaped horns, which were capable of producing a surprisingly loud volume.

FACTORY IN FRANCE (c. 1907)
Compagnie française du Gramophone had been founded in 1898 as an independent subsidiary of The Gramophone Company. Pressings of French recordings were initially made in Hanover, Germany, until 1907 when a dedicated factory was set up at Ivry-sur-Seine, a suburb in the southeast of Paris.

SPREADING EAST (c. 1928)
As the gramophone became increasingly popular, factories were set up across the globe. Japanese record label Nipponophone was founded in 1910 and acquired by Columbia in 1927; it became part of the newly formed EMI four years later. This set of engineering photographs were marked up in the UK and sent to Japan to ensure that plant equipment would be correctly calibrated.

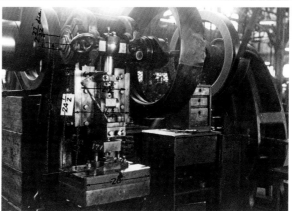

first wave : ACOUSTIC ERA

110.111

PHONOGRAPHES PATHÉ

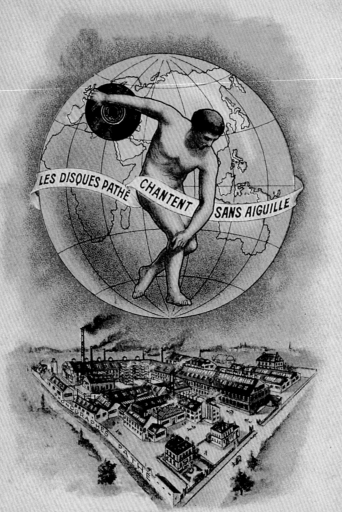

LES DISQUES PATHÉ CHANTENT SANS AIGUILLE

RÉPERTOIRE DES
DISQUES PATHÉ

MAI 1908

opposite

PHONOGRAPHES PATHÉ CATALOGUE
(1908)
This French record catalogue was
distributed by Carpentier Laga,
an agent for The Gramophone and
Typewriter Company. Cabinetmakers
were central to the development
of the form and design of the
early gramophones.

right

ODEON RECORDS CATALOGUES
(1920-36)
Based in Berlin, Odeon Records
was founded in 1903 by Max
Straus and Heinrich Zuntz of
the International Talking Machine
Company. It was named after
a Parisian theatre and took as
its logo a classical dome; it
is visible in all the German
record catalogues shown here.
Odeon Records was one of the
first labels to issue double-
sided records, and in 1909 made
what is thought to have been
the first recording of a large-
scale orchestral work. Odeon was
an early pioneer of what might
now be referred to as 'world
music'; recording engineer John
Daniel Smoot travelled the world
making new musical discoveries.
By 1905 Odeon claimed to have
recorded more than 11,000 titles
from Eastern Europe to northern
Africa and the Middle East,
even establishing bases
in South America and Asia.

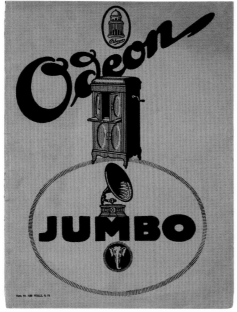

Complete Dance Catalogue

FOXTROTS
WALTZES
TANGOS
&c.

ONE-STEPS
TWO-STEPS
LANCERS
&c.

Waltzes
Fox Trots
Tangos
One Steps
&c.

Blues
Lancers
Two Steps
Quadrilles
&c.

Complete Catalogue of
"HIS MASTER'S VOICE"
DANCE RECORDS

The Latest Dances

ON

"HIS MASTER'S VOICE"

SEPTEMBER · · · 1921

GEMS FROM THE GIPSY PRINCESS

and the Latest Dances

ON

"HIS MASTER'S VOICE"
RECORDS

NUEVOS DISCOS
MARCA
GRAMÓFONO

LA VOZ DE SU AMO
MARCA REGISTRADA

JUNIO - JULIO 1920

MIKIPHONE POCKET PHONOGRAPH (c. 1926)

The Mikiphone is actually a miniature gramophone. When folded, the circular aluminium case - a little over 4 inches (10 cm) in diameter - is designed to resemble a large pocket watch. When opened, the case acts as a base, with the motor mechanism activated by turning the key. An extendable tonearm is fitted to a soundbox and connects to the base. The sound emerges via a two-part circular celluloid 'horn' slotted together and then fixed to the soundbox. The Mikiphone could play standard 10-inch (25-cm) gramophone records, although the audible sound was low both in volume and fidelity. Built by System Vadasz in Switzerland, it was sold predominantly in the United Kingdom. Well-preserved examples are now highly collectible.

POULSEN'S
TELEGRAPHONE (1903)
A magnetic version of
a phonograph, Poulsen's
telegraphone used a cylinder
wrapped with steel wire,
which became magnetized.

It could be used as either
an answering or dictating
machine. However, it proved
unreliable and it was not until
the 1950s that a satisfactory
answering machine became
widely available.

FRICTION LINK 1920

TIME 1920

NAME FRICTION LINK 1920

ASSEMBLY 1920?

DATE Nov. 7 10. DR'N W.K.B.R. CHK'D CR6

VICTOR TALKING
CAMDEN, N.J.

SCALE 2—1

2185-E

MATERIAL
DRAWING STEEL

ALTERATIONS

DIMENSION A CHANGED FROM 180" TO .208" B 7/17/11
.088 .025 .036
MATERIAL CHANGED FROM SYMBOL 5G
TO DRAWING STEEL B. 11-24-11
WIDTH OF SLOT CHANGED FROM .0610.0634 4-20-12
DIAM. OF HOLE CHANGED FROM .1875 TO .201 4-20-12
DIA. OF LEATHER HOLDER CHANGED FROM .31 TO 33 5-14-12
RADIUS ADDED N.L. 5-27-12
SHAPE OF SLOT CHANGED 5-6-15

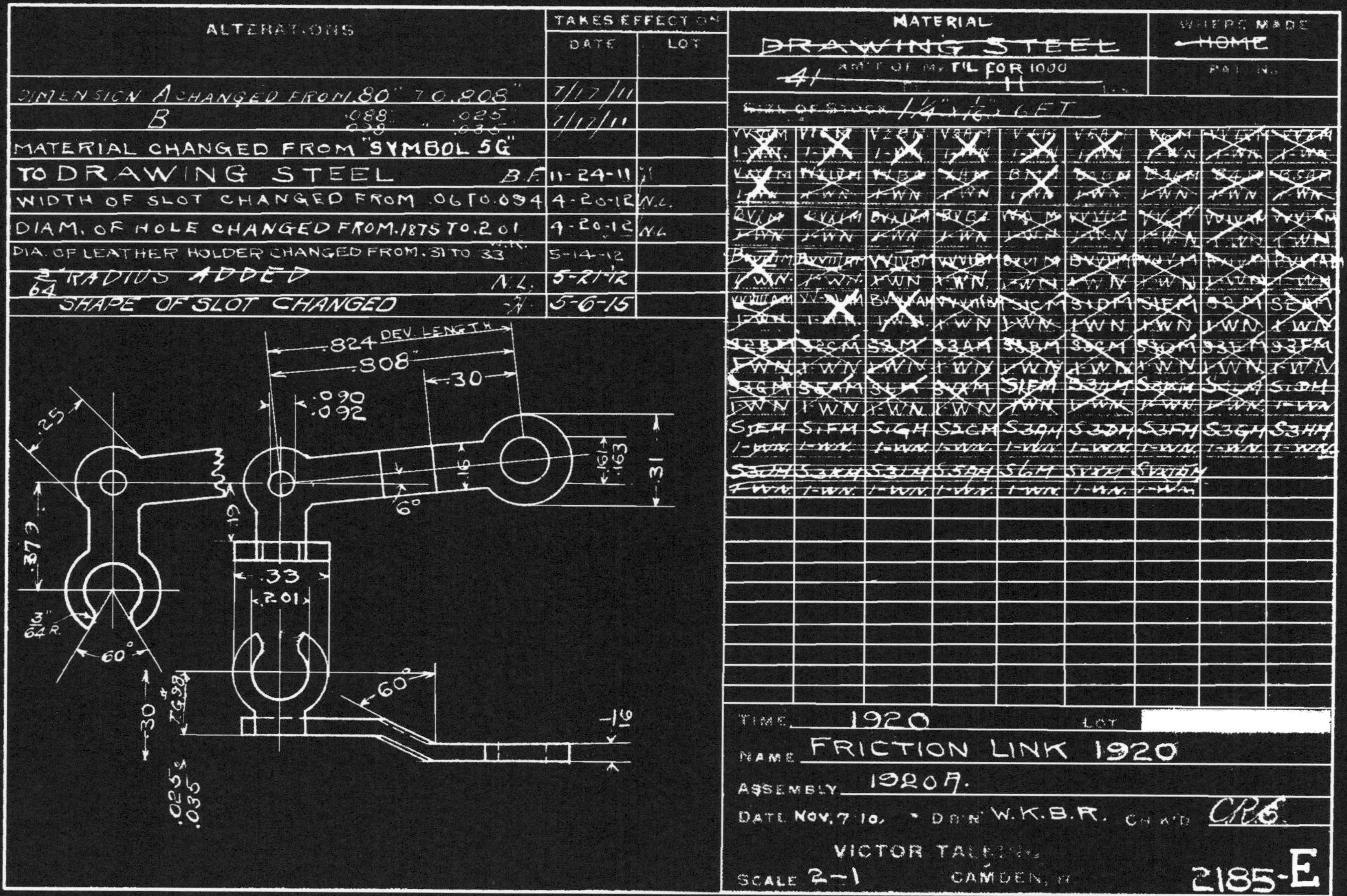

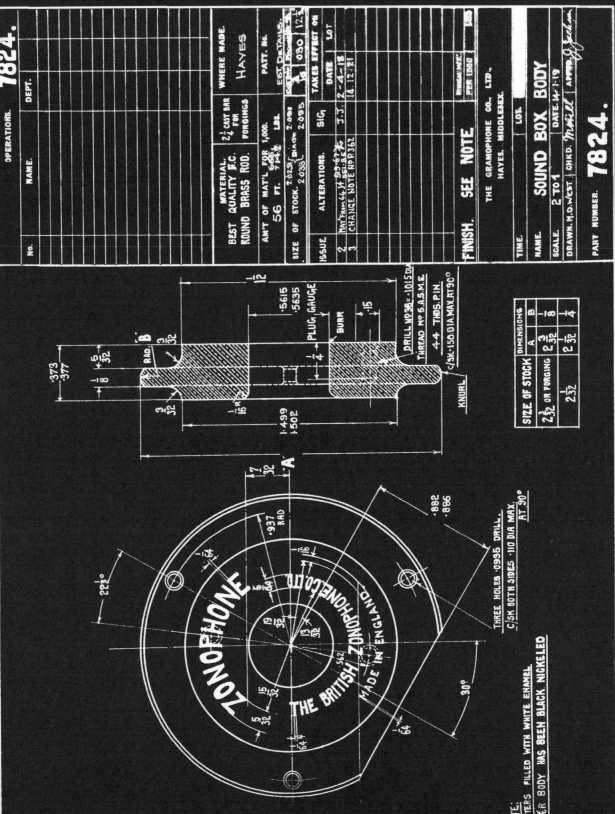

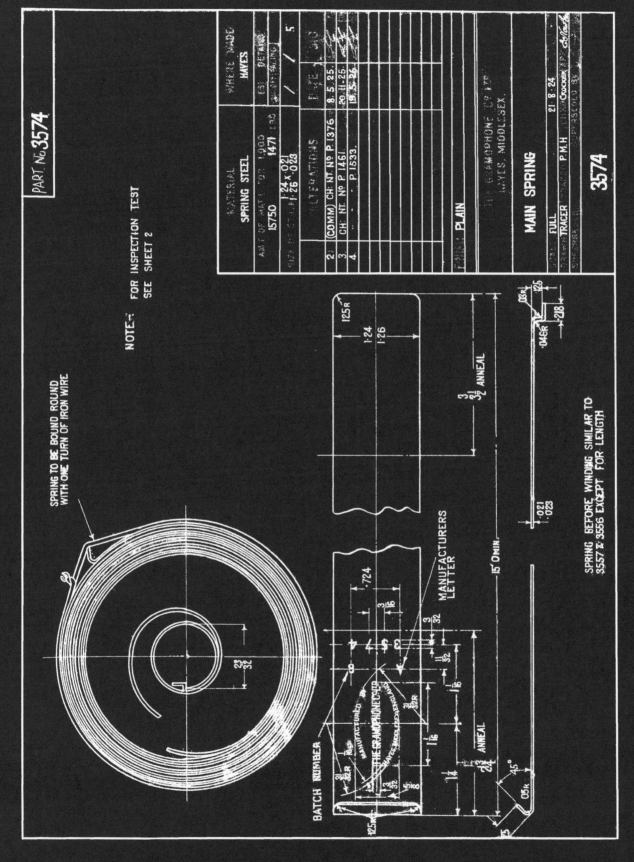

PART No. 3574

NOTE:- FOR INSPECTION TEST
SEE SHEET 2

SPRING TO BE BOUND ROUND
WITH ONE TURN OF IRON WIRE

SPRING BEFORE WINDING SIMILAR TO
3557 & 3556 EXCEPT FOR LENGTH

MANUFACTURERS
LETTER

BATCH NUMBER

MATERIAL	WHERE MADE
SPRING STEEL	HAYES

MAIN SPRING

3574

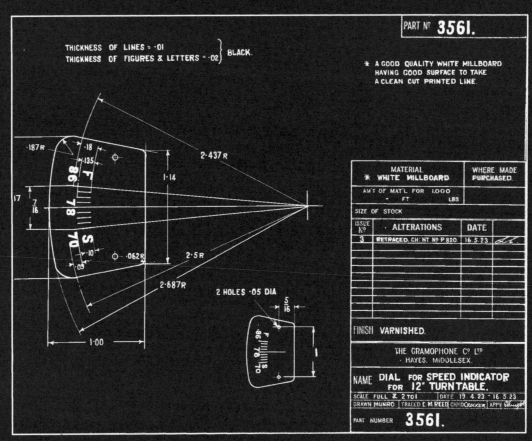

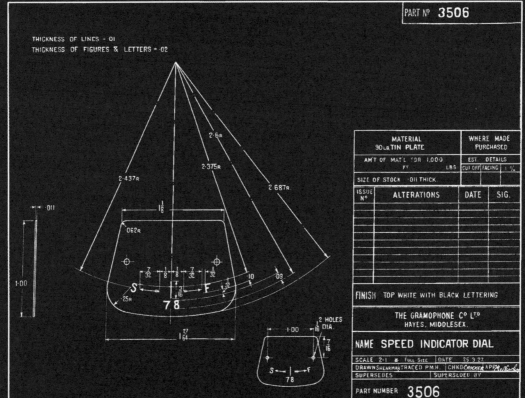

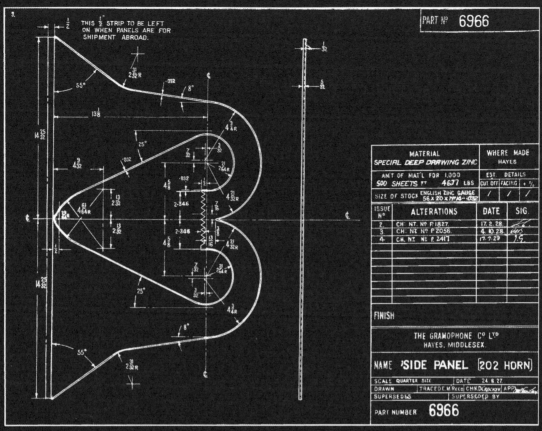

THIS 1½ STRIP TO BE LEFT ON WHEN PANELS ARE FOR SHIPMENT ABROAD.

PART Nº **6966**

MATERIAL		WHERE MADE
SPECIAL DEEP DRAWING ZINC		HAYES

AM'T OF MAT'L FOR 1,000		EST.	DETAILS	
500 SHEETS FT	4677 LBS	CUT OFF	FACING	+ %
SIZE OF STOCK ENGLISH ZINC GAUGE 56 X 20 X ⁷⁄₈ = ·032		/	/	/

ISSUE Nº	ALTERATIONS	DATE	SIG.
2.	CH: Nᵀ Nº P.1827.	17.2.28.	
3.	CH: Nᵀ Nº P.2056.	4.10.28.	
4.	CH: Nᵀ Nº P.2417	17.7.29.	

FINISH

THE GRAMOPHONE Cº LTD
HAYES, MIDDLESEX.

NAME SIDE PANEL (202 HORN)

SCALE QUARTER SIZE	DATE 24.6.27.
DRAWN TRACED E.M.Reed	CHKD CROCKER APP'D
SUPERSEDES	SUPERSEDED BY

PART NUMBER **6966**

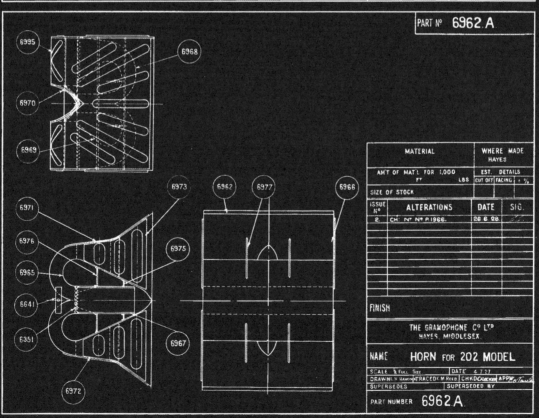

PART Nº **6962.A.**

MATERIAL		WHERE MADE
		HAYES

AM'T OF MAT'L FOR 1,000		EST.	DETAILS	
FT	LBS	CUT OFF	FACING	+ %
SIZE OF STOCK				

ISSUE Nº	ALTERATIONS	DATE	SIG.
2.	CH: Nᵀ Nº P.1966.	26.6.28.	

FINISH

THE GRAMOPHONE Cº LTD
HAYES, MIDDLESEX.

NAME HORN FOR 202 MODEL

SCALE ½ FULL SIZE	DATE 4.7.27
DRAWN H.Hancox TRACED E.M.Reed	CHKD CROCKER APP'D
SUPERSEDES	SUPERSEDED BY

PART NUMBER **6962.A.**

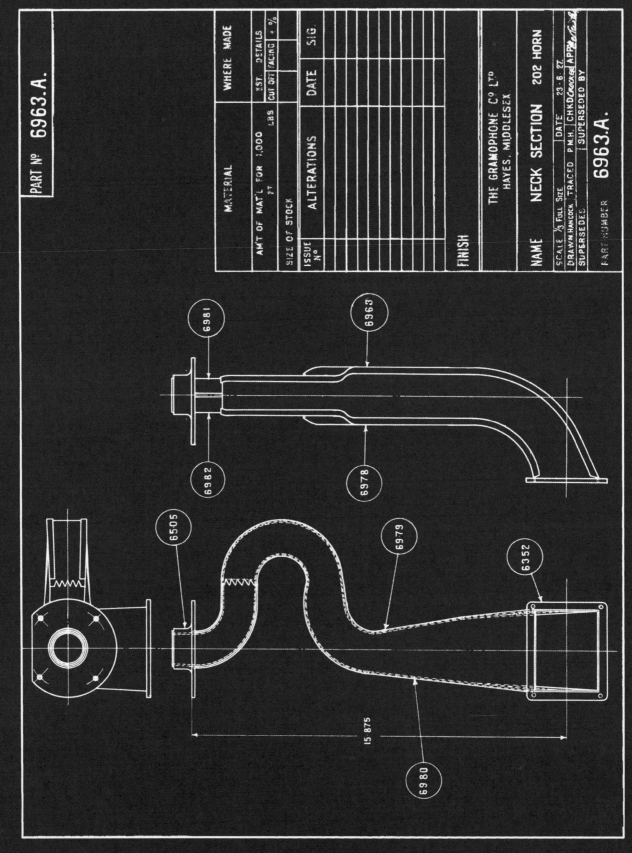

PART Nº **6963.A.**

MATERIAL

AMT OF MAT'L FOR 1,000   LBS   FT

SIZE OF STOCK

WHERE MADE

EST. DETAILS

CUT OFF | FACING | ± %

ALTERATIONS   DATE   SIG

ISSUE Nº

FINISH

THE GRAMOPHONE Cº LTD
HAYES, MIDDLESEX

NAME   NECK SECTION   202 HORN

SCALE ⅓ FULL SIZE   DATE 23·6·27
DRAWN HANCOCK   TRACED P.M.H.   CHKD CHECKED APP
SUPERSEDES   SUPERSEDED BY

PART NUMBER   **6963.A.**

6981

6963

6982

6978

6505

6979

6352

6980

15·875

1927: NECK SECTION FOR 202 HORN NO. 6963A

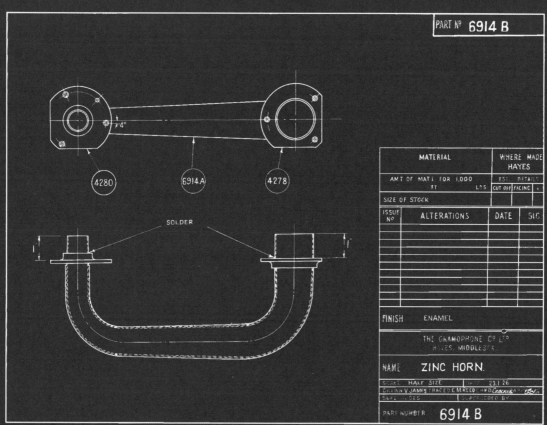

PART N° 6914 B

MATERIAL		WHERE MADE HAYES		
AM.T OF MAT.L FOR 1,000 FT	LBS	EST.	DETAILS	
		CUT OFF	FACING	+
SIZE OF STOCK				
ISSUE N°	ALTERATIONS	DATE	SIG	

FINISH   ENAMEL

THE GRAMOPHONE C° L.TD
HAYES, MIDDLESEX.

NAME   ZINC HORN.

SCALE HALF SIZE	DATE 23.1.26	
DRAWN V JAMES	TRACED E.M REED	CH.K.D Crocker APP.D
SUPERSEDES	SUPERSEDED BY	

PART NUMBER   6914 B

SOLDER

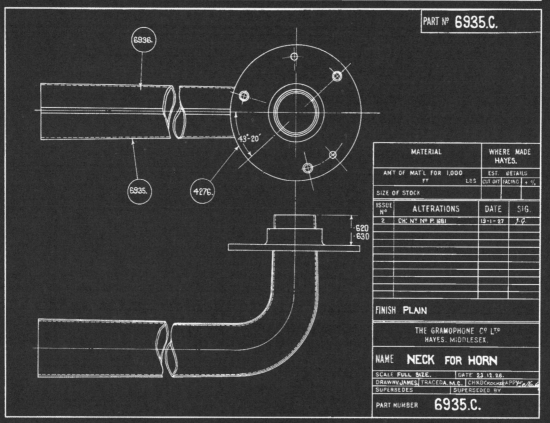

PART N° 6935.C.

MATERIAL		WHERE MADE HAYES.		
AM.T OF MAT'L FOR 1,000 FT	LBS	EST.	DETAILS	
		CUT OFF	FACING	+ %
SIZE OF STOCK				
ISSUE N°	ALTERATIONS	DATE	SIG.	
2	CH. N.T N° P. 1681	19-1-27	J.C.	

FINISH PLAIN

THE GRAMOPHONE C° L.TD
HAYES, MIDDLESEX.

NAME   NECK FOR HORN

SCALE FULL SIZE.	DATE 23.12.26.	
DRAWN V.JAMES	TRACED A. M.C.	CH.K.D Crocker APP.D
SUPERSEDES	SUPERSEDED BY	

PART NUMBER   6935.C.

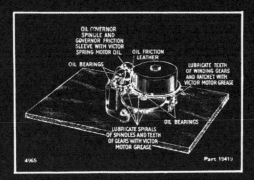

CUT 3 5/16" X 2 3/16"

ALTERATIONS	DATE	AUTHORITY

PART No. *19419*

NAME *OIL LABEL*

SUPERSEDES _____ SUPERSEDED BY _____

DATE *8-31-27* DR'N *MacCloskeY*

DATE _____ TRACED _____ CH'K'D *HO 9-16-27*

VICTOR TALKING MACHINE CO.
CAMDEN, N. J.

6135 - E

SCALE _____

5

Be Careful

Before inserting any Radiotrons in the Sockets, turn Battery Setting Knob to left until pointer rests on "Off," and press Filament Switch down to "Off" position.

Improper setting of this Pointer will injure your Radiotrons.

Read your Instruction Book carefully— it will save you expense and trouble.

6859   Part 17500

3 1/4"

ALTERATIONS	DATE	AUTHORITY

PART No. *17500*

NAME **WARNING TAG**

SUPERSEDES *7979 D* SUPERSEDED BY _____

DATE *8-31-27* DR'N *MacCloskey*

DATE _____ TRACED _____ CH'K'D *HO 9-15-27*

VICTOR TALKING MACHINE CO.
CAMDEN, N. J.

6143 E

SCALE _____

14
6143

second wave
ELECTRICAL ERA

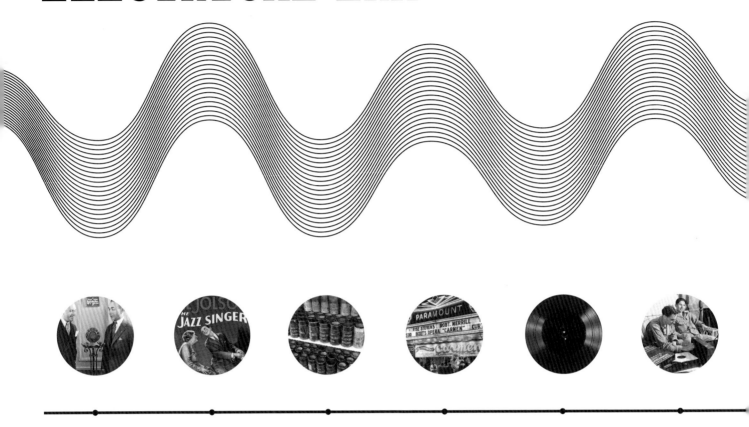

1925

The invention of electrical recording allows all the major labels to start using microphones in studio sessions.

1927

The first commercial talking picture is released. *The Jazz Singer*, starring Al Jolson, uses Vitaphone sound recorded on discs that are synchronized with the moving picture.

1929

The flat gramophone record wins the first audio format war as production of cylinders draws to a close.

1931

Alan Blumlein develops binaural sound (now known as stereo sound) at the Central Research laboratories at EMI.

1934

Lacquer-coated blank discs are introduced, making instant recording possible for broadcast and home recording.

1934

The American Federation for the Blind and RCA Victor records make long-playing audio books for the sight impaired.

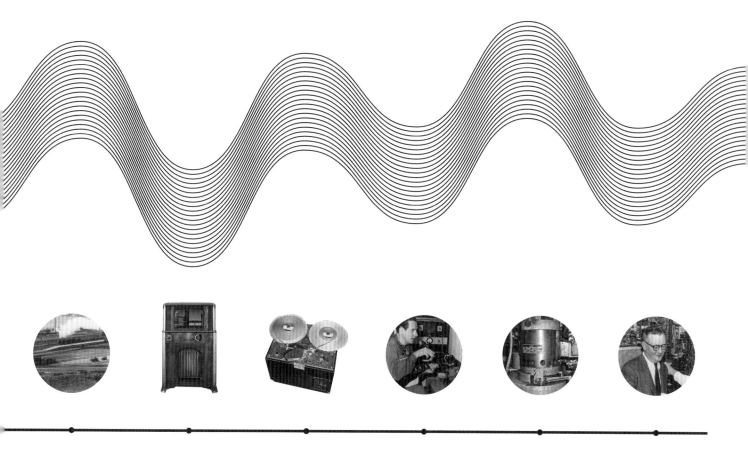

1935

The first film footage is shot in stereo. *Trains at Hayes Station* is produced by prolific engineer and innovator Alan Blumlein.

1935

Rock-Ola, Seeburg and Wurlitzer sell multiple-selection nickel juke boxes in post-Prohibition grilles and taverns in the US.

1935

The AEG Magnetophon K1 – the first effective tape recorder – is demonstrated at the Berlin Radio Show.

1940

The guitarist Les Paul experiments with sound-on-sound recordings, leading to the development of four- and eight-track recordings.

1941

High-frequency biasing is developed by Weber and Von Braunmühl at AEG, improving the quality of the Magnetophone.

1945

Paul Klipsch patents the Klipschorn folded horn speaker, contributing to the birth of the 'hi fi' era of sound production.

Until the 1920s, all sound recording was produced by mechanical means. The invention of the thermionic triode valve heralded a new dawn. Developed in 1906 by Lee de Forest (building on the work of the physicist John Ambrose Fleming), this device would play a fundamental role in the electrification of every aspect of sound recording, reproduction and broadcasting. Without the valve, there would have been no radio and television, microphones, amplification or 'talking pictures'. And all these innovations converged during the first three decades of the 20th century.

John Ambrose Fleming, a professor at University College, London, had worked for ten years as a consultant for the Edison Electric Light Company and so was familiar with the idea of thermionic emission. In 1901, he had designed the transmitter used by Guglielmo Marconi for the first transatlantic transmission of radio waves; the Morse code signal for the letter 'S' was sent from the tip of Cornwall to Newfoundland, although the receiver had difficulty in distinguishing it from atmospheric radio noise. In 1904, Fleming used the principles of thermionic emission in his 'oscillation valve' to create a more sensitive receiver. It was immediately put to use in Marconi's Morse code telegraph units. A year later, American engineer Lee de Forest read Fleming's paper on the oscillation valve and in 1906 he created his own three-element vacuum tube, the Audion valve (or triode) – the first electronic amplifying device – which would have such important ramifications for the future of electronics. [1]

Marconi's 'wireless telegraphy' had only been able to transmit and receive Morse code signals rather than sound. There had been experiments with the wireless broadcasting of music as far back as 1904 when Dr. Nussbaumer of the University of Graz in Austria was said to have yodelled a folk tune into a crude experimental transmitter which was received

[1]
LONG-RUNNING FEUD
Fleming and De Forest would thereafter engage in decades of costly litigation regarding patent validity, which would only be settled in De Forest's favour in 1943, two years before Fleming's death.

2 in an adjoining room. And more publicly, in 1910, De Forest himself had organized a heavily publicized transmission by Enrico Caruso from the Metropolitan Opera House in New York. But it was not until 1912 that De Forest's Audion valve was used to create the first true amplifying radio receivers. Before this time, radio receivers had been crude devices using crystal 'cat's whisker' detectors. They were unreliable, prone to frequency drift and had no amplification. The Audion valve enabled the creation of amplified receiver sets that could be heard through a loudspeaker, and hence paved the way for public broadcasting. On 15 June 1920, 2MT a radio station based at the Marconi Research Centre in Chelmsford, England, transmitted a performance by the celebrated soprano Dame Nellie Melba; 2MT would, thereafter, be the first regular broadcaster of live musical performances. Two years later the British Broadcasting Company (BBC) was created; after receiving a Royal Charter in 1926, it would become the world's first national radio broadcaster.

By the early 1920s, the advances in electronics that had enabled the birth of the broadcasting industry were having a similar impact on the way in which sound was recorded. The idea of electrical recording had been among Thomas Edison's original experiments for improving the sound of his cylinder phonograph. He had attached a tiny stylus to a telephone receiver so that the signal would vibrate the stylus and cut a groove in the cylinder.

3 By the end of World War I, when valves first became commercially available outside research laboratories, some engineers began to consider the idea of using an electrical signal from a microphone to drive a disc-recording device. In theory, by inserting a triode valve the microphone's weak signal could be stepped up to drive a cutter. This concept became more realistic in 1916, when Edward Wente developed the condenser microphone. This incorporated two parallel plates, each with an

---

2
AUDION TRIODE VALVE
By 1913 it had been discovered that by cascading large numbers of Audion valves, the weakest of signals could be amplified, making long-distance telephone calls possible. In July 1914, American Telephone and Telegraph (AT&T) president Theodore Vail was able to make the first successful coast-to-coast telephone transmission - a full year before the heavily publicised 'official' inaugural transcontinental call between Aleander Graham Bell in New York City and Thomas West in San Francisco.

3
A FALSE START
With telephone technology still in its infancy, however, there was no satisfactory way of amplifying the signal. While the principle worked, it proved far less effective than simply making a loud noise into an acoustic recording horn, and Edison eventually abandoned the idea.

electric charge (one fixed; one mobile). The front plate moved according to the pressure from the audio signal, causing a small change in capacitance between two plates and allowed a change in the flow of current. This created a very low output, but with the addition of a valve amplifier a strong signal could be produced. Although originally designed for long-distance telephone transmission, the condenser microphone showed exceptional acoustic capabilities when compared to existing carbon microphones – notably, a top frequency of 6 kHz at a time when even the best mechanical disc-cutting process could only reproduce up to 2.5 kHz.

It was clear that an improved disc-cutting process was needed. The first electrical system was developed in the UK by Lionel Guest and Horace O. Merriman using a carbon microphone. It was used in the earliest surviving electrical recording – the hymn 'Abide with Me', recorded on 11 November 1920 during the burial service for the Unknown Soldier at London's Westminster Abbey.

The same year, Bell Laboratories set up two research teams under the supervision of physicist and electronic pioneer Dr Harvey Fletcher. One team was to develop an electrical recording system, while the other worked on a sound system for cinema theatres. The result was the Western Electric recording system, which combined an improved condenser microphone (enabling a frequency range of 250 Hz to more than 15 kHz), with an amplifier and an electromechanical disc-cutting arrangement. Commercialized as the Westrex system (Western Electric was the commercial arm of Bell Labs), it was shown to executives of the Victor and Columbia recording companies in 1924. Columbia's former British subsidiary (which bought out its ailing American parent in 1925) drove the move towards the Westrex process, with both companies electing to license the system.

4

A QUALIFIED SUCCESS
As radical as the principle might have been, the results of Guest and Merriman's system were considerably poorer than would have been possible using existing acoustic technology – excepting, perhaps, that recording such a large group of people using an acoustic horn would have been difficult.

The equipment was installed at Victor's headquarters in Camden, New Jersey, on 3 February 1925. The first recording session using the Westrex system was for a 'A Miniature Concert' performed by a vocal group credited as 'The Eight Popular Victor Artists'. On 29 April that year, the first commercial orchestral recording to use the system was made: Saint-Saën's *Dance Macabre* by the Philadelphia Orchestra conducted by Leopold Stokowski. At the same time, Columbia began using the Westrex system for recordings by popular radio singer Art Gillham.

In 1926, Victor began to promote their 'electrical' recordings using the name 'Victor Orthophonic' and marking labels with the 'VE' logo. Columbia followed suit, with its self-designated 'Viva-tonal Electrical Process'. In Britain, the Columbia Gramophone Company would merge with The Gramophone Company in 1931 to produce Electric and Musical Industries Ltd (EMI). It produced records under the brand 'His Master's Voice', with an iconic logo featuring the painting of Nipper the dog listening to a gramophone record. The Columbia brand continued to be used in the United States. A year later, to avoid the need to pay royalties for using the Westrex system, a similar process was adopted that had been developed in-house by former Columbia researcher Alan Blumlein and which incorporated a moving-coil microphone. It is possible to tell which system was used from looking alongside the matrix number on the record label: the circled letter 'W' denotes Westrex, while 'C' stands for Columbia.

The development of the Westrex and Blumlein systems revolutionized the possibilities for recorded sound. The ability to handle musical instruments below the 200 Hz range meant that the bass drum could be heard for the first time on recordings, as could the lower-end frequencies of the string bass, which previously had to be augmented with other bass instruments such as the tuba.

5

ELECTRICAL VS ACOUSTIC
At first, neither company had publicized their use of this superior new technological process, for fear of damaging sales of existing acoustic records.

6

THE BIRTH OF STEREO
In 1931, Blumlein would also be responsible for the development of stereophonic sound as well as a method for cutting stereophonic gramophone records, although the first commercially available stereo releases would not appear until 1957.

7

More significantly, by the early 1930s musicians were no longer necessarily required to position themselves around a single recording device; rather, a number of microphones could be used and their respective volumes altered to 'mix' the sound. This gave a new lease of life to instruments that traditionally struggled to be heard in an ensemble, such as the guitar. This period of innovation also saw the appearance of the first amplified musical instruments, with magnetic pick-ups fitted to guitars, as well as new instruments such as the theremin and electric organ.

It was perhaps vocal music that was most affected by these developments, though. In the acoustic era, the recording medium was most suited to strong, powerful voices – those performers capable of projecting from the stage to the rear seats of a theatre. The development of the condenser microphone and the ability to mix sound levels meant that quieter singing voices could now be accommodated, even when backed by a band or orchestra. This innovation saw the evolution of a softer, more personalized style of singing and a new generation of popular 'crooners'. Among the creators of the style were Al Bowlly and Art Gillham, though the era's first great heart-throb was Rudy Vallée, whose good looks and romantic singing style inspired the tagline 'Men Hate Him! Women Love Him!' for his first feature film. The most popular crooner of all, however, was Bing Crosby, who was America's most successful singer in the 1930s, and would become one of the biggest box-office stars in cinema history. Crosby was also an unlikely player in the future of recorded sound, as one of the driving forces behind its next phase of evolution – magnetic recording.

The advances in gramophone recording technology were not reflected in the living rooms of the consumer, who increasingly looked to the new radio broadcasts for musical entertainment. In fact, from the mid-1920s gramophone record sales began to fall.

7
INSTRUMENTAL CHANGES
Players such as Eddie Lang and Django Reinhardt were quick to take advantage of these new possibilities, and were all but responsible for inventing the jazz guitar.

Although the playing apparatus had evolved during the first two decades of the 20th century, gramophones were still acoustic/mechanical devices armed with heavy 100-g needles that would eventually shred the grooves of any record if played enough times. Nonetheless, some manufacturers experimented with devices that not only used electricity to amplify the sound but also to power the motor rotating the platter. The first serious electric gramophone was the Brunswick Panatrope, made in the USA in 1925. Four years later, RCA, America's largest radio company, bought the Victor record company and began selling combined radio-gramophone units, or 'radiograms'. These were not cheap, however, and well into the 1940s the majority of gramophone players found in the households of America and Europe were essentially improved versions of the 'wind-up' gramophones that 8 had existed since the beginning of the century.

One of the most significant developments of this period was the emergence of 'talking pictures'. As far back as 1919, inventors and engineers had looked for ways of synchronizing sound and 9 vision. It was Lee de Forest who developed the first sound-on-film technology, via which a soundtrack 'strip' was added to the movie. Two years later, Western Electric gave a demonstration of a system that combined film with a mechanically synchronized gramophone turntable for the playback of discs. Sufficiently impressed by the process, Warner Brothers commissioned its use for the John Barrymore adventure *Don Juan*, the first major motion picture to boast a synchronized soundtrack.

Although there had been some scepticism in the industry about the need for sound in the cinema, all doubt was swept aside in 1927 with the success of Al Jolson's *The Jazz Singer*. Ultimately, the major Hollywood studios agreed among themselves to a sound-on-film standard that could be adopted by all movie theatres. By 1930, the silent cinema era was over.

8
POST-WAR DEVELOPMENTS
The electric 'record player' would not become popular with consumers until after World War II, and into the following decade, when the market for gramophone records took off among teenagers with the birth of rock 'n' roll.

9
PATENT PROBLEMS
As with many of De Forest's innovations, he would lose valuable headway in a bitter legal battle over a patent with one of his employees, Freeman Harrison Owens.

136.137

opposite

HMV MODEL 460 LUMIÉRE
GRAMOPHONE (1925)

The Model 460 saw the usual
amplifying horn replaced with
a Lumiére pleated diaphragm,
eliminating the need for a tonearm
and soundbox. The diaphragm was
too fragile and the model was
dropped a year later.

above

MARCONIPHONE MODEL 105
LOUDSPEAKER (1927)

An early relic of the electrical
era, the Model 105 was a moving
iron-cone loudspeaker fitted
in a drum-shaped walnut veneered
plywood cabinet. An oxidized
metal grille covers the
speaker aperture.

opposite

PADEREWSKI ADVERT (1920s)

Diplomat Ignacy Jan Paderewski was a famous pianist and composer, with a vast gramophone discography. In 1919, he became newly independent Poland's first prime minister.

below

ODEON ELECTRIC RECORDINGS

In September 1926, Odeon began using the Westrex electric recording system in Berlin. In 1945 most of Odeon's archive was wiped out when Berlin fell at the end of World War II.

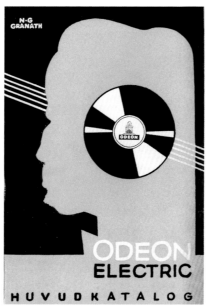

LEE
DE FOREST

RADIO AND
TELEVISION
PIONEER

Lee de Forest – the self-appointed 'father of radio and grandfather of television' – lived a colourful life. A flamboyant self-promoter, he was married four times, was a notoriously poor businessman and spent huge amounts of money and energy on patent lawsuits. He boasted that he'd made, and lost, fortunes four times over; by the time of his death he was virtually penniless. Many of his rivals denounced his inventions as derivative, leaning heavily on the work of others. Yet beneath the bluster there was a

1 prolific inventor. His principle development, the Audion vacuum tube, made live radio broadcasting a reality, and would play a key role in the development of the telephone, television, audio and computer industries.

The son of a preacher, De Forest grew up in rural Alabama, an enthusiastic builder of mechanical gadgets. Expected to follow his father into the clergy, De Forest instead took a place at the Sheffield Scientific School at Yale University. Working his way through college, although an undistinguished undergraduate, he went on to earn a PhD in physics in 1899: inspired by the work in Europe of Heinrich Hertz and Guglielmo Marconi, his doctoral thesis was titled *The Reflection of Hertzian Waves from the Ends of Parallel Wires*. After Yale, De Forest sought employment both with Nikola Tesla and Marconi himself, but eventually joined Western Electric's telephone laboratory in Chicago, where, refining the work of two German scientists, he developed a new receiver. Finding working for others unproductive, in 1902 he started his own business, the American De Forest Wireless Telegraph Company, which sold radio equipment and demonstrated new technology by broadcasting Morse code signals. Although the business thrived, within four years he found himself in conflict with his backers and was forced to sell his stock.

De Forest quickly re-established himself as an independent inventor and in 1906 he and former American De Forest salesman

1
TALENT FOR INVENTION
De Forest had almost
200 patents to his name.

James Dunlop Smith incorporated the Radio Telephone Company to promote his inventions. It was at this time that he patented his most famous creation, the Audion vacuum tube.

In 1904, British physicist John Ambrose Fleming had developed what he called an 'oscillation valve' (later re-christened the 'diode'). It is universally recognized as the first true electronic device. De Forest built on Fleming's important invention, adding a control grid to create the Audion vacuum tube. Designed initially as a radio receiver detector, it was only after further research that its important amplification capabilities were established; De Forest had created a valve that not only rectified the AC current, but also boosted it.

An outraged Fleming accused De Forest of stealing his idea. But De Forest had made a very significant improvement. The Audion contained the same filament/cathode and plate/anode design as Fleming's valve, but inserted a zigzag of wire – the 'grid'. When a small electric current was applied to the grid, greater current would move from the filament to the plate, making it effectively the first electrical amplifier. With its three active electrodes, the Audion valve was the first triode. This valve remained in everyday use until the 1960s when it was gradually superseded by the transistor, developed at Bell Labs in 1947. While the triode became a practical triumph, the lawsuits continued unabated until 1943 when the United States Supreme Court ruled finally that Fleming had no claim over De Forest's patent.

De Forest's commercial aptitude fluctuated for the rest of his life. New companies emerged and declined, yet he continued to innovate. In the early 1920s he created Phonofilm, one of the first sound-on-film processes, and in 1960 was awarded an honorary Academy Award in recognition of 'his pioneering inventions which brought sound to the motion picture'.

LEE DE FOREST
Born: 26 August 1873,
Council Bluffs, Iowa, USA
Death: 30 June 1961, Hollywood,
California, USA

second wave : ELECTRICAL ERA

2
A TECHNOLOGICAL LANDMARK
The Audion valve would be central to most of the important developments in electronics over the fifty years that followed. Indeed, without the triode, Marconi's pioneering work in long-distance signal transmission would not have evolved into radio and television broadcasts, and the development of radar and the earliest computers could not have happened.

3
BELATED RECOGNITION
In 1946, the importance of the triode was acknowledged when De Forest was awarded the prestigious Edison Medal of the American Institute of Electrical and Electronics Engineers (IEEE).

142.143

CONTEMPORARY MODEL OF A RE-ENTRANT TONE CHAMBER (1927)

The Exponential Re-entrant Tone Chamber or Horn was introduced in November 1927 and used in Models 163, 193, 202 and 203. The horn was made of sheet zinc with an enamel finish. The sound travelled through a series of folded curves, enabling a larger sound chamber to be installed in a cabinet below the turntable. At all points along the length of the chamber, the cross-sectional areas were proportional to each other so that an exponential rate of expansion was maintained. This created an improved sound, and eliminated what the makers described as 'the last traces of what was formerly known as "gramophone tone"'.

MOBILE RECORDING SYSTEM (1927)

Two years after the installation of an electrical recording system at The Gramophone Company's headquarters in Hayes, the first mobile recording system arrived. A compact recording suite built onto a Lancia van chassis, it enabled recordings of large-scale ensembles to be made on location.

THE ROYAL MICROPHONES
(1923-37)

From the earliest days of electronically amplified sound, when members of the British royal family were called upon to address the nation, or a large gathering, they used their own personalized microphones. The gilt-rimmed circular microphone (below) was built by Marconi-Sykes for King George V. An inscription plaque on the top of the microphone lists the royal occasions on which it was used, beginning with the opening of Liverpool Cathedral on 19 July 1923. King George V was the first monarch to be widely heard by his subjects. It was the development of valve technology that made both electronic amplification and radio broadcasts possible. EMI gave King George V the Marconi-Reisz carbon microphone (opposite left) for use during his Silver Jubilee celebrations in 1935. The reign of King George VI began in 1936. His silver moving-coil permanent magnet microphone (opposite right) was based on the EMI PM 201 model and was first used in 1937 at the opening of the Maritime Museum in Greenwich.

above

ELECTROLA RECORDS

The Electrola label was
founded in Berlin in 1925 and
recorded many of Germany's most
celebrated classical musicians.

opposite and overleaf

THE GLOBAL VOICE (1930s)

A selection of catalogue
covers is shown here from
Switzerland (opposite), Greece
and South Africa (overleaf).

pages 152–53

GRAMOPHONE AND MUSIC SALOON,
CALCUTTA (1930s)

His Master's Voice became one of
the most instantly recognizable
brands in Asia in the 1930s.

SCHWEIZER
AUFNAHMEN
1 9 3 O

"His Master's Voice"

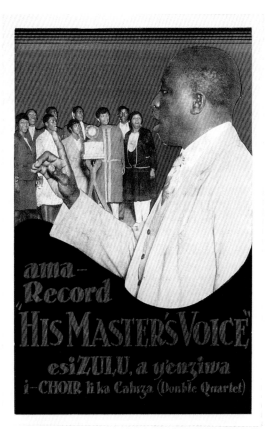

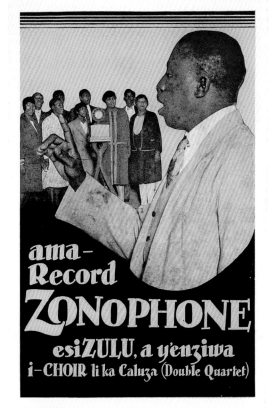

GUGLIELMO MARCONI

Inventor and engineer Guglielmo Marconi was born into a wealthy Italian family. He was educated at home by private tutors, and later attended the Technical Institute in Livorno and the University of Bologna, but never received any formal qualifications. He took a particular interest in the work of German physicist Heinrich Hertz, in particular Hertz's demonstration that electromagnetic radiation (radio waves) could be generated and detected. In 1894, the twenty-year-old Marconi began conducting his own experiments into 'wireless telegraphy'.

In the late 19th century, the prevailing scientific view was that radio waves were a short-range phenomenon, limited to the visual horizon – and so not suited to communication over a long distance. Marconi discovered that a greater range was possible if the shape of the transmitting antenna was changed to a straight rod (a monopole antenna), it was raised in height, and both the transmitter and receiver were grounded. In the summer of 1895, in the grounds of his parents' estate in Bologna, he achieved a transmission distance of 2 miles (3.22 km). Marconi wrote to the Italian government, explaining his work and its practical potential and requesting funding for research. Receiving no response, he was advised to move to England. In 1896, Marconi found interested backers in London, among them William Preece, the Chief Electrical Engineer of the British Post Office. Within a year, Marconi was able to transmit and receive up to a distance of 12 miles (19.31 km), and applied for his first patent. In 1899, [1] Marconi's signals crossed the English Channel. The same year, he sailed to the United States at the invitation of the *New York Herald* newspaper. He sent telegraph messages on the progress of the America's Cup yacht race from off the coast of New Jersey.

Marconi continued to improve and refine his equipment in pursuit of his ultimate goal: to make the first ever transatlantic broadcast. On 12 December 1901, using a 500-ft (152-m)

[1]
AN ASTUTE SELF-PROMOTER
Marconi publicized his work by staging a number of newsworthy demonstrations. In 1898, he set up a wireless station on the Isle of Wight that enabled Queen Victoria to send messages to her son Prince Edward aboard the royal yacht.

antenna supported by a kite, a faint three-dot signal (Morse code for the letter 'S') broadcast from a transmitter in Poldhu, on Cornwall's Lizard Peninsula, was picked up in St John's on Newfoundland some 2,100 miles (3,380 km) away. In 1909, Marconi was awarded the Nobel Prize for Physics, which he shared with German inventor Karl Ferdinand Braun for 'their contributions to the development of wireless telegraphy'.

Marconi began to build high-powered transmitters on both sides of the Atlantic to communicate with transatlantic shipping, making it possible to send or receive navigation reports or distress signals in the middle of the Atlantic. Marconi radios had become standard on most liners, manned by trained operators known as 'Marconi Men'. When RMS *Titanic* struck an iceberg on 14 April 1912, the ship's operator was able to send out a distress signal to RMS *Carpathia* which was able to attend the scene and rescue 710 survivors who otherwise would have perished. The tragedy shocked the world and raised public awareness of the value of Marconi's work.

Despite Marconi's initial groundbreaking work, it had not been possible to transmit actual sounds, such as an audible human voice, but 'spark-gap' signals that produced the dots and dashes used in Morse code communication. It was only the invention of the thermionic diode and triode valves by John Ambrose Fleming and Lee de Forest respectively that would pave the way for the first radio transmissions of speech and music.

In 1913, Marconi and his family returned to Italy where, a year later, he joined the Italian Senate. He embraced the policies of dictator Benito Mussolini when the Italian Fascist party came to power in 1922, and was later appointed a member of the Fascist Grand Council. In 1935, he toured Europe defending the fascist ideology and Mussolini's invasion of Abyssinia.

2 He died two years later, following a series of heart attacks.

GUGLIELMO MARCONI
Born: 25 April 1874,
Bologna, Italy
Died: 20 July 1937,
Rome, Italy

2
SILENT TRIBUTE
Marconi was given a state
funeral in Italy and honoured in
the UK when all BBC transmitters
closed down for two minutes.

MARCONIPHONE

Model 292

The world's finest radio-gramo-phone — a 9-valve 12-stage superheterodyne with Automatic Record Changer, Silent-Speed tuning, magnificent Multi Functional speaker, Variable selectivity and every conceivable refinement. Walnut cabinet of the very highest quality; for A.C. Mains only.

52 GNS.

previous pages

MARCONIPHONE POSTERS (1934)

In 1929, the Marconi Company
sold its Marconiphone brand to
The Gramophone Company. As these
Art Deco posters attest, models
such as the Marconiphone 292
radio-gramophone were marketed
to wealthy, urbane consumers.
The price tag of 52 guineas would
be the equivalent of more than
£3,000 ($4,000) today.

opposite

HIS MASTER'S VOICE NATIONAL
TRAIN SHOW (1934)

In 1934, EMI decked out a train
in 'His Master's Voice' livery
for a trip to dozens of towns
and cities around Great Britain.
The train is shown at Paddington
Station at the start of the
2,750-mile (4,426-km) tour.
Prime Minister Ramsay MacDonald
looks on in a pale suit.

above

COVERING THE GLOBE (c.1930)

By the beginning of the 1930s,
His Master's Voice was a
recognizable brand even in remote
parts of the world. Here 'The
Symbol of Supremacy', is seen
in a country district of Portugal
on the back of a Model T Ford
van beneath the Nipper trademark.

below

BLUMLEIN MICROPHONE (1932)

Shown here are two views of one of Blumlein's binaural ribbon microphones, one of which has the 'crinkled' ribbon and cover grille removed. The matching output transformer is housed in the black base casting. The microphone has a permanent magnet and aluminium ribbons. A pair of these microphones was used in conjunction with a pair of HB microphones for Blumlein stereo tests.

opposite

BLUMLEIN MICROPHONE (1934)

EMI's Alan Blumlein was a central figure in the history of sound recording. A binaural ribbon microphone, this is a stereo model with a pair of orthogonal ribbon velocity elements designed to maintain a uniform field between two spaced loudspeakers, thereby avoiding a 'hole' in the middle of the sound.

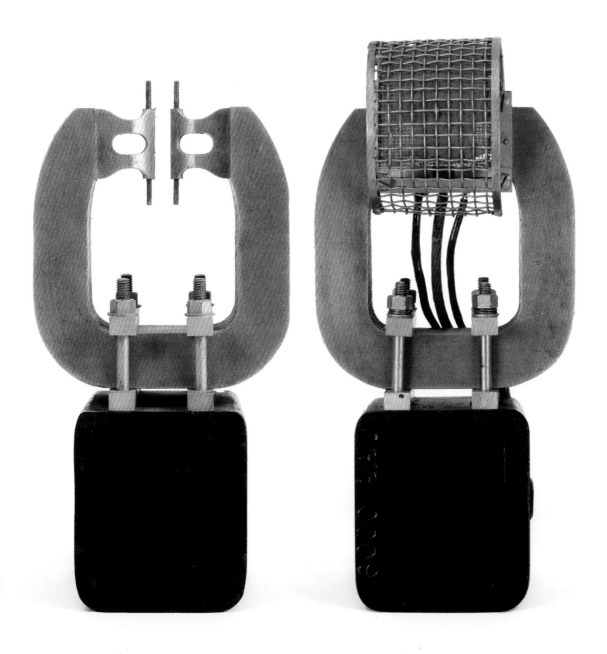

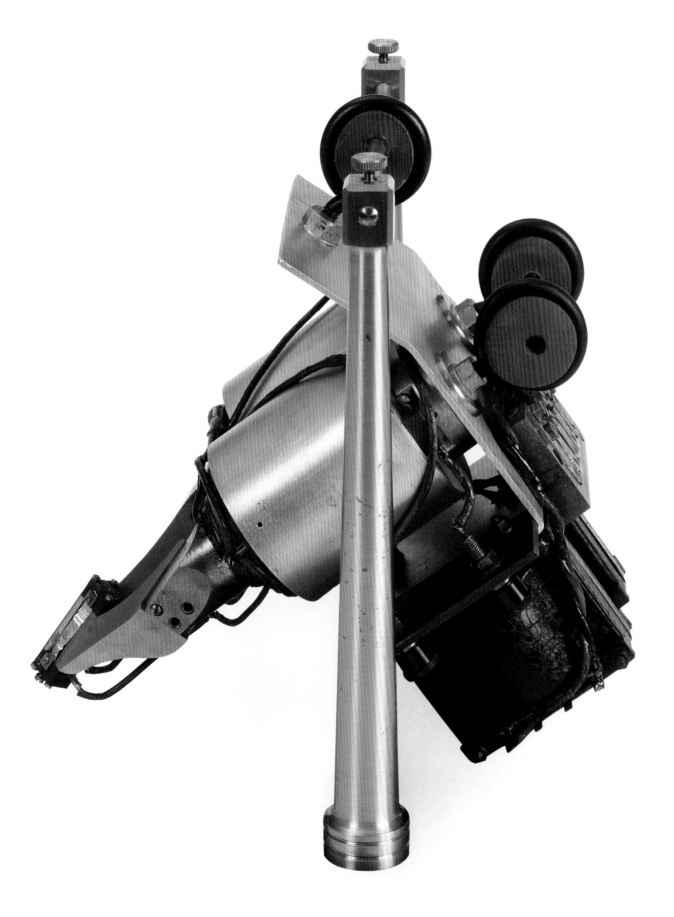

previous pages, left

THE UBIQUITOUS RECORD STORE
(c. 1915-29)

By the end of the 1920s, the
gramophone store was a familiar
sight in many towns and cities
across Europe. The proprietor
stands before the specialist
gramophone dealer, Paris-Phono,
on the Rue de Rivoli, Paris,
in 1915 (above). Dressed for
Christmas, HMV's Paris flagship
store (below) advertises the
newly fashionable 'appareils'
and 'discs' in its window.

previous pages, right

CHRISTMAS WITH HIS MASTER'S
VOICE (1935)

The first HMV shop, located
at 363 Oxford Street, London,
was opened on 20 July 1921 by
celebrated composer Sir Edward
Elgar. Seen here decorated for
Christmas 1935, it remained the
largest HMV store until it was
destroyed by fire on Boxing Day
1937. Rebuilt two years later,
there remains an HMV music
store at this address today.

right

VINYL CENTRE LABELS
(1930-58)

78-rpm records were sold in
generic sleeves, with only
record-company information
printed on them. The centre
label was used to identify
the contents of the record:
not only did it contain
the artist, song and matrix
information, but also the
composer, publisher and
sometimes a broad description
of the style of music or the
vocal range of the singer.

SERENADE
(Don Pasquale)
LENGHI-CELLINI,
Tenor, Aria with
Orch. Acc.
Sung in Italian
No. 5082

Piccadilly

IMPERIAL
BRITISH MADE

VOCAL 2921-A

LOVE LOCKED OUT

NOT FOR SALE

CRYSTALATE GRAMOPHONE
RECORD MFG. CO. LTD LONDON E.C.1

TRADE MARK

Parlophone

28180
SPEED 78   MO 107

MUSIC OF THE ORIENT
15. BALI
(BOESOENGBIEO)
Gamelan Gong "Lagu Kebiar"

Melodisc
MADE IN ENGLAND

Disc New York   1141
(D 201)

RAMBLING BLUES

WOODY GUTHRIE

(Vocal and Guitar)

MADE IN ENGLAND

Capitol

THE DECCA   RECORD CO. LTD

I TOLD YA I LOVE YA, NOW GET OUT
(Frigo, Ellis, Carter)
STAN KENTON & HIS ORCHESTRA
Vocalist : June Christy

CAP.2368   CL
B   13030

SUPRAPHON
LION WITH LYRE

42109   22714

IN THE MOOD
Polka
Jan Hlaváč
MILITARY BRASS BAND
Conductor: VACLAV THIER

MADE IN CZECHOSLOVAKIA - COPYRIGHT SUPRAPHON PRAGUE

Oriole

(O.309) (YB9086)
Francis, Day and
Hunter Ltd.   CB. 1160
Instrumental

TI-PI-TIN
(Grever)
JERRY MURAD'S HARMONICATS
and
JAN AUGUST
A Mercury Recording

MADE IN ENGLAND BY ORIOLE RECORDS LTD.

PHILIPS

ALL RIGHTS OF THE MANUFACTURER

P26010H
AA 26010 1H   P.B.108
78 r.p.m. Green

I LIVED WHEN I MET YOU
(Billy Reid)
VINCENT ROBERTO
with GERALDO and His
Orchestra

BILLY REID
PUBLICATIONS
LTD

NOT TO BE PUBLICLY PERFORMED WITHOUT LICENCE

Paxton

PR.637   H.256
CRIMOND (Arr. E. Siebert) 1.29 mins.
BLAENWERN (Rowlands, arr. E. Siebert) 1.25 mins.
THE "ALL-STAR" (CONCERT) BRASS
BAND   Cond.: Harry Mortimer
Recorded by Levy's Sound
Studios Ltd., London

W. PAXTON & CO LTD 36-38 DEAN ST LONDON W.1. MADE IN ENGLAND

ORIOLE

Speed 78 rpm.   CB 1352

Recdg. First Publd. 1957

THE COTTON SONG
(Trad. arr. McDevitt)

THE CHAS McDEVITT
SKIFFLE GROUP

BRADBURY WOOD

TRADE   MARK

Parlophone
MADE IN ENGLAND

الشرق Part. 19128 78
VDL. 177
VOIX DE L'ORIENT SERIES

NADIA HAMDI ET KREIDIE
Zaffat el Oursane

THE PARLOPHONE CO. LTD.

Kay

NEW CHRISTOPHONIC SOUND
HIGH-FIDELITY TRINIDAD RECORDING

OEF.10344 78   Made in England
CRS.019.A

THE QUEENS' CANARY—CALYPSO
(S. Francisco)
CYRIL DIAZ & ORCHESTRA
Vocal by Mighty Sparrow

PRODUCED BY CHRISTOPHER RECORDING SERVICE, PORT-OF-SPAIN, TRINIDAD, B.W.I.

opposite

ULTRAPHON TWIN-PICKUP GRAMOPHONE (1925)

Founded in Berlin in August 1925, Ultraphon existed initially to serve as a commercial outlet for Heinrich J. Küchenmeister's unique new gramophone design. Housed in an attractive Bauhaus-style circular cabinet, the Ultraphon featured a spring-driven motor and was fitted with two pickups and two horns positioned at right-angles to one other. The Ultraphone could play standard 78-rpm gramophone records, the second pickup replaying the sound 0.07 seconds after the first pickup to create a spatial 'pseudo-stereo' sound effect. Although the system provided superior sound quality and received the approval of no lesser figure than composer Arnold Schoenberg, it was not a commercial success.

right

HMV EXTENSION LOUDSPEAKER UNITS (1930-35)

Towards the end of the 1920s, when paper cone loudspeaker drivers were introduced, the first dedicated loudspeaker units began to appear. These two HMV models are typical of the period, each comprising a single speaker mounted in a wooden enclosure. Most cabinets had no in-built amplifying electronics but were connected to an existing radio or gramophone; the principle advantage of fitting a speaker in a large wooden enclosure was in emphasizing the bass frequencies.

BRITISH RADIO RECEIVER SETS (1934-49)

During the 1930s, broadcast radio became the most popular medium for listening to music, so much so that the sale of gramophone records went into decline. The HMV Model 442 (1934; left) was commonly found in wealthier British households of the period; with its elegant Art-Deco stylings and a rare PX4 triode used in its output stage, the Model 442 is now collectible. The Philips 580A (1935; below left) was the company's first superheterodyne ('superhet') radio set, and was also found in their radiogram models of the time. A long-established London electronics company, in 1937 Ferguson introduced the Model 603 table-top radio unit (opposite above). Like most domestic radios, this eight-valve, twin-rectifier unit could pick up long-wave and medium-wave broadcasts. Sir Michael Sobell was a prominent British businessman who became wealthy during the 1940s, having been awarded lucrative government contracts to provide radio equipment to the British military; the Sobell 511W (1949) (opposite below) was also able to pick up shortwave radio broadcasts.

overleaf

PRODUCTION LINE (1935)

Dozens of skilled electricians are shown here constructing valve radio sets at the EMI factory in Hayes. The rise of broadcast radio, along with the severe economic conditions of the early 1930s, resulted in a fall in the sale of gramophone records.

above

HB1B MICROPHONE (1930)
Royalty payments to Western
Electric for the use of their
Westrex recording system were so
high that Alan Blumlein created
the Columbia MC1A recorder as
an alternative. As part of the

system, this electro-acoustic
high-frequency HB (Holman-
Blumlein) microphone was
developed. Used in the EMI and
BBC recording studios, where
it was very popular, it was still
in wide use two decades later.

opposite left

RM1A RIBBON MICROPHONE (1933)
The first EMI-designed electromagnetic ribbon microphone
contained little spacing between
the rigid 2.5-inch (6-cm) ribbon
and the pole pieces, making
the frequency response limited.

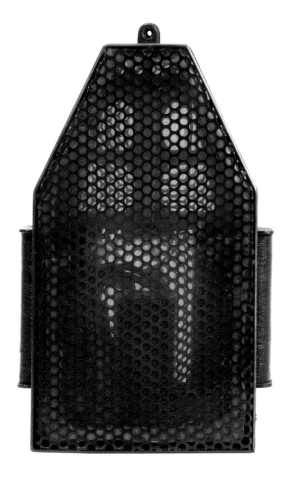

right

<u>EMI RM1B MICROPHONE (1934)</u>

Used by EMI Studios and the BBC
at Alexandra Palace TV Studios,
the RM1B features a 'horseshoe'
magnet with a thin aluminium foil
ribbon. An output transformer is
housed at the base of the magnet
within the bronze case.

overleaf

<u>VARIETY IN SOUND</u>

Even in the 1930s, the makers
of gramophone records were looking
for the next vogue. Parlophone
sought to introduce music from
around the globe with 'more than
17 separate national repertoires
searched each month' (page 174);
Regal Zonophone opted for the
'novel and unusual' (page 175).

PARLOPHONE
The
RECORD of QUALITY
More than 17 separate national repertoires are searched each month to provide the music lover at home with the finest records of the finest artistes in the world—cn
Parlophone Records
For the lover of Real Music the Parlophone Catalogue is a Treasure House of Musical Masterpieces interpreted by the Master Musicians of the world. Ask your dealer for a copy.
TRADE MARK

REGAL ZONOPHONE

THE BIGGEST SELLERS •

ALWAYS THE MOST NOVEL AND UNUSUAL IN RECORDS •

BAL (3) FINE
BAL (1)
FOCUS
FREE
X AMP
Y AMP
VOLTS
EMI
0.5mA
TIME
200 μS
4 mS
40 μS
40 mS
COARSE GAIN
TIME SCALE
X SHIFT
D.C.
A.C.
A.C. 1:1
A.C. 10:1
D.C. 10:1
D.C. 1:1
ZERO
INPUT SEL
FREE RUNNING
DRIVEN
SYNC EXT −VE
SYNC EXT. +VE
SYNC INT. −VE
SYNC INT. +VE
TRIG INT. +VE
TRIG INT. −VE
TRIG EXT. +VE
TRIG EXT. −VE
SYNC SEL
FIELD SYNC SEP.
NORMAL
MAINS
OFF
ON
TWO
INPUT 2
EARTHY
EXT. TRIG.
0·5
0·15
0·05
1·5
5
15
50
150
500

SELF AND MUTUAL
INDUCTANCE BRIDGE

Electrical engineers at
the EMI Research Laboratory
in Hayes, designed and built
their own test equipment for
use in the sound recording
process.This is a Self and
Mutual Inductance Bridge,
designed by M. T. Terry at
the EMI Research Laboratory
in 1937. Inductance is a
measure of the amount of
magnetic flux produced for
a given current.

TYPE 5 GAIN SET

The EMI Type 5 Gain Set was
standard test equipment for
measuring the gain of amplifiers
or even whole channels. Specific
sending levels of signal were
set for overall checks. The
signal sending level would have
been supplied from a pair of
Line Attenuators, one adjusting
the level in 1-dB steps, the
other in 10-dB steps. Fractions
of a decibel in both the sending
and receiving levels could then
be read from the Gain Set meter.

LIGHT ENTERTAINMENT

The star acts of the Parlophone
label were among Britain's
most popular performers of the
1930s. Harry Roy specialized in
popular risqué jazz numbers such
as 'She Had to Go and Lose it at
the Astor'. Parlophone Records
had been founded in Germany as
'Parlophon'. It became well known
for its trademark 'pound' symbol,
which had actually evolved from
a stylized 'L' used in Germany to
denote Parlophone's founder (and
parent company) Carl Lindström.

BRITAIN'S BRIGHTEST
BROADCASTING BAND

HARRY
ROY AND HIS
DANCE
ORCHESTRA
From the MAY FAIR HOTEL
LONDON

Millions Enjoy
us alike
on Radio and
Parlophone

Now **1/6** each

RECORDS ONLY FOR—
PARLOPHONE

Obtainable from

BRITAIN'S GREATEST TRUMPETER

NAT GONELLA
AND HIS GEORGIANS

1/6
EACH

For Details
of Records
see overleaf

Personnel

NAT GONELLA—Trumpet and Vocalist
Bob Dryden—Drums
Pat Smuts—Saxophone
Harold Hood—Piano
Chas. Winters—Bass
Jimmy Messini—Guitar

Photo : 20th Century Studios

RECORDS ONLY FOR—
PARLOPHONE

Obtainable from—

African
MUSIC
RHYTHM IN THE JUNGLE
Vol. 1

Recorded by LAURA C. BOULTON on
the Straus West African Expedition
of Field Museum of Natural History.

VICTOR RECORDS

WORLD MUSIC

From 1929, Laura C. Boulton made a number of field trips to remote parts of Africa to study the distribution of animal and plant life. She took with her a phonograph and made a series of groundbreaking recordings of indigenous music from the continent, little of which had ever been heard in the West. Some of these - now prized archive pieces at Harvard and Columbia universities - were issued by RCA Victor on the Victor Records label under the title 'Rhythm in the Jungle'.

BEAUTIFUL BODIES

It wasn't until the 1970s
that the proliferation of
workout programmes reached
a mainstream peak, but the
first dedicated women's fitness
regimes appeared in Victorian
times. In 1939, RCA Victor
launched 'Streamlining'
on Victor Records (above),
denoted by dark-green centre
labels, as part of its
'Instructional' series. Designed
by fitness expert Wanda Bowman-
Wilson, it comprised nineteen
exercises on four 78-rpm records,
an instruction booklet and
a diagram sheet.

overleaf, left

ELECTRICAL RECORDING POSTER
(c. 1928)

Record companies emphasized the
inherent superiority of the new
recording processes. This poster
for a new version of *Die Walküre*
gives the 'Electrical Recording'
system greater prominence than
the composer, Richard Wagner.

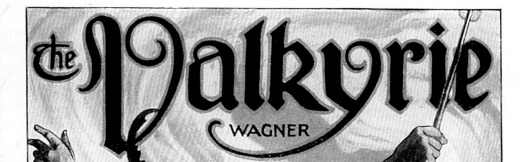

The Valkyrie

WAGNER

"His Master's Voice"

"His Master's Voice"

Electrical Recording

J.H.G.

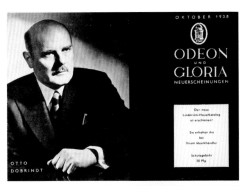

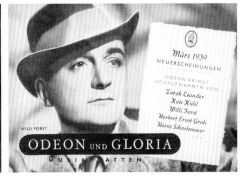

DISQUES

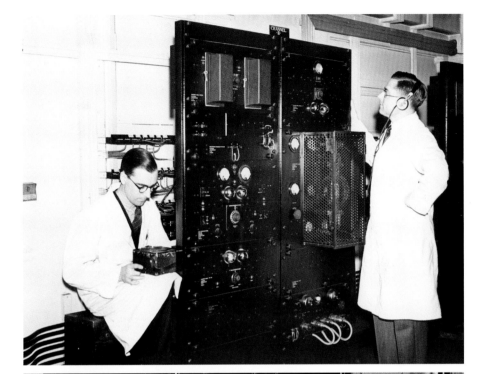

opposite

MEN IN WHITE COATS

EMI's famed Abbey Road Studios
in north London were founded
in 1931, but early photographs
show scenes more reminiscent
of a science laboratory. At this
time there was no such formal
profession as a sound engineer,
and those operating the equipment
were often employed in the
research laboratory. Until well
into the 1960s, engineers working
at Abbey Road would be required
to wear a shirt and tie and
a white lab coat.

right

GETTING THE LEVELS

Before the existence of the first
mixing desks in the late 1940s,
huge pieces of valve technology
were required to achieve the
correct audio output levels.
Since almost no commercial market
for recording equipment existed
at that time, it was usually
designed and built by scientists
at the EMI Research Laboratory
in Hayes.

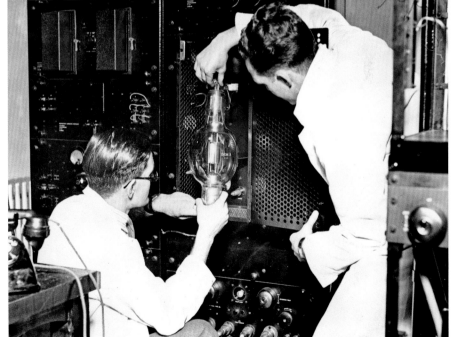

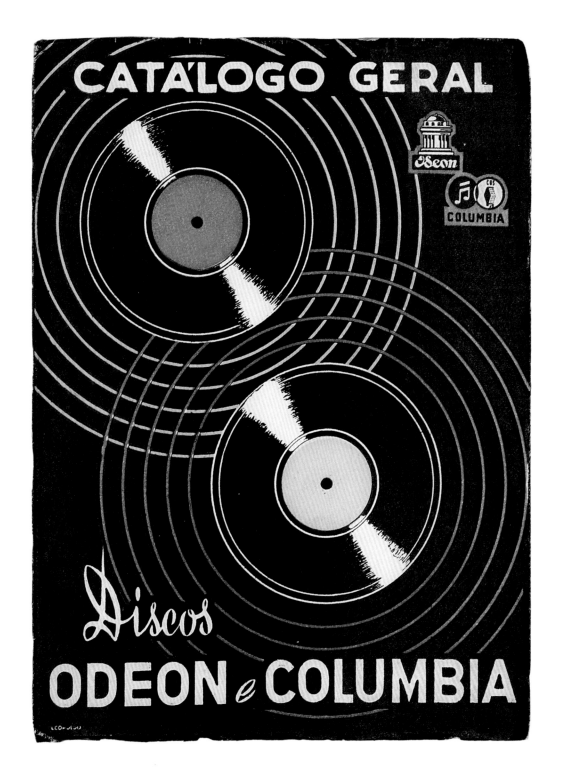

previous pages

ODEON AND COLUMBIA RECORD
CATALOGUES (1940s)
A South American Odeon record
catalogue from 1941 (left)
features popular French jazz
bandleader, Ray Ventura, and
his band on the cover. Odeon
and Columbia published a combined
record catalogue in 1945 for
the Brazilian market (right).

right

1940s RECORD CATALOGUES
Throughout the 1940s Odeon and
Columbia published combined
record listings in Brazil. The
style was distinctive: printed
in a single colour, nearly every
one featured a photograph of a
leading musician or singer of the
time combined with a drawing of
a smiling woman, dancing couple
or orchestra enticing prospective
buyers of the records to join
in the fun and lift their mood.

ALAN BLUMLEIN

For more than half a century, music buyers have been accustomed to listening to records, tapes or CDs presented through a pair of loudspeakers or headphones. This allows a piece of music to be heard not from a single direction but to be spread along a stereophonic 'field' between the two speakers, so that individual sounds can be heard coming from different positions. In fact, the impetus to create stereophonic sound came not from any desire to change the way music was reproduced – at that time monophonically, with a single loudspeaker – but to improve cinema sound.

Modern stereophonic sound was developed by British electronics engineer Alan Dower Blumlein. He was a poor school [1] student, but excelled in electronics, graduating with first-class honours from London's Imperial College. A prolific inventor – he earned 128 patents in a mere seventeen years – working for Columbia he developed the first moving-coil disc-cutting head. In 1931, Columbia merged with The Gramophone Company to form EMI and Blumlein was appointed senior sound engineer at a new research laboratory in Hayes outside London.

The idea for stereophonic sound came to Blumlein during a visit to the cinema with his wife in 1931. At a time when cinema sound typically came from a single set of loudspeakers, Blumlein became aware of the dislocation between the position of the actor on the screen and the voice coming from the loudspeaker, and sought to find a way in which the sound of the voices on the screen could follow the actors as they moved around. His idea was what he called 'binaural' sound and the patent he filed on 14 December 1931 contained many of the ideas that still form the basis of stereophonic sound in use today.

French inventor Clément Ader had, in fact, demonstrated a working two-channel audio system fifty years earlier. At the 1881 International Exposition of Electricity in Paris, Ader positioned

1
ACADEMIC STRUGGLES
Blumlein was apparently unable
to read until the age of thirteen.

multiple telephone transmitters along the front of the stage at the Paris Opera; listeners at the Palais de L'Industrie, more than a mile and a quarter (2 km) away, were then able to hear a form of stereophonic sound through two separate earpieces.

Blumlein's experiments with his binaural sound idea quickly evolved. In 1934, he made a pioneering stereophonic recording at EMI's Abbey Road Studios of Mozart's 'Jupiter' Symphony performed by the London Philharmonic Orchestra. He also devised a means of cutting the two necessary channels of sound into a single groove on a phonograph record using the two walls of the groove. It would be a further twenty-five years, however, before this became standard for producing stereophonic LPs. And in 1935, Blumlein realized his aim of making cinema sound 'move' on the screen in the world's first stereophonic film, in the form of two test shorts: *Trains at Hayes Station* and *Walking and Talking*. The soundtracks were recorded using a pair of microphones and played back through two separated loudspeakers.

It would be two decades before EMI was able to benefit from this pioneering work, when the first commercial stereophonic gramophone records began to appear. Blumlein's research was thereafter focused on the new medium of television, to which he would make similarly important contributions.

Following the outbreak of World War II, Blumlein worked on the development of the H2S radar system, intended to aid accuracy when bombing targets. On 7 June 1942, while engaged in a secret test flight, he and two of his colleagues were killed when their Halifax bomber crashed following an on-board fuel fire. He was thirty-eight years old.

Although he was barely known outside the EMI research facility during his lifetime, Alan Blumlein is now regarded as one of the key figures in the history of British audio engineering.

ALAN BLUMLEIN
Born: 29 June 1903,
Hampstead, London, UK
Died: 7 June 1942,
Welsh Bicknor, UK

2
STEREO FOR THE RICH
The system was later commercialized under the name Le Théâtrophone, as a means of enabling subscribers to listen to theatre and opera performances that they were unable to attend. Popular among wealthy Parisians, by the 1920s the system had become redundant with the onset of radio broadcasting.

3
NO STEREO
Although impressed with Blumlein's work, EMI saw limited commercial use in it, not least because the idea of cinema 'talkies' played through a single speaker was still regarded as a novelty at this time.

MC4 MONOPHONIC DISC CUTTER
(1932)

Alan Blumlein designed the
improved MC4 disc cutter to
supersede the original MC1.
It featured lighter rubber
mounting blocks to aid suspension,
replacing the steel springs
used on the earlier version.
This lower mass enabled higher
frequencies to be recorded.

EXPERIMENTAL RECORDING HEAD
(1933)

This cutter was used by
Alan Blumlein in his first
binaural stereophonic gramophone
experiments. It was built using
a pair of Western Electric
monaural disc cutters, coupled
to provide horizontal and
vertical movements to the
recording stylus.

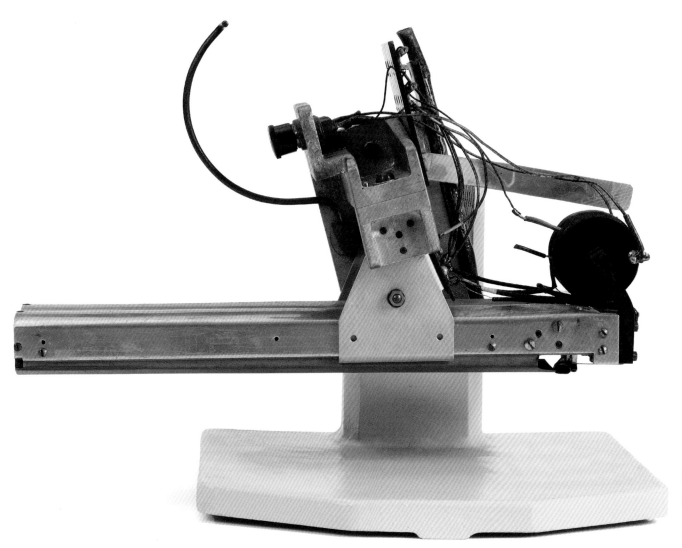

below

COLUMBIA MOVING-COIL LATHE (1922-25)

The first stage in the creation of a gramophone record, the lathe mechanism was used to cut audio signals into the blank wax disc. The lathe was originally used for acoustic recording, but later converted to take an electronic cutter head.

overleaf

NIPPER THE CELEBRITY

By the end of the 1930s, more than four decades after his death, Nipper had reached a level of canine celebrity perhaps matched only by Hollywood's Rin-Tin-Tin. Super-sized plastic models of Nipper were mass-produced for display in gramophone stores worldwide.

<u>WATERS CONLEY</u>
<u>GRAMOPHONE (1940)</u>
Long after the development of
electric-powered gramophones,
these Waters Conley acoustic
wind-up models were built
for the United States Army,

for use in war zones where
there was no access to a power
supply. Built in a robust
military green casing, they
were still in use as late
as the Korean War in the
early 1950s.

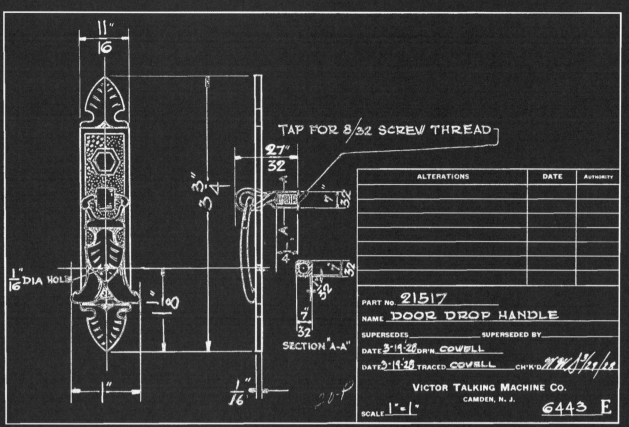

TAP FOR 8/32 SCREW THREAD

$\frac{11"}{16}$

$\frac{27"}{32}$

$3\frac{3}{4}"$

$\frac{1}{16}"$ DIA HOLE

$1\frac{1}{8}"$

$1"$

$\frac{1}{16}"$

SECTION "A-A"

$\frac{7}{32}$

ALTERATIONS	DATE	AUTHORITY

PART No. 21517
NAME DOOR DROP HANDLE
SUPERSEDES_____ SUPERSEDED BY_____
DATE 3-19-28 DR'N COWELL
DATE 3-19-28 TRACED COWELL CH'K'D W.W.S 3/22/28
VICTOR TALKING MACHINE CO.
CAMDEN, N. J.
SCALE 1"=1"   6443 E

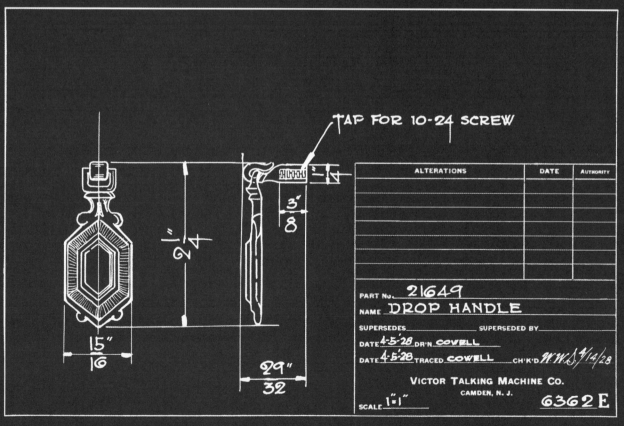

TAP FOR 10-24 SCREW

$2\frac{1}{4}"$

$\frac{3}{8}"$

$\frac{15"}{16}$

$\frac{29"}{32}$

ALTERATIONS	DATE	AUTHORITY

PART No. 21649
NAME DROP HANDLE
SUPERSEDES_____ SUPERSEDED BY_____
DATE 4-5-28 DR'N COWELL
DATE 4-5-28 TRACED COWELL CH'K'D W.W.S 4/14/28
VICTOR TALKING MACHINE CO.
CAMDEN, N. J.
SCALE 1"=1"   6362 E

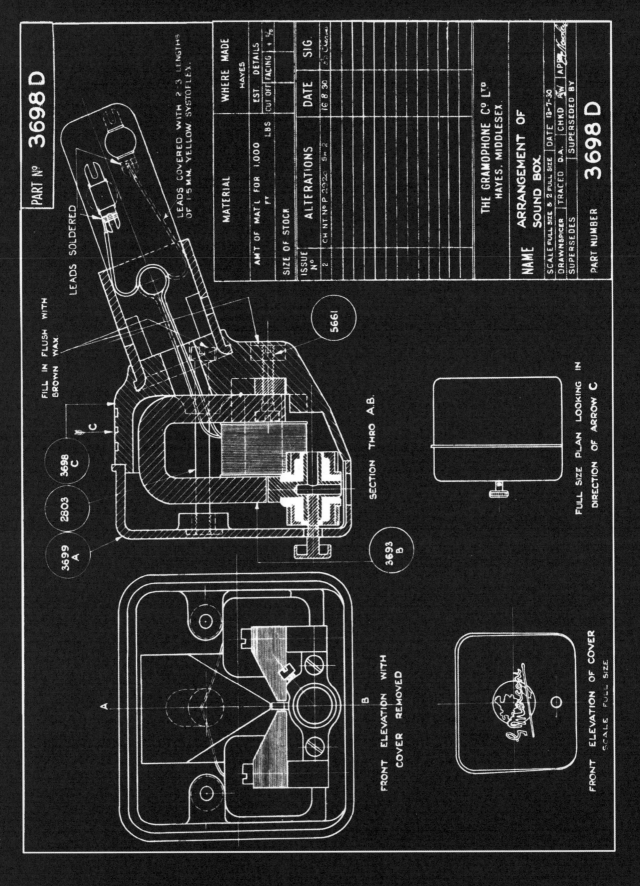

PART N? **3698 D**

LEADS COVERED WITH 2-3 LENGTHS
OF 1-5 M.M. YELLOW SYSTOFLEX.

LEADS SOLDERED

FILL IN FLUSH WITH
BROWN WAX.

SECTION THRO A.B.

FULL SIZE PLAN LOOKING IN
DIRECTION OF ARROW C

FRONT ELEVATION WITH
COVER REMOVED

FRONT ELEVATION OF COVER
SCALE FULL SIZE.

MATERIAL	WHERE MADE
	HAYES

	EST DETAILS	
AMT OF MAT L FOR 1,000	CUT OFF	FACING	+ ⅝
	FT	LBS	
SIZE OF STOCK		

ISSUE N°	ALTERATIONS	DATE	SIG.
2	CH NT N° P 2920 5-2	16 8 30	

THE GRAMOPHONE C? L?
HAYES. MIDDLESEX.

NAME **ARRANGEMENT OF
SOUND BOX.**

SCALE FULL SIZE & 2 FULL SIZE	DATE 13-7-30
DRAWN SPICER	TRACED D.A. CHKD A/w APP Needle
SUPERSEDES	SUPERSEDED BY

PART NUMBER **3698 D**

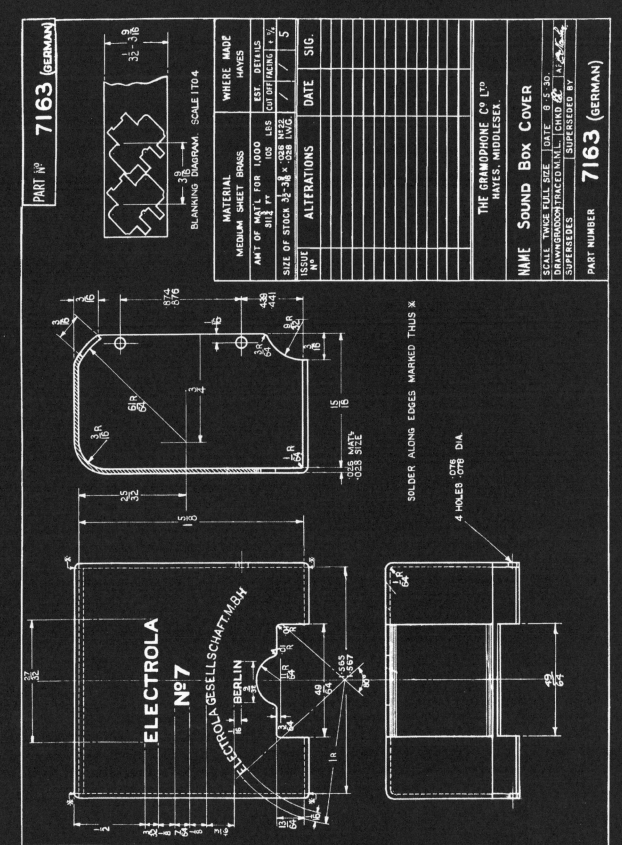

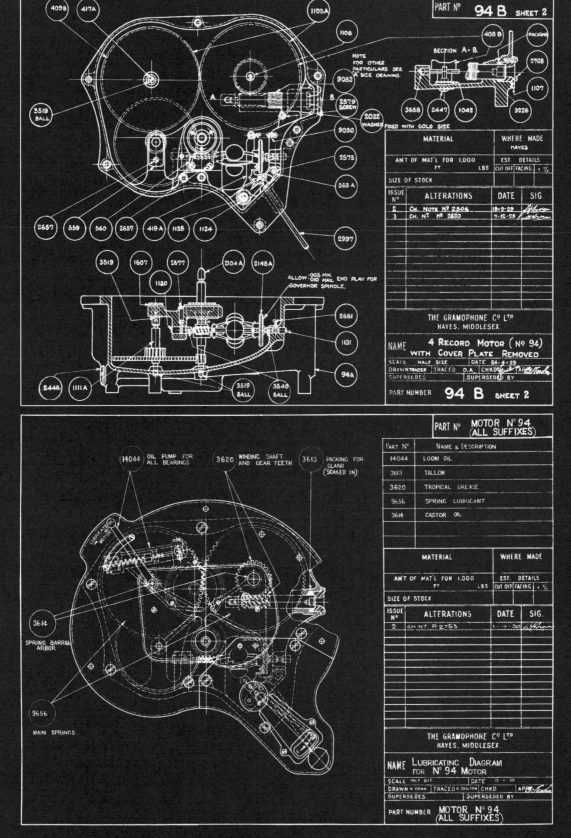

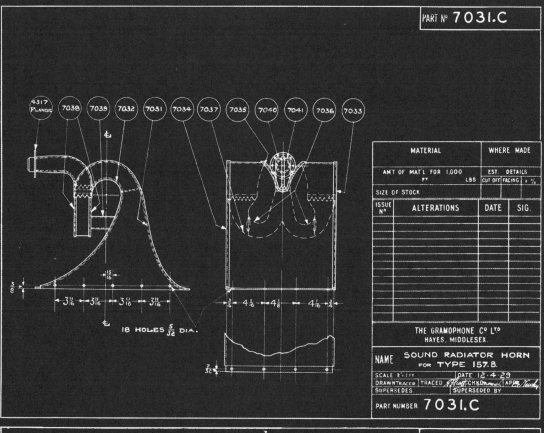

PART № 7031.C

4317 FLANGE	7038	7039	7032	7031	7034	7037	7035	7040	7041	7036	7033

18 HOLES $\frac{5}{32}$ DIA.

MATERIAL		WHERE MADE
AMT OF MAT'L FOR 1,000 FT	LBS	EST. CUT OFF / DETAILS FACING / + %
SIZE OF STOCK		

ISSUE N°	ALTERATIONS	DATE	SIG.

THE GRAMOPHONE C° L™
HAYES, MIDDLESEX.

NAME SOUND RADIATOR HORN FOR TYPE 157.B.

SCALE 2″=1FT DATE 12·4·29
DRAWN TRACER TRACED CHKD APP.
SUPERSEDES SUPERSEDED BY

PART NUMBER 7031.C

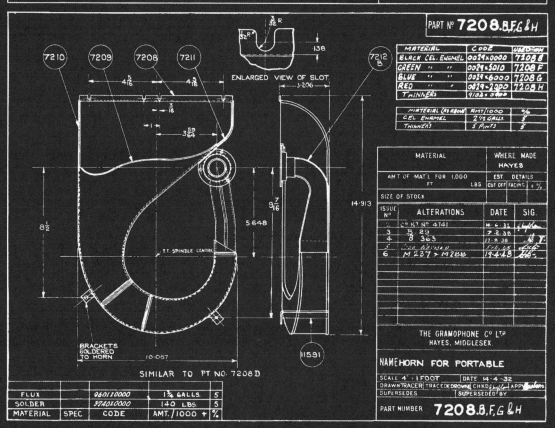

PART № 7208.B,F,G&H

ENLARGED VIEW OF SLOT.

SIMILAR TO PT NO. 7208D

BRACKETS SOLDERED TO HORN

T.T. SPINDLE CENTRE

MATERIAL	CODE	USED ON
BLACK CEL. ENAMEL	0024X0000	7208 B
GREEN " "	0024X5010	7208 F
BLUE " "	0024X6000	7208 G
RED " "	0024X7000	7208 H
THINNERS	9102X0000	

MATERIAL (AIRBORN)	AMT/1000	%
CEL. ENAMEL	2½ GALLS	5
THINNERS	5 PINTS	5

MATERIAL		WHERE MADE HAYES
AMT OF MAT'L FOR 1,000 FT	LBS	EST. CUT OFF / DETAILS FACING / + %
SIZE OF STOCK		

ISSUE N°	ALTERATIONS	DATE	SIG.
2	C° NT N° 4741	14·6·32	
3	B. 29	7·2·36	
4	B 363	17·8·38	
5		5·6·45	
6	M 237 & M 288	19·4·48	

THE GRAMOPHONE C° L™
HAYES, MIDDLESEX.

NAME HORN FOR PORTABLE

SCALE 4″=1FOOT DATE 14·4·32
DRAWN TRACER TRACED DRAWN CHKD APP
SUPERSEDES SUPERSEDED BY

PART NUMBER 7208.B,F,G&H

FLUX		960110000	1¾ GALLS.	5
SOLDER		374010000	140 LBS.	5
MATERIAL	SPEC.	CODE	AMT./1000 +	%

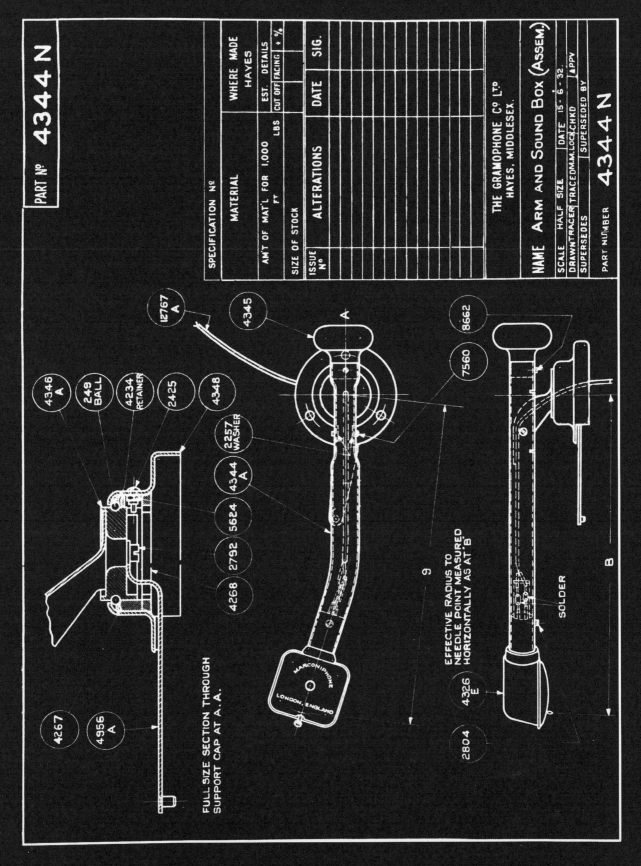

1932: ARM AND SOUNDBOX (ASSEMBLY) NO.4344N

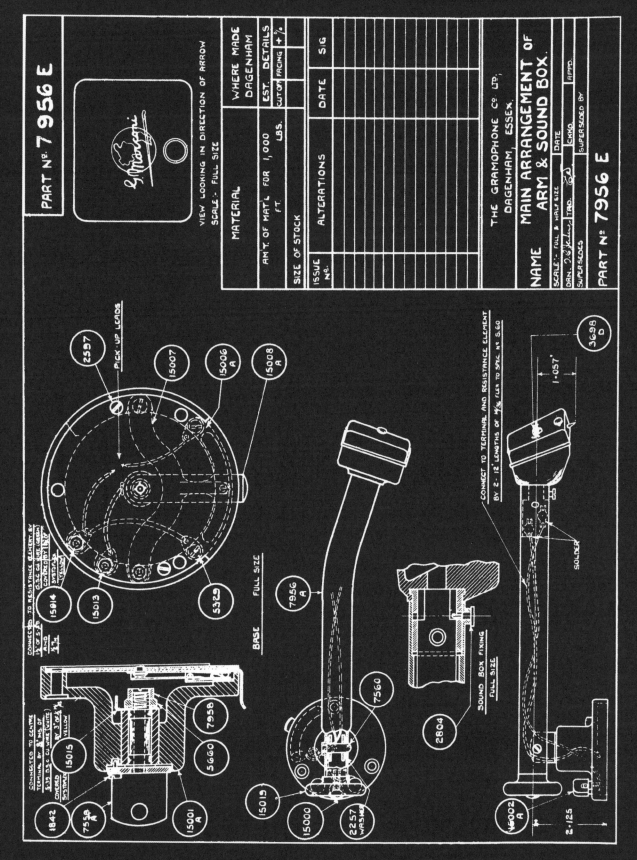

MAIN ARRANGEMENT OF ARM AND SOUNDBOX NO.7956E

206.207

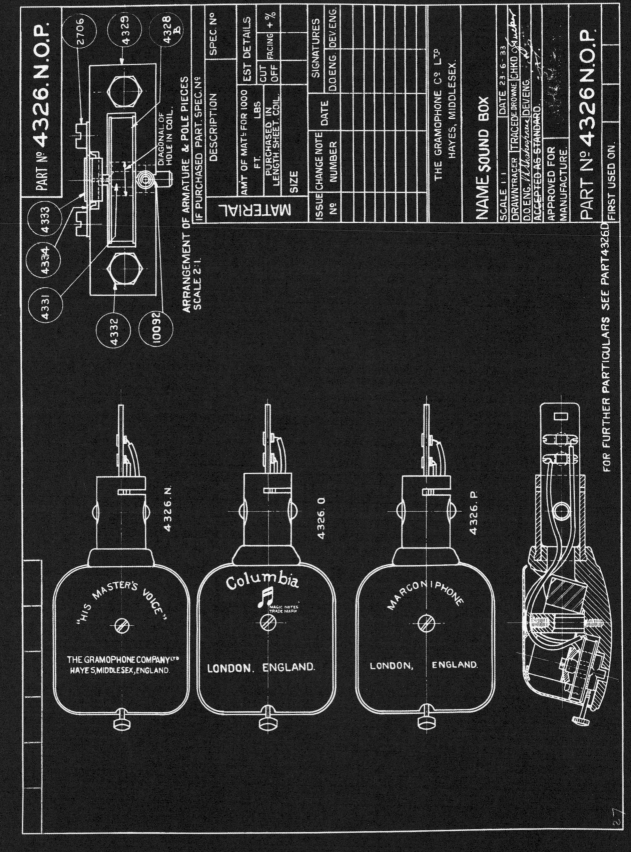

third wave
MAGNETIC ERA

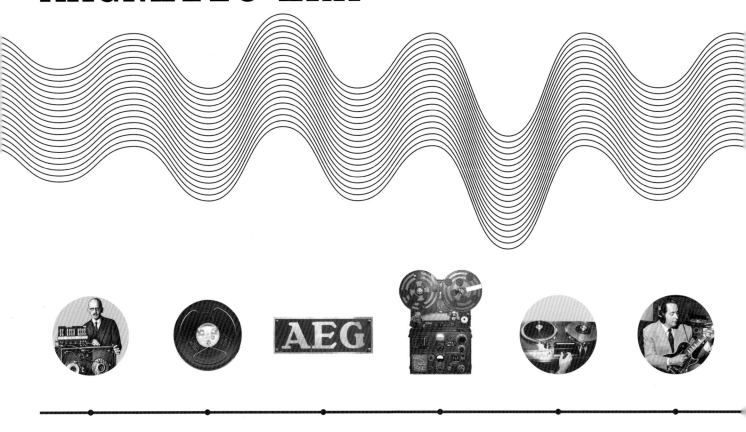

1928

Fritz Pfleumer receives a patent for magnetic tape recording in Germany. The tapes become widely used over the next decade.

1934

Building on the work of Fritz Pfleumer, BASF (part of I. G. Farben) produces recording tape comprising carbonyl iron powder on plastic film.

1935

Designed and built in Germany, the AEG range of Magnetophon tape machines provides a template for audio recording over the next fifty years.

1945

Allied forces capture Magnetophon magnetic tape recorders in Frankfurt. Far superior to existing US counterparts, the machines are taken back to the States, analysed, and inspire a revolution in recording technology.

1948

The Ampex Model 200A becomes the first commercial reel-to-reel tape recorder. Singer Bing Crosby, who had invested $50,000 in its development, gives the second machine produced to his friend Les Paul. The same year Columbia Records introduces the 12-inch (30-cm), 33⅓-rpm, long-playing microgroove album.

1949

'Lover (When You're Near Me)' is released on Capitol Records. It features eight individual guitar parts played by musician Les Paul – the first time the guitarist had released a multi-track recording. Also that year, RCA Victor introduce the 45-rpm record to compete with new Columbia's 12-inch (30-cm) album.

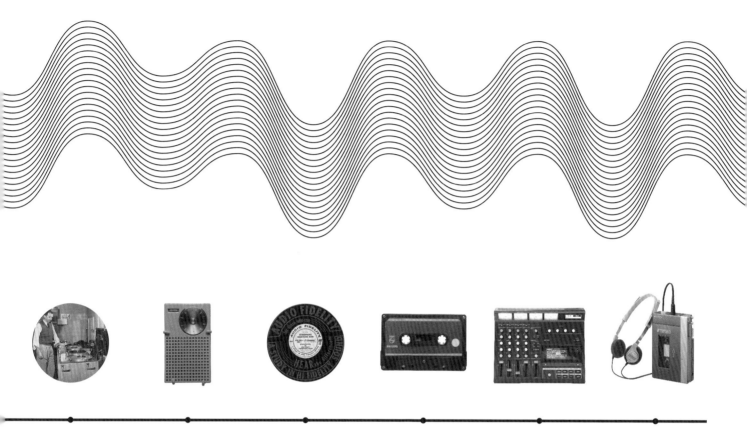

1951

Bing Crosby Enterprises gives the first demonstration of a video recorder on 11 November.

1954

The first commercially produced transistor radio – the Regency TR-1 – goes on sale.

1957

In November, the Audio Fidelity label issues the first mass-produced stereophonic long-playing records. These are initially given to music-store owners for demonstration purposes.

1962

Philips produces the Compact Cassette.

1979

Japan's TEAC Corporation revolutionizes creative home recording with the 144 Portastudio, a four-track cassette recorder with an in-built mixing desk.

1979

On 1 July, Sony releases the Sony Walkman TPS-L2, retailing at $150. It is the first personal stereo tape player.

A lthough the magnetic tape recorder would not have a major impact on the world of audio technology until the late 1940s, its basic principles were evolving at the same time that the phonograph and gramophone were fighting out the first consumer format war.

Engineer Oberlin Smith had visited Edison's laboratory at Menlo Park in 1878. A music lover, Smith was frustrated by the poor sound quality of the foil-covered cylinder. He proposed using the mouthpiece from one of Alexander Graham Bell's telephones to convert sound into electrical signals: current would run through a magnetic coil, creating a series of magnetic pulses. The pattern would be imprinted on a 'thread' as it passed through the coil. A successful businessman, Smith had little free time to develop his idea. Instead, on 8 September 1888, he published an article on the subject in the science journal *The Electrical World*, entitled 'Some Possible Forms of Phonograph'. He detailed a magnetic wire recording machine and provided diagrams depicting the basic mechanism. Even though he built no working prototype, Smith appears to have been the first person to have described the principles of magnetic tape recording.

Danish engineer Valdemar Poulsen created the first 1 operational system, the Telegraphone. A ribbon (in this case a spool of steel piano wire) was pulled at a constant speed across a magnetic recording head at the same time that sound captured through a mouthpiece was converted to electrical pulses. The recording head imposed these pulses as a pattern of magnetization onto the wire. The wire could then be passed across a playback head that detected changes in the magnetic field stored on the wire; in a mirror process, the electrical pulses could be converted back to audible sound.

Poulsen sold his patent to a group of investors who founded the American Telegraphone Company. The machines produced

1

HISTORIC PRECEDENT
Although Poulsen was granted
a patent for his device in 1898,
there can be little question
that he was familiar with
the Oberlin Smith article
of ten years before.

were marketed primarily for business uses, such as office dictation. The technology proved useful for other purposes too, though: at the start of World War I in 1914, the German navy used recorders bought from American Telegraphone (America was adopting a neutral stance at this point) to transmit speeded-up messages from the eastern seaboard to submarines in the Atlantic. A crude form of encoding, these messages could only be made intelligible when played back at the correct speed on a similar machine.

Wire-based magnetic recording underwent significant improvements during the 1920s. Using De Forest's Audion valve technology, German engineer Curt Stille developed an electronic amplifier and integrated it with a wire recorder to create his own superior dictation machine. Stille also came into contact with S. Joseph Begun, a young graduate from Berlin's Institute of Technology, who invented the Dailygraph recorder – arguably a precursor to the compact cassette – and in 1933 the Textophone, widely used within the Nazi government. Begun's final innovation at this time was the Stahltone-Bandmaschine, a mobile steel tape recorder.

Audio fidelity would always remain an issue with wire recording systems, but a promising solution came from an unexpected source when German inventor Fritz Pfleumer perfected a method of coating cigarette papers with bronze powder. Pfleumer had a keen interest in sound recording, and applied the same principle to iron oxide powder. On 1 January 1928, he was granted a patent for his 'sounding paper'. In practice, though, his thin strips of paper 'tape' were ineffective and tore easily when used.

The idea interested Hermann Buchner, Chairman of Allgemeine Elektricitäts-Gesellschaft AG (AEG), who in 1932 signed an agreement with Pfleumer to develop a new type of

2
DOCUMENTING FASCISM
The Stahltone-Bandmaschine was adopted for outside radio broadcasts and was used extensively during the 1936 Berlin Olympics. Shortly afterwards, like many other German Jews, Begun fled the Nazis to start a new life in the USA.

3
AURAL PROPAGANDA
Later, improved models were used by the Nazis in war-time broadcasting, the quality reaching such a level that it became impossible for the Allies to tell if propaganda speeches were being made live at a specific location or were recordings.

magnetic recorder with chemist Friedrich Matthias from BASF. The result was the AEG Magnetophon K1, the first practical tape recorder. A portable machine – the letter 'K' stands for *koffer* ('suitcase') – the K1 was a self-contained unit incorporating an in-built amplifier and loudspeaker. Matthias, meanwhile, created a radical new recording medium based around cellulose acetate tape with a bonded layer of carbonyl iron powder. Over the course of three years, this collaboration produced what amounted to a blueprint for every analogue magnetic tape recorder that followed.

While AEG seemed to have perfected the format, in Britain, Japan and the United States engineers were pursuing the idea of recording on steel tape. In 1935, the Marconi-Stille recorder appeared, offering the first onboard tape-editing block; steel tape was brittle and prone to snapping, so a method for spot-welding broken tape was built into the recorder. It was not a practical system, though; the 2,700-m spools of tape weighed approximately 15 kg each and were too heavy for most operators to lift and mount.

In Germany, AEG and BASF continued to move the technology forward although, with the outbreak of war, many of the developments that took place were hidden from the Allies and actively used as part of the Nazi war effort. BASF continued to experiment with the chemical make-up of the tapes, in 1939 settling on the use of ferric oxide powder and different types of plastic base for the tape itself. Other Magnetophon models were produced, among them a field version – the Tonschreiber ('soundwriter') – designed for the German military.

More surprisingly, perhaps, AEG engineers were also known to have produced more than 200 wartime stereophonic recordings – the first to be made on magnetic tape. The principles of stereo had been developed in the UK in the early 1930s by Alan Blumlein as a way of improving clarity in cinema sound, but

WORLD LEADER
By 1943, the Magnetophon had become the de facto high-fidelity recording system, outperforming the gramophone in almost every way. Such was its pre-eminence that 'Magnetophon' became a generic word for a tape recorder in many European languages.

it quickly became clear that it could also be used with music to recreate the effect of hearing a live concert.

The commercial development of magnetic tape recording in America was due in no small way to the efforts of John T. ('Jack') Mullin and singer Bing Crosby. Serving in the US military in Germany at the end of World War II, Mullin would listen to what appeared to be live radio broadcasts and wonder how it was possible for full orchestras to be performing at all hours of the night. His answer came when he discovered a pair of seized Magnetophons and boxes of magnetic tape, which he then had sent back to the United States. Mullin carried out numerous modifications and in 1947 was introduced to Alexander Poniatoff, the owner of a progressive young electrical company called Ampex. Mullin also became acquainted with the singer Bing Crosby. At this time, Crosby performed his popular Philco radio show twice on the same evening to accommodate the time differences within the United States. Ampex had already built the first Model 200A tape recorder, and were able expand production when Crosby invested $50,000 in the company. In 1948, the great crooner was able to record his west-coast show live on an Ampex tape deck, then play back the recording later that evening for the east-coast broadcast.

One of the many advantages of recording with magnetic tape was that it was possible to creatively edit performances by physically cutting and re-joining the tape. The practice began in the world of classical recording, where an audible mistake necessitated abandoning a recording and starting again from scratch. With magnetic tape, however, it was possible to 'splice' together sections from different recordings to produce a composite performance. Eventually it would become standard practice to make multiple recordings then 'comp' together the best parts of each one.

5

AHEAD OF HIS TIME
Ampex would later also develop the first practical videotape recorder, which in 1956 Crosby began using to pre-record his television shows.

6

COMPING AND POP
Many of Elvis Presley's best-known songs from the 1950s feature verse and chorus sections recorded at different times; British producer Joe Meek took this idea even further, sometimes recording different parts of the same song with different sets of musicians before splicing together a final master version.

MAGNETIC ERA

The 1950s saw the birth of multi-track recording. Guitarist Les Paul and other experimentally minded musicians had pioneered the use of 'sound-on-sound' recording to play multiple parts on the same piece of music. By inserting an additional playback head, Paul could play along with a previously recorded part; both recordings could then be mixed onto a second track. For greater control, he began to use a second tape recorder, capturing a performance on the first deck, then recording himself on the second deck playing along with the mixed-in sound from the first deck. Paul's early 1950s recordings astounded listeners, who couldn't comprehend how one musician could play six different guitar parts at once.

The first Ampex tape recorders were either single-channel (mono) or two-channel (stereo) machines. In 1952, Ampex demonstrated the first genuine multi-track machine, which featured three discrete channels. It functioned in much the same way as a regular machine, but the heads were each split so that three separate lines of recordings could be made on the same tape at the same time; rather like three synchronized single-channel tape recorders. Individual channels could be recorded while others were being monitored, allowing for 'overdubs' alongside parts that had already been recorded. It was commonly used to record instrumental parts on two channels and vocals on a third. The three channels could then be mixed down to produce a master. Ampex produced the first eight-track tape recorder as early as 1957, but three- and four-track tape recorders were the norm in recording studios until well into the 1960s. During the 1970s, 16- and 24-track systems became the norm in professional studios. Ampex tape recorders were aimed firmly at the professional market, although during the 1950s other manufacturers emerged to produce cheaper domestic models that found favour with the general public until the arrival of the compact cassette.

7

THE FAB FOUR-TRACK
As late as 1967, The Beatles'
*Sgt. Pepper's Lonely Hearts
Club Band* album was recorded
on four-track recorders
at EMI's Abbey Road
Studios in London.

Philips introduced the compact cassette in 1963. It was intended as a consumer medium and designed for convenience: the user no longer had to come into direct contact with the tape, as it was held in place in a small plastic cartridge that slotted into the player. The format made its public debut just as the transistor, a solid-state replacement for the thermionic triode valve, began to have an impact on the way technology was designed. Accompanying the first compact cassettes were small battery-powered portable cassette players and recorders a fraction of the size of a domestic reel-to-reel unit. The cassette format initially produced inferior sound. The tapes were narrower and thinner, and the playback speed was slow. With improvements in both equipment and tape, however, it found a place in the 'hi-fi' world, mainly because of the inclusion of the Dolby B noise-reduction system, which reduced background tape hiss.

Developed at around the same time as the compact cassette, the eight-track tape was also a cartridge-based system but intended for use in cars. The cartridge contained a continuous loop of tape and was so-named because the music was recorded as four parallel pairs of stereo tracks on a single piece of tape. Switching between tracks was achieved automatically by mechanically altering the height of the playback head so that it aligned with the correct piece of music.

The compact cassette remains the most popular consumer medium for audio recording in history. But while there was once a global market for pre-recorded cassette tapes, these never truly won the affections of the audio connoisseur, for whom the vinyl record would always sound superior. The magnetic era began to decline in the 1980s, with the rise of the digital compact disc. Yet in the same way that a niche market continues to flourish for lovers of vinyl, pre-recorded compact cassettes are still produced and bought, albeit in small numbers.

8

9

8
ON THE ROAD
The eight-track format flourished into the 1970s, mainly because many US car manufacturers offered eight-track players as a standard feature in their cars. Some eight-track decks did make their way into domestic hi-fi systems, but as they offered no facility for recording, the format was not directly comparable with the compact cassette.

9
DECKS APPEAL
It is a testament to the enduring affection for compact cassettes that the last car to feature a built-in cassette deck was produced relatively recently – the 2010 Lexus C430 convertible.

right

AEG TONSCHREIBER 'B' MAGNETIC TAPE RECORDER (1939)

AEG/Telefunken built the first Magnetophon tape recorders in 1934. The company made enormous technological progress in this area although, during the build-up to the outbreak of World War II in 1939, this was hidden from scientists and engineers in Britain and America. The Tonschreiber 'b' was developed for military monitoring purposes, but was also widely used in German radio broadcasts throughout the war. Like other Magnetophon models, the Tonschreiber 'b' provided a template for all tape recorders built over the next five decades.

opposite

BING CROSBY WITH THE AMPEX 200A TAPE RECORDER (1947)

Bing Crosby played a significant role in the popularization of the tape recorder in the entertainment business. A $50,000 interest-free loan from the singer enabled the tiny Ampex company to produce and market the 200A tape recorder, which Crosby used in the recordings of his coast-to-coast Philco radio show from 1947.

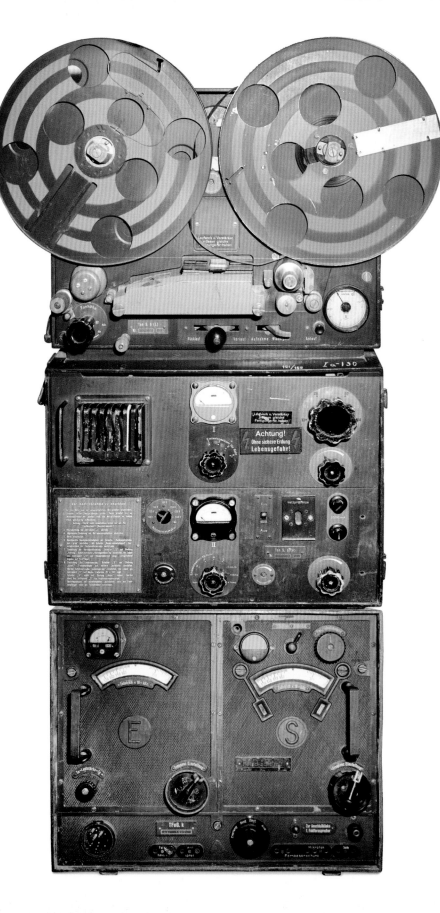

LES PAUL

Part musician, part engineer, part inventor, Lester William Polsfuss (Les Paul) was one of the most remarkable figures in the evolution of music technology, combining a successful career as a guitarist and entertainer with the development of several important technical innovations.

Les Paul's enduring fame can be attributed to his involvement in 1952 with the famous Gibson electric guitar that still bears his signature on the headstock. Although his specific role in the design of that guitar is debated, he was undoubtedly one of a small number of pioneers in the 1940s who came up with the idea of building an electric guitar with a solid – rather than hollow – body. His prototype model, 'The Log', was a 4 × 4-inch (10 × 10- cm) block of pine fitted with pickups and a homemade tremolo arm, attached to a guitar neck; he later added two halves of an Epiphone archtop guitar either side of it, for a more conventional look.

A successful and well-regarded jazz guitarist, during the 1940s Paul had played with artists such as The Andrews Sisters and Nat 'King' Cole, and provided the memorable guitar accompaniment for Bing Crosby's 1945 hit 'It's Been a Long, Long Time'. During this time, he also experimented with a rudimentary sound-on-sound technique for building up multiple overdubs on the same song made by recording directly to acetate records. He would record the first part onto a disc, and then record a second part alongside the sound from the first disc. In this way, he was able to create multiple guitar harmonies, a sound characteristic of many of his future recordings.

Les Paul's friendship with Bing Crosby proved to be valuable. One of the world's most popular singers, Crosby also played a pivotal role in the commercial development of the tape recorder. During the final months of World War II it became evident that German engineers had developed a recording format superior to anything known by the Allies. Serving in the US Army Signal

1

1

SOLID IMPROVEMENT
The greater body mass of
'The Log' reduced vibration,
so it was less likely to cause
howling feedback than a hollow-
bodied guitar.

Corps, 'Jack' Mullin was assigned to investigate Nazi technology. Mullin came across a pair of AEG Magnetophon tape recorders and fifty reels of a plastic-backed magnetic tape. He had them shipped back to the United States, where he spent the next year making modifications and improvements to audio sound. In 1947, he gave a series of 'blind' demonstrations, in which an audience was invited to compare a live performer with a tape recording hidden behind a curtain. Crosby was deeply impressed, realizing that this would enable him to record his popular weekly radio shows in advance rather than live. He made Mullin his technical director and invested $50,000 in a six-man company called Ampex to build Mullin's tape recorders.

2

In 1948, Crosby gave Les Paul one of the first Ampex Model 200A one-track tape recorders. He immediately began experimenting, placing an additional playback head before the existing set of erase/record/playback heads. This enabled him to combine an original track with a new part that he played live, to create a new mono track. The technique was essentially destructive: each time a new layer was recorded, it erased the previous layer; one mistake would render the recording useless. Paul overcame this problem by obtaining a second Model 200A

3

and copying from one tape recorder to another. Newly married to singer Mary Ford, he used this technique not only on his guitar parts but also on Ford's vocals, and together as a duo in the early 1950s they were among America's most popular artists.

Les Paul continued to combine music and technical innovation for the rest of his life. He was actively involved in the development of the first Ampex eight-track system, worked on designs for an early synthesizer, and continued to come up with modifications to his guitars, some of which were implemented by Gibson. But he remained a musician to the very end, playing weekly Monday-night sessions at a New York City jazz club well into his nineties.

LES PAUL
Born: 9 June 1915,
Waukesha, Wisconsin, USA
Died: August 13 2009, White
Plains, New York. USA

2
TAPING BING
Crosby himself received Ampex model numbers 1 and 2. They were first used to record the 27th instalment of his show's 1947-48 season.

3
A GROUNDBREAKING RELEASE
One of Paul's first experiments was issued by Capitol Records: the instrumental 'Lover' featured eight different guitar parts, some recorded at different speeds to create unusual effects.

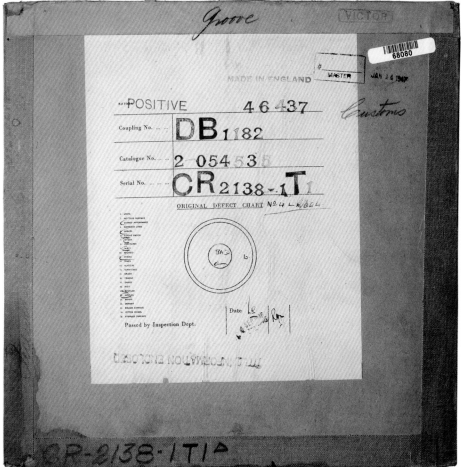

GRAMOPHONE RECORD PRESSING PROCESS (1930s)

The original recording made by the cutting lathe from a highly polished wax 'blank' was the wax master or 'positive' (above). Although playable, these were extremely delicate and easy to damage until they were 'fixed' in an electrotyping bath by being brushed with graphite powder and lowered into a tank of nickel or copper solution. When the metal had set, it was peeled away from the wax master, leaving a metal 'negative' (opposite left) - an inverse copy of the record. This was placed in an electrotyping bath to create the 'mother' (opposite right) - a playable metal gramophone record. From this, the stamper was made, from which the final gramophone records were mass-produced.

opposite

<u>GRAMOPHONE RECORD</u>
<u>MANUFACTURE IN CALCUTTA,</u>
<u>INDIA</u> (1940s)

India's first gramophone-record-
pressing plant was set up in
1908 in Dum Dum, a suburb north
of Calcutta. These photographs
show Indian workers at an EMI
plant in Calcutta. In the Indian
subcontinent, 78-rpm gramophone
records were hugely popular and
EMI continued their production
until 1968 - long after their
decline in the West. EMI even
produced Indian 78s by The
Beatles on the Parlophone label.

right

<u>GRAMOPHONE STORES IN BOMBAY</u>
<u>AND CALCUTTA</u> (1940s)

Typically, music salons in
India were small stores selling
gramophones and records. The
posters on the store shutters
of the Bombay Music Mart can
be seen to advertise record
labels such as Kohinoor and
Maxitone. Originally set up
as local independents, they
were eventually consumed by the
mighty His Master's Voice empire.

1-3

4-6

7-9

TOP ROW (1-3)

1. The engineer takes a wax blank and places it on the cutting lathe. 2. He starts the lathe and controls the recording levels. 3. When the recording is finished, the newly cut master disc is made electrically conductive; here it is coated with a fine bronze powder.

CENTRE ROW (4-6)

4. The metallized wax is fitted to a spindle to provide an electrical contact. 5. It is immersed in an electro-plating bath where it is revolved to give an even copper coating. 6. The copper shell that has 'grown' on the wax is removed; this negative imprint is the 'master'.

BOTTOM ROW (7-9)

7. A positive 'mother' is grown from the master. 8. This is strengthened by fixing to a rigid backing plate. The matrix/stamper is made from this plate. 9. The material from which the records are pressed is made from slate powder, carbon black, shellac, copal and resin.

10-12

13-15

16-18

TOP ROW (10-12)

10. The materials are ground
separately, mixed and ground
once again. 11. When mixed, the
warm pressing compound comes out
as a pliable 'blanket'. 12. The
material is compressed, cooled
and then marked into what are
called 'biscuits' - the amount
needed to press one record.

CENTRE ROW (13-15)

13. The two stampers (one for
each side of the record) and
the centre labels are applied
to each side of the press.
14. The 'biscuit' is rolled out
on a hotplate ready for insertion
into the press. 15. The rolled
'biscuit' is inserted before
the hydraulic press is closed.

BOTTOM ROW (16-18)

16. The press is opened to reveal
the finished gramophone record.
17. A sample selection of the
records is tested for pressing
quality. 18. Each record is given
a final polish before being
placed in its sleeve.

ARTHUR MURRAY TEACHES THE FOX TROT, GRAMOPHONE ALBUM SET (1946)

America's most famous dance instructor, Arthur Murray is best remembered for his franchised dance schools, more than 200 of which still exist. In 1938, he was responsible for turning the English Lambeth Walk into a national dance craze in America. In 1946 the Musicraft label - early mixed-media specialists - produced an instructional album to teach the popular foxtrot dance. It featured gramophone records with both spoken instruction from Murray and suitable music with which to practise at home, and a 28-page book with photographs and diagrams. The set also entitled the buyer to a private lesson at any of Murray's dance studios.

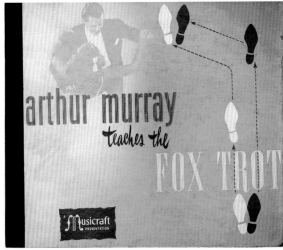

Record 3 · Side 1

THE PATTERN FOR THE MAGIC RIGHT

The Magic Right Turn is another very popular variation of the Magic Step. This step is of great value when you want to turn smoothly. Before doing the actual Magic Right Turn, let us learn the *pattern* of the step.

1. On the first count step straight *back* on the left foot, placing your entire weight on that *left* foot.

2. For the second count, step straight *forward* on your right foot.

3. Now place the *left* foot about twelve inches to the *left* side, count *three.*

4. Bring the right foot up to the left, count *four.*

10

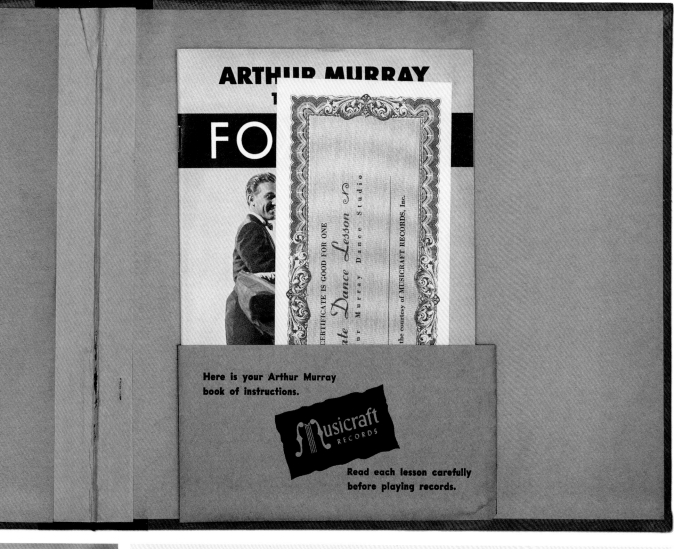

ARTHUR MURRAY

FO

THIS CERTIFICATE IS GOOD FOR ONE
Private Dance Lesson
at any Arthur Murray Dance Studio
presented through the courtesy of MUSICRAFT RECORDS, Inc.

Here is your Arthur Murray
book of instructions.

Musicraft RECORDS

Read each lesson carefully
before playing records.

THIS CERTIFICATE IS GOOD FOR ONE
Private Dance Lesson
at any Arthur Murray Dance Studio

NAME

presented through the courtesy of MUSICRAFT RECORDS, Inc.

© GOES-451

RADIOS AND RADIOGRAMS
(1930-56)

From 1930 radios could receive both medium- and long-wave broadcasts. The HMV model, dating between 1930 and 1940 (top) was also able to receive a channel called 'K'. Mounted in a mahogany-veneered cabinet, it features a glass-fronted tuning scale and bakelite dials. The 1946 HMV Model 115 radio (above) weighed only 12 lb and was designed to be easily transportable. It could operate from DC or AC mains and received broadcasts using an in-built internal aerial. The 1950s Philips radio (opposite, above right) features a bakelite chasis. Add-on units, such as the 1956 HMV model 1252 VHF adaptor (opposite centre), were produced to enable existing radios to receive very high-frequency FM broadcasts. The 1935 radio with bakelite case and four dials (opposite, below right) could receive short-, medium- and long-wave broadcasts, and could also be plugged into a gramophone. Radiograms, such as the 1953-55 HMV models 1508 and 1507 (opposite, above left and below left) boasted a 5-valve, 3-band radio with an epicyclic tuning system. They had two internal aerials, and a socket for an external one. The gramophone unfolds from the rear, and the turntable has a counter-balanced and pivoting tonearm; it plays at 33, 45, and 78 rpm. The 1507 model is portable with rexine covering and plastic grille.

VALDEMAR POULSEN

CREATOR OF
THE FIRST MAGNETIC
RECORDING SYSTEM

The principles of magnetic recording were first considered in the late 19th century, when American engineer Oberlin Smith published *Some Possible Forms of Phonograph*. In this 1888 article, he touched upon the possibility of using permanent magnetic impressions in the recording of sound. Although Smith was unable to build a working model, Danish engineer Valdemar Poulsen used many of his ideas when he developed the first magnetic recording system, the Telegraphone.

Poulsen had shown an interest in science from an early age, but although he studied at the University of Copenhagen he was unable to complete his degree. After working briefly in local machine shops, he became an assistant engineer at the Copenhagen Telephone Company, where he began his pioneering research.

In principle, the Telegraphone worked in a similar way to later magnetic tape recording systems. A motorized transport assembly pulled a spool of fine steel piano wire at a constant speed across a magnetic recording head. Here the sound was converted to electrical pulses that imposed a pattern of magnetization onto the wire, reflecting the original signal. When rewound, the wire passed across a playback head that detected changes in the magnetic field stored on the wire – these were converted back to a continuous electrical signal that could then be heard. The assembly moved the wire at a speed of 84 inches (213 cm) per second, and could record continuously for 30 seconds. The contents of the wire could be erased and reused. The Telegraphone was extremely low in audio fidelity, but since Poulsen had only ever envisaged its use with the human voice this was not deemed to be especially important.

[1] Poulsen patented his invention in 1898 and two years later gave a demonstration at the World Exposition in Paris, where he was able to record the voice of Emperor Franz Joseph of Austria.

[1]
WORLD-RECORD RECORDING
This is the oldest surviving magnetic audio recording and is stored in the Danish Museum of Science and Technology.

Poulsen was awarded the Grand Prix for scientific invention, but at first had limited success selling licences for production in Europe. He moved to the United States and rights to the Telegraphone were bought by a group of investors who founded the American Telegraphone Company. Wire-based magnetic recording evolved during the first half of the 20th century, reaching a point where the sound quality was on a par with a 78-rpm record, and it found some use in radio broadcasting.

German-Austrian engineer Fritz Pfleumer was involved in a very different line of research, but was familiar with Poulsen's ideas. Pfleumer developed Poulsen's work, creating the first magnetic tapes. During the 1920s, luxury cigarette brands were decorated with costly gold leaf at the tips; Pfleumer had successfully created a process by which cigarette paper could be imprinted with cheap powdered bronze to give a gold-like effect to the tip. With an understanding of Poulsen's work, Pfleumer thought he could use the same method to fix magnetic iron oxide powder to a thin strip of paper or film. He was granted a patent for the idea in 1928.

In 1932, Berlin's AEG company signed an agreement with Pfleumer to produce a recording system based on his magnetic tape. In 1934, in collaboration with German BASF company, 31 miles (50 km) of cellulose acetate tape backed with a lacquer of iron oxide was manufactured. At the 1935 Radio Fair in Berlin, AEG unveiled the Magnetophon K1, the first true magnetic tape recorder, but it was costly and intended only for professional use.

In 1936, the German National Court cancelled Pfleumer's patent, claiming that his idea of coating paper with iron dust had, in effect, been covered by Poulsen's original patent for the Telegraphone. But although Poulsen is rightly identified as the inventor of magnetic recording, Pfleumer's work played an important contributory role in the birth of audio tape recording.

VALDEMAR POULSEN
Born: 23 November 1869,
Copenhagen, Denmark
Died: 23 July 1942,
New York City, USA

2
MUTED SUCCESS
The machines produced by the American Telegraphone Company were promoted as office dictation units or telephone message recorders. Although quite popular, the sound was poor and low in volume. Moreover, the wire itself was delicate, prone to breaking, and built into the machine, making it of little use for long-term audio storage.

MINIFON P55S PORTABLE WIRE RECORDER (1955)

Using the same basic principles developed more than fifty years earlier by Valdemar Poulsen, the Minifon P55S wire recorder was produced in Germany by Protona GmbH from 1955 to 1960. Designed as a portable dictation machine, using extremely fine wire (0.038 mm) it could record up to 200 minutes of audio at a speed of 13½ inches (34 cm)/second. A long-play model, the P55L, was also available and could record five hours of audio at a slower speed of 9 inches (23 cm)/second.

WEBSTER-CHICAGO 18-1R WIRE RECORDER (1949)

In 1945, Webster-Chicago purchased the rights to produce wire recorders in the United States. The sturdy metal-cased 18-1R was a desktop model that could record up to 60 minutes in a single wire spool. The transport mechanism could be controlled by hand or by using a foot pedal. Anticipating that the wire recorder was on a path to swift obsolescence, by 1955 Webster-Chicago had switched to magnetic tape production.

L2 PORTABLE TAPE RECORDER (1953)

The EMI Model L2 Tape Recorder was the world's first commercial battery-operated portable tape recorder. It was extensively used for a variety of purposes, including location filming, on-the-spot news reporting and interviews. In spite of its size (14 × 8 × 7 inches; 35.5 × 20 × 18 cm), it was a rugged professional machine. The lid secures to the base using suitcase-style latches, as does the battery pack at the side. It is housed in a wooden case with green rexine covering and a shoulder strap. A circular nickel speaker grille is visible on the front of the case.

EMI L4A PORTABLE TAPE RECORDER (1962)

A later, more sophisticated version of the EMI L2, the L4A was a twin-speed model with two separate microphone inputs, each with its own gain control, and a line-level input socket. A bass-cut switch could be used to reduce low frequencies. The unit also had an additional socket enabling it to take power from an external battery source.

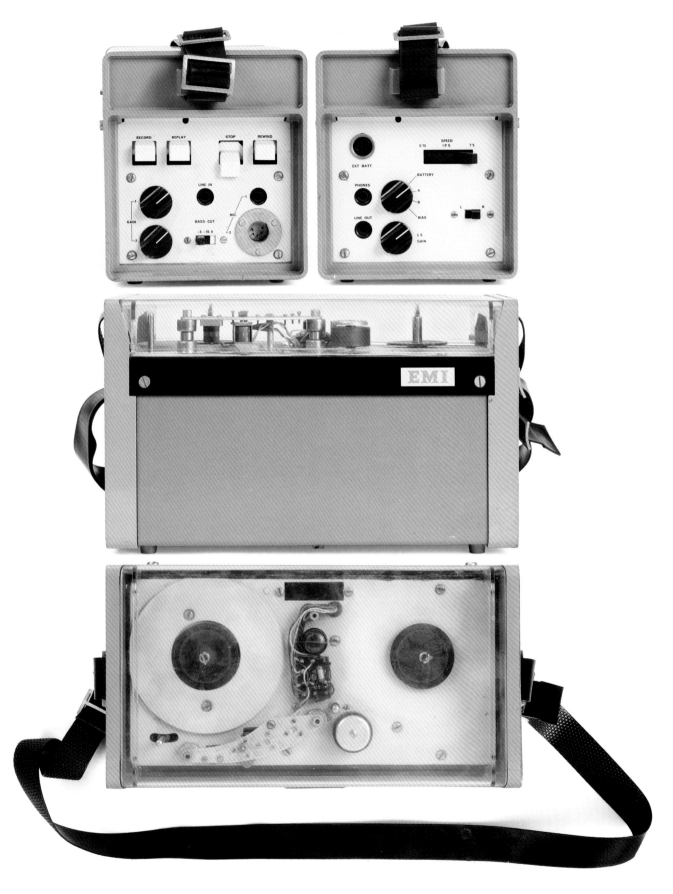

EMITAPE

Manufactured by

E.M.I. FACTORIES LTD. HAYES. MIDDX. ENGLAND

(CONTROLLED BY ELECTRIC & MUSICAL INDUSTRIES LTD.)

XHAX 22

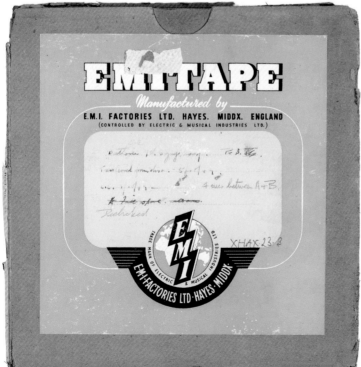

EMITAPE

Manufactured by

E.M.I. FACTORIES LTD. HAYES. MIDDX. ENGLAND

(CONTROLLED BY ELECTRIC & MUSICAL INDUSTRIES LTD.)

XHAX 23

E.M.I. ABBEY ROAD LONDON

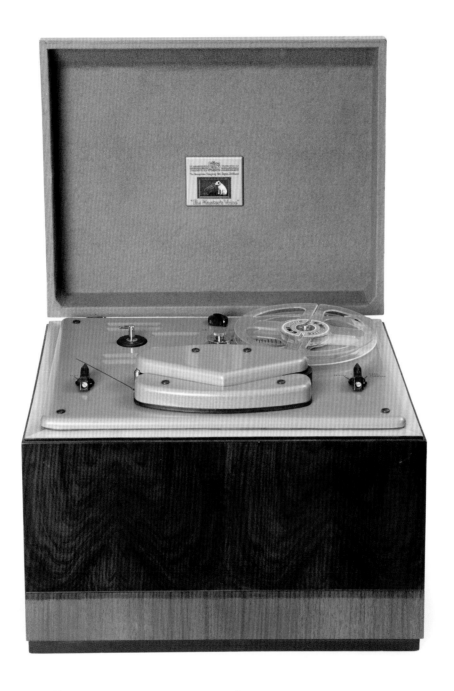

opposite

EMI ALUMINIUM SPLICING BLOCK (c. 1952)

To join two pieces of tape, both
were slotted into the cradle,
a razor blade passed through one
of the cutting channels, and the
pieces joined using editing tape.

above

HMV 3031 OPEN-REEL TAPE PLAYER (1956)

Built into a plush wooden case,
this high-fidelity unit - based
on the professional EMI TR series
- will only play open-reel tapes.
It cannot be used for recording.

HANSEL
AND
GRETEL
FOR CHILDREN 5 TO 8
Sung by
EARL ROGERS

RED ROBIN SERIES RR-3

HANS CHRISTIAN ANDERSEN'S
THE UGLY
FOR CHILDREN 4 to 7
DUCKLING
Story adaptation and original music by
HECKY KRASNO and PETER STEELE
RONNY LISS, Narrator
with
TED DALE and Orchestra

RED ROBIN SERIES RR-

Mother
GOOSE
SONGS
FOR CHILDREN 3 TO 6
Sung by
EARL ROGERS

RED ROBIN SERIES RR-1

Songs of
AMERICA
FOR CHILDREN 7 TO 10
Sung by
EARL ROGERS

RED ROBIN SERIES RR-5

THE STORY OF
CHICKEN LICKEN
AND
The Little Red Hen
FOR CHILDREN 3 to 6
NARRATED AND SUNG BY
GLORIA STORY

Story adaptation and original music by
HECKY KRASNO and PETER STEELE.

RED ROBIN SERIES—RR8

THE STORY OF
THE THREE BEARS
FOR CHILDREN 3 to 6
CAST
GLORIA STORY
VIRGINIA DWYER
MORDY BAUMAN
with String Ensemble

Story adaptation and original music by
HECKY KRASNO and PETER STEELE

RED ROBIN SERIES—ALBUM RR7

SONGS
and SINGING
GAMES
FOR CHILDREN 5 TO 8
Sung by
EARL ROGERS

RED ROBIN SERIES RR-4

ROBIN
HOOD
FOR CHILDREN 7 TO 10
Told by
CRANE CALDER

RED ROBIN SERIES RR-8

HAPPY TIMES
TUNES
FOR CHILDREN 3 TO
Sung by
EARL ROGERS

RED ROBIN SERIES RR-

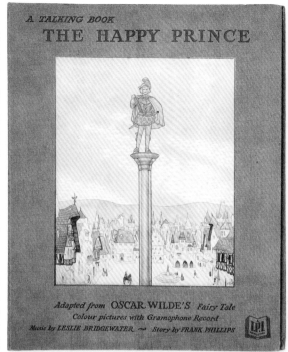

opposite

MUSICRAFT CHILDREN'S RECORDS
(1936-48)

The market for children's records
goes back almost as far as the
start of the gramophone era.
The popular Musicraft series
mixed storytelling with music.

above

TPL PRODUCTIONS A TALKING
BOOK SERIES (1948)

Each instalment of the British
Talking Book series included a
hardback illustrated storybook
and 78-rpm record narrated by
BBC newsreader Frank Phelps.

opposite

STANDARD TELEPHONE AND CABLE
COMPANY 4021 MICROPHONE
(1945)
This omni-directional microphone
was widely used at the BBC where,
due to its shape, it was dubbed
the 'apple and biscuit'. The 4021
served as an outdoors ambient
microphone, although this example
sat on an announcer's desk.

above left

HMV 2350H MICROPHONE (1949)
The 2350H ribbon microphone was
in use at the BBC as a general
announcing microphone right up
until the 1960s.

above right

STEREO CAPSULE MICROPHONE
(1954)
Built by EMI researcher Reg
Willard for making stereophonic
recordings, it was combined with
a pair of Neumann M49 capsules
mounted at right angles to each
other. It was first tested in May
1954 at Abbey Road Studio 2 with
Norrie Paramor and his orchestra.

AMERICA'S GREATEST POP RECORDING STARS ON

Capitol

REGD TRADE MARK CAPITOL RECORDS INC
REGD USER E.M.I. LTD.

JOHN RAITT

HARRY JAMES

PAULETTE SISTERS

"TENNESSEE" ERNIE FORD

FRANK SINATRA

VICKY YOUNG

LES PAUL *and* MARY FORD

BUNNY PAUL

JUNE CHRISTY

MARGIE RAYBURN

ELLA MAE MORSE

NAT "KING" COLE

CAPITOL ARTISTES.. ...CAPITAL ENTERTAINMENT!

Capitol

REGD. TRADE MARK CAPITOL RECORDS INC.
REGD. USER E.M.I. LTD.

SHOWBILL

FRANK SINATRA The fabulous voice on Capitol records bringing you all the greatest hits

Les Paul ☆ Mary Ford

A sparkling blend of phantom guitars—a gentle voice with its own reflection—in unforgettable melodies

NAT 'KING' COLE The King of vocalists—the husky voice that thrills fans with every new record

MARGARET WHITING One of Capitol's most popular and alluring young singers. Vivacious Margaret constantly brings you great songs

JUNE CHRISTY 'Cool' or 'Hot' this intriguing blonde vocalist brings you something interesting

MARGIE RAYBURN A contribution to the entertainment world. Watch for her latest releases

STAN KENTON The Genius of modern jazz.

GORDON MacRAE The voice with a heart in it

TENNESSEE ERNIE FORD The nation's most popular singer of such hit tunes as "Sixteen Tons" – "His Hands" – "Give Me Your Word," etc.

ELLA MAE MORSE The Capitol girl singer with zest and drive

Take the Stars Home!

★ **CAPITOL ARTISTES... CAPITAL ENTERTAINMENT**

Capitol

REGD TRADE MARK CAPITOL RECORDS INC
REGD USER E.M.I. LTD.

Smash Hits!

"OFF THE GROOVE"

SIXTEEN TONS You don't have to be a baby to cry "Tennessee" Ernie Ford
CL 14500 · 45-CL 14500

Oh, my darlin'
Burn that candle
The Cues
CL 14501 · 45-CL 14501

LOU BUSCH ORCHESTRA ZAMBEZI
Rainbow's end
CL 14504 · 45-CL 14504

TEXAS LADY Alabama bound
Les Paul & Mary Ford
CL 14502 · 45-CL 14502

FRANK SINATRA
Love & Marriage
Look to your heart
CL 14503 · 45-CL 14503

CAPITOL ARTISTES...
CAPITAL ENTERTAINMENT

Capitol

REGD TRADE MARK CAPITOL RECORDS INC
REGD USER E.M.I. LTD.

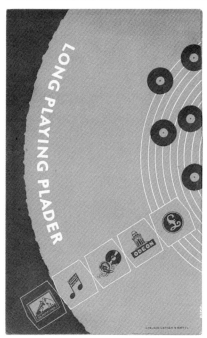

previous pages
**CAPITOL RECORDS MAGAZINE
ADVERTISING (1955-56)**
Founded in 1942 by songwriter
Johnny Mercer, by the end of the
decade Capitol Records was one
of the biggest labels in the
USA. In 1955, EMI bought Capitol
Records and marketed it in the UK
as the glitzy home of America's
greatest singing stars.

below

CAPITOL RS101 RECORD PLAYER (1959)

By the end of the 1950s,
stereophonic sound was finding
its way into American homes.
The stylish Capitol RS101 came
equipped with stereo cartridge
and a pair of matching speakers.
For full effect, both the record
player and the speakers were
mounted on screw-in legs.

JAZZ AT THE PHILHARMONIC
ALBUM SETS (1945-49)

Promoter Norman Granz was a key
figure in the rise of post-war
jazz in the USA, and many of
its greatest exponents recorded
for his Clef, Norgran, Verve
and Pablo labels. Granz made his
reputation in 1944 when he staged
the first of a series of large-
scale jazz concerts at the Los
Angeles Philharmonic Auditorium.
Recordings made at these concerts
were released as 'albums' of
78-rpm gramophone records.

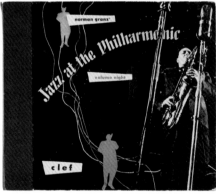

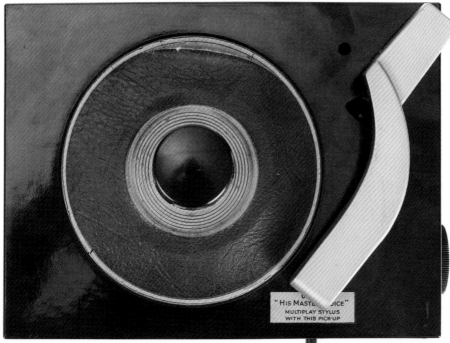

left

MARCONIPHONE 4306 RADIOGRAM (1963)

A suitcase-style portable unit
in a red leatherette casing, the
4306 was a combined gramophone
and radio. Lifting the lid
reveals the turntable with
an autochange mechanism. The
front panel features a volume
control that doubles up as an
on-off switch, a radio waveband
selector and rotary tuning dial.

below left

HMV MODEL 2107 RECORD PLAYER (1952)

The HMV Model 2107 was similar
to the RCA Victor Victrola
Model 45-J-2 and was essentially
an adapter that added 45-rpm
capability to existing record
players or radiograms. Housed
in a bakelite casing, the
unit also allowed multiple
45-rpm records to be stacked
on the spindle and drop
down automatically. It has
no speakers, and had to be
attached to an existing radio
or gramophone with an auxiliary
input to be heard properly.
Produced by HMV under licence,
these miniature turntables were
originally designed and built
in 1949 by RCA Victor in the USA.

opposite

DANSETTE MAJOR RECORD PLAYER (1958)

Manufactured in London by
J & A Margolin Ltd, the Dansette
was a staple of teenage life in
Britain during the 1960s, where
more than one million units were
sold until production ended in
December 1969. The Dansette was
both expensive and fashionable,
and its styling set the tone
for other cheaper 'suitcase'
record players of the period.

below

RECORDS PRODUCED BY PHIL SPECTOR (1962-70)

Gene Pitney, 'Every Breath I Take' (1961) / The Crystals, 'Da Doo Ron Ron' (1963) / Ike And Tina Turner, 'River Deep, Mountain High' (1966) / The Beatles, 'Get Back' (1969) / The Beatles, 'Let It Be' (1970) / The Beatles, 'The Long And Winding Road' (1970) / John Lennon/Plastic Ono Band, 'Instant Karma! (We All Shine On)' (1970) / John Lennon/Plastic Ono Band, 'Mother' (1970) / George Harrison 'My Sweet Lord' (1970).

opposite

PHIL SPECTOR (c. 1963)

Spector is shown here at the famous Gold Star studio in Los Angeles. Seated at the bespoke 12-channel mixer is his engineer Larry Levine, a key figure in the realization of Spector's signature 'Wall of Sound'.

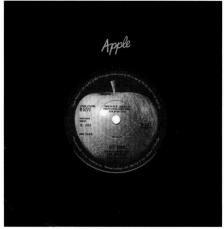

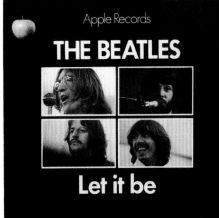

PHIL SPECTOR

LEGENDARY
'WALL OF SOUND'
RECORD PRODUCER

The role of record producer can take on a wide variety of guises. As Brian Eno put it in 2014: 'It's a very difficult job to define because it really covers a lot of territory. There are some famous producers from the seventies who [would just] take bags of drugs into the studio....But then at the other end there were producers like Phil Spector who effectively invented the music and then got people in to do it for them.' Indeed, Spector not only controlled the engineering and mixing of recording sessions, but acted as creative director, composing or selecting the material to be recorded, and generally masterminding all phases of the studio process. Eccentric and single-minded, he was the first of the auteur producers, and was directly responsible for some of the greatest pop music ever made.

Spector was born into a first-generation Ukrainian-Jewish family in the Bronx district of New York City. His father committed suicide in 1949; four years later, his mother moved the family to Los Angeles. While still in high school, Spector composed a song for his teenage vocal group, The Teddy Bears. In 1958, 'To Know Him is to Love Him' rose to the top of the Billboard Hot 100 chart. Just nineteen years old, he had already written, arranged, performed on and produced an international best-seller. [1]

While adept as a singer and guitarist, Spector knew that his talents would be best served away from centre stage. He quickly gained studio expertise working for songwriters Leiber and Stoller, in 1960 co-writing the classic 'Spanish Harlem' for Ben E. King. He also worked regularly with audio engineers Stan Ross and Larry Levine and a group of top Los Angeles session musicians who became his de facto house band, 'the Wrecking Crew'.

It was the 1964 hit 'You've Lost That Lovin' Feelin'' by The Righteous Brothers that gave rise to the term 'Wall of Sound', a description of Spector's dense production technique and complex multi-layered musical arrangements. Making full use [2]

[1]
SPECTOR'S FIRST HIT
Poignantly, the song's title was inspired by the words on his father's gravestone: 'To know him was to love him'.

[2]
THE 'WALL OF SOUND'
In fact, by 1964 Spector's signature production style was already familiar from earlier hits such as 'Be My Baby' by The Ronettes and The Crystals' 'Da Doo Ron Ron'.

of the natural reverberation chambers at Gold Star Studios in Los Angeles, Spector and the Wrecking Crew built up the sound for The Righteous Brothers' hit layer by layer, first four acoustic guitars, then three pianos, three basses, two trumpets, two trombones, three saxophones and then the drums. After the lead and backing vocals had been completed orchestral strings were added. The effect was a brooding atmospheric pop epic that American musicologist Robert Palmer described as 'Wagnerian rock 'n' roll with all the trimmings'.

Spector continued to enjoy hits with his characteristic sound, himself citing 1966's 'River Deep, Mountain High' by Ike and Tina Turner as the pinnacle of his production career. Meanwhile, the influence of the 'Wall of Sound' could also be heard in the music of other artists, such as The Beach Boys, whose 1966 masterpiece *Pet Sounds* saw them evolving from surfer beat group to purveyors of pop music as an art form.

The end of the 1960s saw Spector's involvement with The Beatles. Brought in to add orchestration and production polish to the band's beleaguered Let It Be project, his efforts yielded the US-chart-topping singles 'The Long And Winding Road' and 'Let It Be'. Both were completed without the knowledge of their composer – Paul McCartney – who was said to be outraged by Spector's additions, but John Lennon and George Harrison happily involved Spector in their fledgling solo careers.

Following a near-fatal car crash in 1974, Spector became an increasingly reclusive and eccentric figure. In 2003, actress Lana Clarkson was found dead from gunshot wounds in Spector's California mansion. After a prolonged court case, a jury rejected his defence that her death was an 'accidental suicide' and he was convicted of murder. With a 'nineteen years to life' sentence, it will be 2027 before Phil Spector even becomes eligible for parole.

PHIL SPECTOR
Born: 26 December 1939,
New York City, New York, USA

3

3
RIGHTEOUS SUCCESS
In 2001, the Recording Industry
Association of America voted
'You've Lost That Lovin' Feelin''
one of the ten greatest songs
of the 20th century.

above

COLUMBIA STEREOSONIC ADVERT
(1955)

EMI's first stereo tape catalogue
targeted the fledgling audiophile
market. Focusing on classical
music, more than 300 Stereosonic
7½ IPS open-reel tape recordings
were issued in all.

opposite

EMITAPE ADVERT (1957)

EMI produced various grades of
open-reel tape in their Emitape
range. The '88' was a general-
purpose tape. The '99' had a
thinner acetate base - more tape
could be wound onto a single
spool and so it ran for longer.

EMITAPE

The Famous '88' 'GENERAL PURPOSE'

and NOW '99' 'LONG PLAY'

STOP PRESS NEWS regarding . . . .

The World's finest range of

MAGNETIC RECORDING TAPE

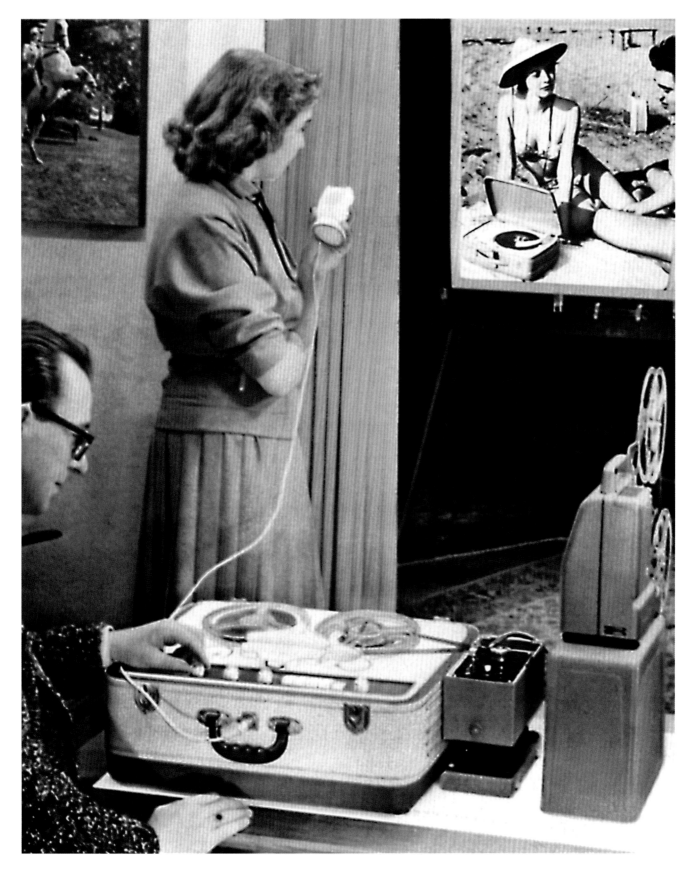

258.259

previous pages

GRUNDIG 'LIFESTYLE'
ADVERTISING FOR OPEN-REEL
TAPE RECORDERS (1950s)

Even a modest open-reel tape
recorder would have been an
expensive purchase for most
families in the 1950s. These
magazine advertisements by
German audio company Grundig
accentuate the aspirational side
of owning a tape recorder. The
image on page 258 even depicts
a young middle-class German
couple recording a synchronized
commentary for home cine films.

right

GRUNDIG TK5 PORTABLE
TAPE RECORDER (1955)

The TK5 was a typical single-
channel portable tape recorder
intended for the domestic
user. It ran at only 3¾ IPS and
featured an in-built 2.5-watt
amplifier and 4-inch (10-cm)
loudspeaker. Even such a basic
model would have been priced
in the UK at 56 guineas - almost
£2,000 nowadays. This particular
machine was used on 6 July 1957
at St. Peter's Church garden
fête in Liverpool to record
The Quarrymen, the band that
evolved into The Beatles.

opposite

EMI VOICEMASTER 65 TAPE
RECORDER (1959)

A British curiosity, the
Voicemaster 65 was not only a
tape recorder but also came with
the option of a record-playing
attachment that fitted over
the top of the tape mechanism
and could play 33- and 45-rpm
gramophone records.

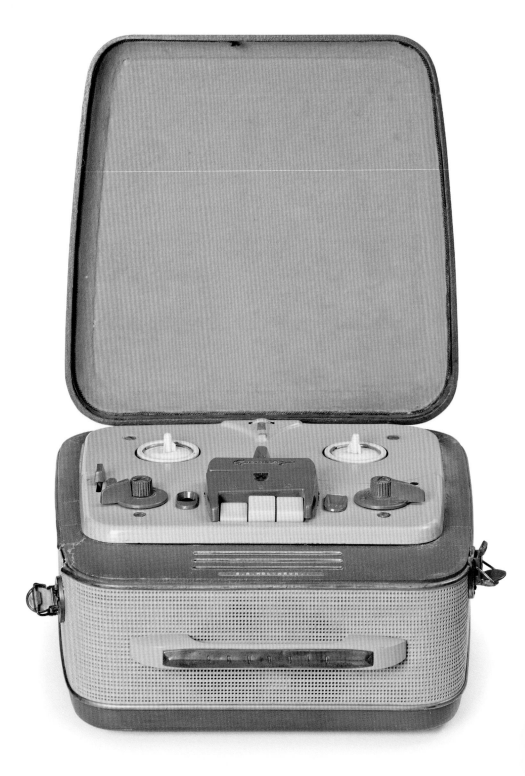

HMV TYPE 2300 MICROPHONE (1960s)

Launched in 1949, these ribbon microphones were designed for professional recording. A Type 2300 microphone was included as part of the HMV Portable Disc Recorder Model 2300.

TAPE DUPLICATION (c. 1959)

Unlike gramophone records, which could be mass-produced by 'stamping' molten vinyl using an inverse metal plate, open-reel tapes had to be recorded in real time. One tape machine plays a master copy that is simultaneously recorded by a large number of connected tape machines. To make the process faster, both master tape and recorders could be set to corresponding higher speeds.

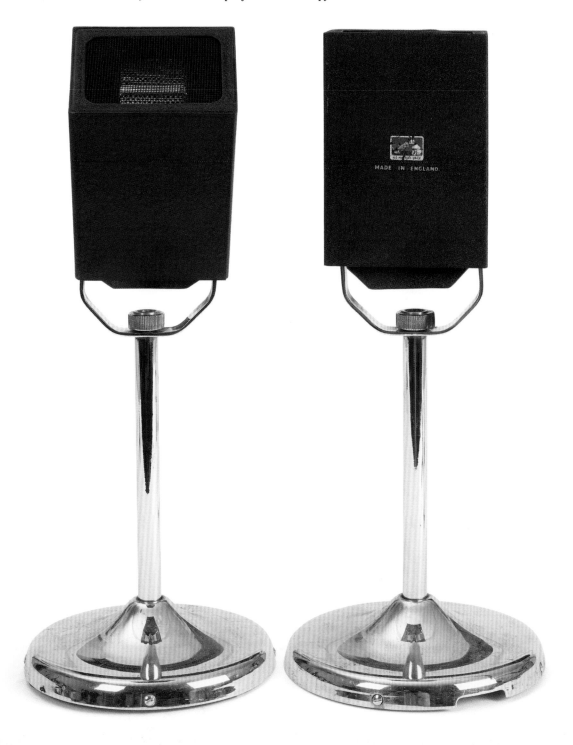

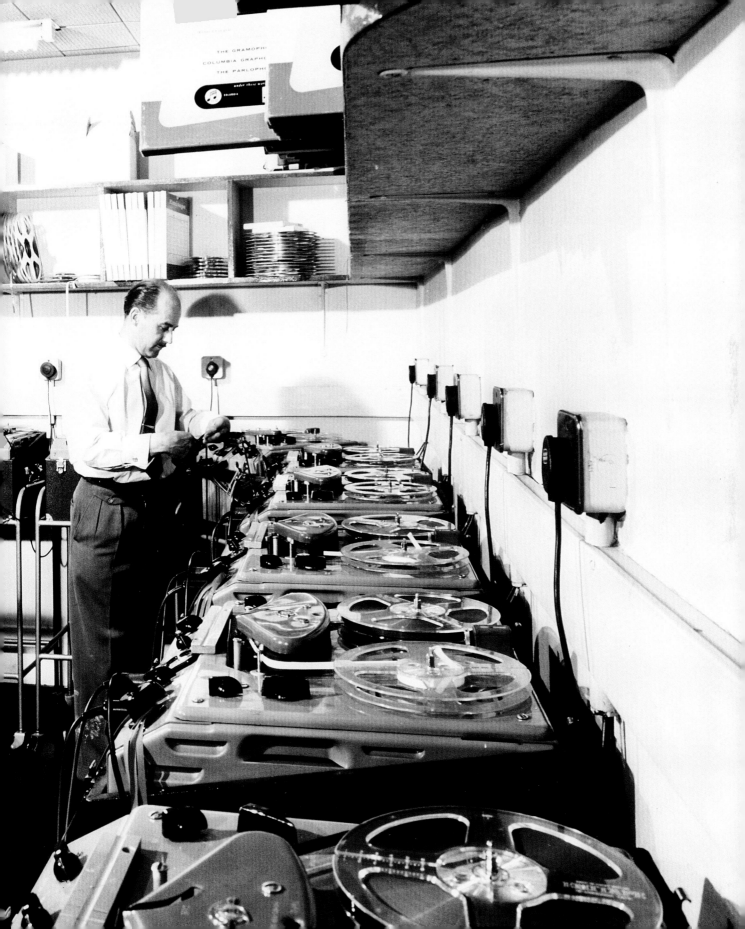

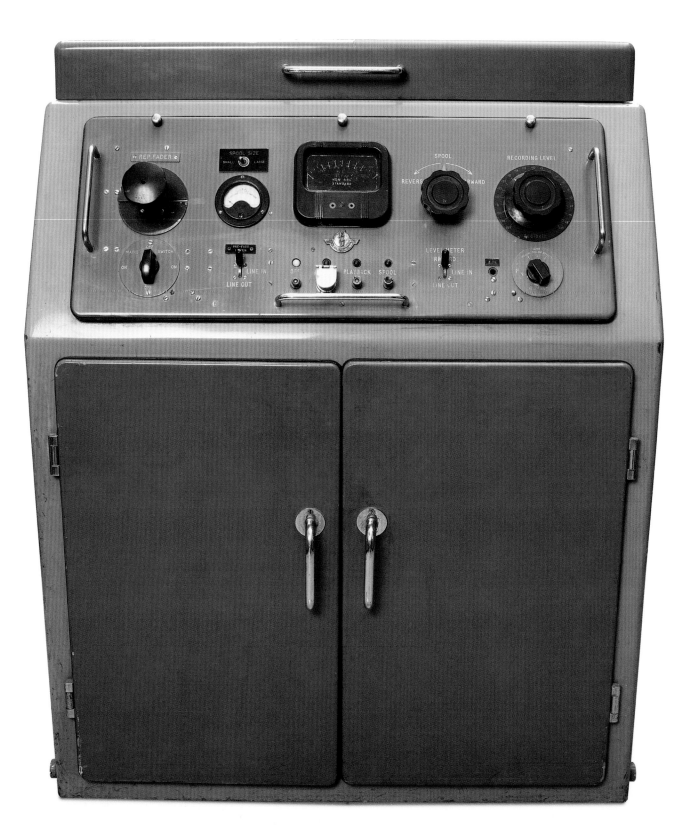

EDIT
TRAIL
SPOOL
PLAY
OFF
REC
REVERSE
REP FADER
REP OFFSET
HEADPHONE
REC
CUE
REP
HEADPHONE
REC
REP
FADER
LOCAL
REMOTE
OR
AUTO
FOLLOW
LH
RH
MONO
STEREO
PH REV
REP LEVEL
NORMAL
OFF
15
1A
3A

previous pages

THE EMI GREEN MACHINES

The first tape recorders to be manufactured in Britain, the BTR1 ('British Tape Recorder') was produced by EMI in 1947. Known because of its colouring as 'The Green Machine', in 1952 it was upgraded as the BTR2 (page 264). Built in large numbers and used in all of EMI's studios, a modified version of BTR2 was produced for the BBC and named the RD4/4 (page 265).

below

LEAK TL/12 'POINT ONE' VALVE AMPLIFIER

In September 1945, H. J. Leak & Company of London launched the first of its 'Point One' valve amplifiers. It represented a significant advancement in amplifier performance (the name derived from the harmonic distortion rate of just 0.1%). The Leak TL/12 'Point One' Valve Amplifier (above) is a classic mono amplifier and the most popular of its time. It was designed for a number of tasks, including laboratory use as a stabilized gain audio frequency power amplifier, studio use in disc recording and as a driver in the speech modulator chain of broadcast transmitters. (The Leak TL/25 'Plus Power' monophonic valve is shown at the bottom of this page.) At 25 pounds and 15 shillings (£25.75) for the power amplifier and an additional 6 pounds and 15 shillings (£6.75) for the preamplifier - around ten weeks' wages for an average worker - the equipment was expensive.

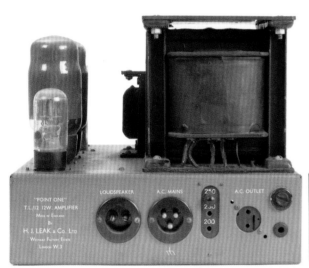

previous pages, right
EL34 VALVES
Used in high-powered audio
amplifiers of the 1960s such
as the Leak monophonic TL/25
and Stereo 60, the EL34 valve
is still used in high-end guitar
amplification. It is particularly
strongly associated with British
manufacturers such as Marshall,
Orange and Hiwatt.

right and opposite
EMI TEST RECORDS
During the 1950s, EMI produced
several sets of records
designed to help in the correct
set-up of audio equipment.
The 'Stereophonic Recording'
demonstrated a combination of
sound effects that made extensive
use of the stereo spectrum
and excerpts from classical
recordings. 'Technical Test
Records' provided recordings
of 'test tones' of specified
frequencies. The records would
be played while the audio
equipment was adjusted.

MADE IN ENGLAND

EMI

CONSTANT FREQUENCY RECORD
SIDE 1

CTPX.16150
SPEED 78

JG.449

c.p.s.	level in db.	c.p.s.	level in db.
20 KC	0	6 KC	0
18 KC	0	4.5 KC	0
16 KC	0	3.5 KC	0
14 KC	0	2 KC	0
12 KC	0	500	—1
10 KC	0	160	—5.5
8 KC	0	70	—12

COPYRIGHT PATENTED RECORD. NOT TO BE PUBLICLY PERFORMED WITHOUT LICENCE, COPIED OR RE-RECORDED

RECORDED BY E·M·I STUDIOS LTD · LONDON · ENGLAND

JOE MEEK

Robert George 'Joe' Meek was one of the first great studio innovators. During the early 1960s, he created a string of classic hits that were all recorded at his home – an apartment above a leather-goods store on London's Holloway Road. Of his 245 singles, twenty-five entered the UK Top Forty, three of them topping the charts.

Meek left school when he was fourteen to begin an apprenticeship repairing radios and televisions. After spending his national service as a radar mechanic in the Royal Air Force, he found work in a recording studio. In 1956, he devised the unorthodox compressed and distorted piano sound on Humphrey Lyttelton's jazz instrumental hit 'Bad Penny Blues'.

In 1960, Meek founded his own independent RGM Productions. Chart success followed quickly when TV heart-throb John Leyton recorded 'Johnny Remember Me'. A classic of audio melodrama, the song tells of a young man haunted by his dead lover; Meek created the powerful chorus hook by drenching the ghostly female voice in cavernous reverberation. [1] Two years later, he enjoyed his biggest success, writing and producing 'Telstar' for The Tornados. Recorded in response to the space launch of the *Telstar* communications satellite that carried the first transatlantic TV broadcasts, the track featured a melody played on a Selmer clavioline keyboard – a precursor to the analogue synthesizer. With electronic sound effects made using radio static, microphone feedback and echo, 'Telstar' came across as nothing less than pop music beamed from the future.

Meek pioneered the idea of using the recording studio as a creative tool in its own right – made possible by his working in his own home studio space, free from interference or the constraints of the clock. The sound of a recording was just as important to him as the song or the performance. His approach to recording was highly unorthodox for the time. Rather than

[1]
TRANSATLANTIC SUCCESS
A global hit, 'Telstar' became the first record by a British pop group to top the American *Billboard* charts.

taping all the musicians together, he separated them, placing players in different rooms; sometimes on different floors. He would often overdub performances separately, sometimes even recording different segments of a song at different times (and with different musicians) before editing together a final master. He pioneered techniques that are now taken for granted, such as close-miking amplifiers or plugging instruments directly into the mixing desk. His recordings made heavy use of compression, echo and reverberation and other mysterious home-brew effects that he'd created himself. And he was one of the first producers ² to distort an audio signal in order to create specific effects.

Joe Meek soon developed a reputation as a 'difficult' character with eccentric views. He regularly attended séances and carried out electronic voice phenomena (EVP) experiments, involving making recordings in graveyards in an attempt to communicate with the dead. He also claimed that he enjoyed conversations in his dreams with the singer Buddy Holly, who had died in 1959.

The final years of Meek's life saw both his business and personal life in serious decline. He was sued for allegedly copying the 'Telstar' melody from a French film soundtrack; the record's substantial royalties were withheld, leaving him in serious debt. Moreover, at a time when homosexuality was still unlawful in the UK, Meek had faced public humiliation with his arrest for 'importuning for immoral purpose'. As the decade progressed, his music became unfashionable; he was overshadowed by young British bands such as The Beatles, who were taking pop music in new directions. He became depressed and developed a spiralling drug problem. On 3 February 1967, in a violent rage, Joe Meek murdered his landlady before turning the shotgun on himself. Less than a month after his death, the plagiarism case that had ³ so troubled him came to end – the court found in his favour.

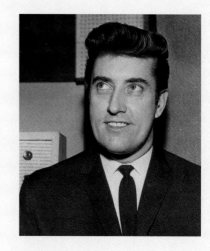

JOE MEEK
Born: 5 April 1929, Newent, UK
Died: 3 February 1967, London, UK

third wave : MAGNETIC ERA

2
THE JOE MEEK STUDIO-GEAR RANGE
In 1993, a line of studio equipment was launched, inspired by and named after Joe Meek. It remains especially popular - fittingly enough - among home-recording enthusiasts.

3
'TEA CHEST TAPES'
Following Meek's death, more than a thousand boxes of tape, featuring unreleased recordings he had made, were discovered. Known as the 'Tea Chest Tapes', these unmarked reels contained early demo recordings by such celebrated British musicians as David Bowie, Tom Jones and Jimmy Page.

270.271

"HIS MASTER'S VOICE" *Classical*

RECORDS FOR JANUARY

78 r.p.m.

Edwin Fischer

GUIDO CANTELLI

JUSSI BJÖRLING

KIRSTEN FLAGSTAD

MOURA LYMPANY

JASCHA HEIFETZ

GERALD MOORE

SENA JURINAC

"HIS MASTER'S VOICE"

The Hallmark of Quality

WORK IN PROGRESS

A designer's rough layout for
the catalogue of forthcoming
classical releases on His
Master's Voice in January 1953.

HMV NO.12 PICKUP (1938)

The pickup (or 'cartridge'
as it later became more widely
known) transforms the physical
motions produced by the record,
turntable, tonearm and stylus
into electrical signals.
Designed at the EMI Research
Laboratory, the No.12 was
a lightweight pickup.

EMI EPU 100 TONEARM AND STEREO PICKUP (1960)

An integrated arm and cartridge
unit, the EPU 100 pivoted on a
single point and pioneered the
(then) unusual idea of a lever
to raise and lower the arm.
The cartridge was stereophonic
and claimed more than 15 dB
of channel separation.

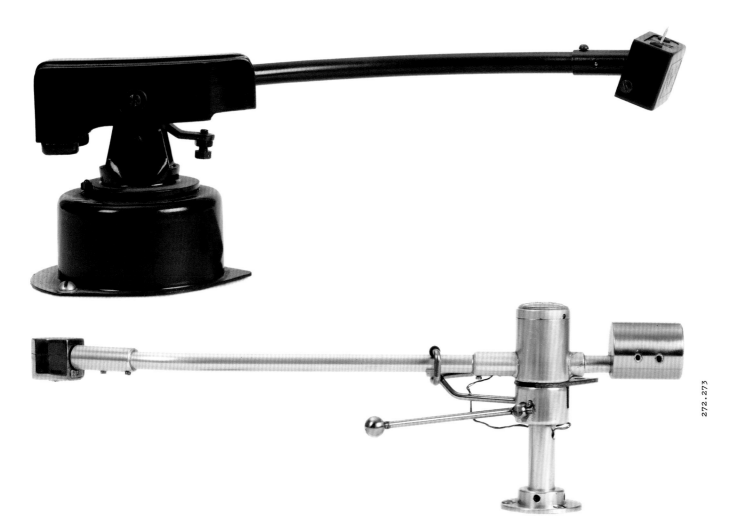

CONSORT *by* HIS MAST

								GF		GNWL	AYCN		
N.S.W.			FC		BL	GB UE KY UWCH SM			MWBEQNLG		2	3
	CR		NUCO NR NB BACY XL GZUHRGADWGNCTM NXPKMGBSVMWN									
	KM ML		BHKP TRANKAGL LM		CAMOHDNZDU LFLTKONMNA RE							UL 2
						QQ							
QLD.		QR		KQ	QG	QY IP	BC	BK BH				4	5
	QL	AT QN		QAOS	RK VKVL RO SBIGMBAK			BU MK	ZR QDSO				
		QW	TO	G QBAYCA MI				GYLM	GM				
				GFWF	WN R	PM IX	KY					6	7
W.A.													
	DL WA NM	AL8KNCA		VA GN	BY TZ GE	WB CI	9PA					SDBU
		8DR 8TC		9RBAMNA KG	MD	8DN		8AL				-S

VOLUME · ON

TONE

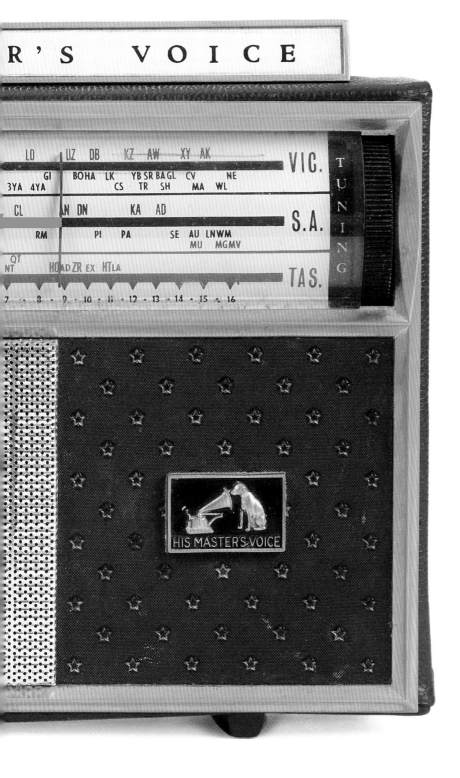

R'S VOICE

left

THE SOLID-STATE REVOLUTION

In 1947, three scientists from
Bell Laboratories in the United
States invented the transistor,
a tiny electronic component that
quickly rendered much existing
valve technology redundant.
By the end of the 1950s, bulky,
valve-radio sets had been
replaced by small, portable
'solid-state' transistor radios.
The HMV Consort (left) was built
in 1963 specifically for the
Australian market. The radio
stations on the dial are grouped
by territory - there is an N.S.W
scale for New South Wales. It
was a battery-operated unit and
featured a circuit board less
than 9 inches (23 cm) in length
containing seven transistors.

overleaf

SUBTLY CHANGING FACE

In March 1931, The Gramophone
Company, with its His Master's
Voice trademark, and the Columbia
Graphophone Company, which
owned the Columbia, Parlophone
and Odeon labels, were merged,
creating Electric and Musical
Industries - or EMI. The EMI logo
remained remarkably consistent,
the only real differences being
perspective scaling and a
typographical shift to simple
san-serif font towards the end
of the 1960s.

the greatest recording organisation in the world

'HIS MASTER'S VOICE'
CAPITOL ★ COLUMBIA
PARLOPHONE ★ M-G-M
RECORDS

'HIS MASTER'S VOICE'
CAPITOL
COLUMBIA
PARLOPHONE &
M-G-M RECORDS

— the greatest recording organisation in the world

HIS MASTER'S VOICE
CAPITOL · COLUMBIA
PARLOPHONE · M·G·M
MERCURY · TOP RANK

...THE GREATEST RECORDING ORGANISATION IN THE WORLD

EMI SUPER 731m 2,400ft
DOUBLE PLAY Recording Tape

EMI SUPER 365m 1,200ft
LONG PLAY Recording Tape

EMI SUPER 182m 600ft
STANDARD PLAY Recording Tape
13 cm 5ins

CATALOGO
GENERALE
DISCHI 1963

EMI

LA PIÙ GRANDE ORGANIZZAZIONE
DISCOGRAFICA DEL MONDO

CATALOGO
GENERALE
DISCHI
1968

catalogo
generale
dischi

CATALOGO
GENERALE
DISCHI 1964

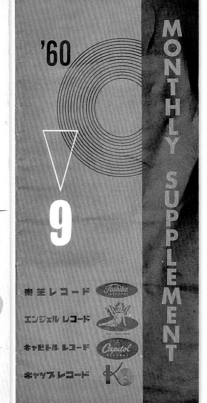

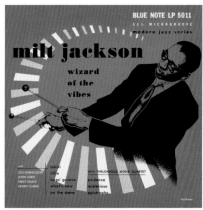

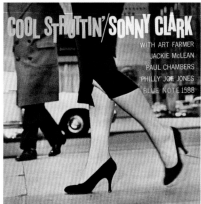

previous pages

CATALOGUES FROM ITALY
AND JAPAN

The design of gramophone
catalogue covers from around
the world generally reflected
the prevailing local fashions
of the time. Interestingly, one
of the Japanese covers (page 279)
shows what appears to be a Santa
Claus figure playing a violin.
The spread of American television
during this time saw the gradual
emergence of secular Christmas
celebration in Japan.

right

THE ART OF THE RECORD SLEEVE

Blue Note Records was founded in
New York City in 1939. The label
took the finest jazz musicians
of their era, recorded them with
the greatest care using state-
of-the-art studio technology
and wrapped the resulting LPs
in beautifully designed miniature
pieces of art. The immediately
recognizable house-design style
was based around the photography
of Francis Wolff and the
typography of Reid Miles. A pre-
celebrity Andy Warhol was one
of the many artists and designers
who contributed to the hugely
influential Blue Note look.

BLUE NOTE 5037
vol. 1

art
BLAKEY
quintet

CLIFFORD BROWN trumpet
LOU DONALDSON alto sax
HORACE SILVER piano
CURLY RUSSELL bass
ART BLAKEY drums

HERBIE NICHOLS TRIO
HERBIE NICHOLS TRIO
HERBIE NICHOLS TRIO
HERBIE NICHOLS TRIO
HERBIE NICHOLS TRIO
HERBIE NICHOLS TRIO
HERBIE NICHOLS TRIO

BLUE NOTE 1519

volume 1 blue note 1515

ju.ta
hipp

at the hickory house

JAY JAY JOHNSON   JACKIE McLEAN   ART BLAKEY   KENNY CLARKE   VOLUME 1   BLUE NOTE

MILES DAVIS

...uke Jordan, Sam Jones, Art Taylor

...NA BROOKS

Art Taylor   Dave Burns
Stanley Turrentine
Wynton Kelly
Paul Chambers
Potato Valdez

STEREO
84047 BLUE NOTE

a.t.'s
delight

STEREO   THE FINEST IN JAZZ SINCE 1939
84043 BLUE NOTE

speakin'
my piece
horace parlan quintet

Stanley Turrentine, Tommy Turrentine, George Tucker, Al Harewood

BST 81081

ART BLAKEY &
THE JAZZ MESS
ENGERSA NIGHT
IN TUNISIA

75261 BLUE NOTE

hub-tones

die
...ubbard

4124 BLUE NOTE

a new perspective
donald byrd band & voices

KENNY BURRELL WITH STANLEY TURRENTINE
MAJOR HOLLEY JR / BILL ENGLISH / RAY BARRETTO

midnight
blue

4123 BLUE NOTE

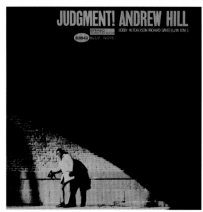

JUDGMENT! ANDREW HILL

BOBBY HUTCHERSON RICHARD DAVIS ELVIN JONES

63842 BLUE NOTE

...NDERSON/ELVIN JONES

N
Y

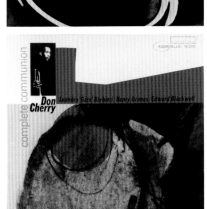

complete communion

4226 BLUE NOTE

Don
Cherry

Leandro Gato Barbieri, Henry Grimes, Edward Blackwell

BLP 4237

UNIT
STRUC
TURES
CECIL
TAYLOR

STEREO

Stanley
Turrentine
Easy
Walker

BLUE NOTE

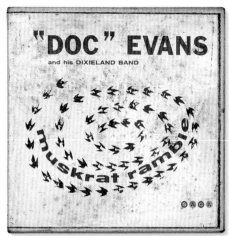

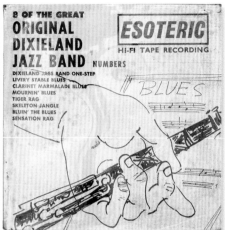

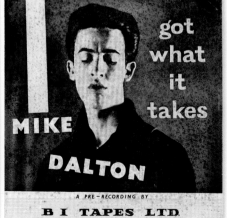

PRE-RECORDED OPEN-REEL TAPES

Evolving at the same time as
the 12-inch (30-cm), 33-rpm
gramophone album format, during
the 1950s pre-recorded open-reel
tapes provided connoisseurs of
hi-fi (then in its infancy) with
the highest-quality domestic sound
options. Magnetic tape was also
more durable than vinyl, which
could easily scratch or warp.

TELEFUNKEN MAGNETOPHON 203

Built from 1965 to 1969, the
Telefunken Magnetophon 203
tape recorder was designed
for use in homes and use in
educational establishments.
It was a stereo machine with
an in-built amplifier and speaker
for standalone use, but could
also be connected to a separate
hi-fi system.

STORING MAGNETIC TAPE

The binding agent that fixes
the oxide to the plastic tape is
susceptible to extremes of heat
or humidity so careful storage
is necessary. In professional
tape archives open-reel magnetic
master tapes are often wrapped in
polythene bags and kept in metal
canisters to protect them from
dust and liquids.

OPEN-REEL TAPE

EMI produced its own brands of
magnetic recording media, from
open-reel Emitape (seen here)
to its Soundhog cassette range.
During the 1970s, 3M's Scotch 256
was also widely used in studios.

THE TELEFUNKEN BRAND

Founded in Berlin in 1903,
in 1941 Telefunken became a
subsidiary of AEG. Post-World
War II, Telefunken became
an important name in audio
recording. Portable Telefunken
tape recorders were widely used
in German homes during the 1960s.

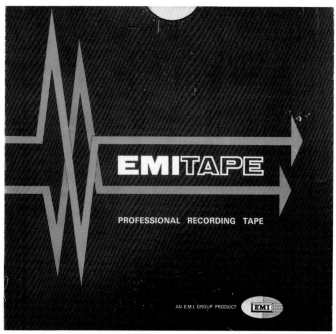

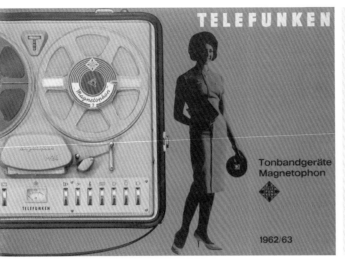

TELEFUNKEN

Tonbandgeräte
Magnetophon

1962/63

Im Namen liegt die Garantie

Wir wissen, daß zu bestimmten Namen ganz bestimmte Qualitätsbegriffe gehören, die unübersehbar beispielsweise mit einem Auto, einem Fernseher oder einem Tonbandgerät verbunden sind. TELEFUNKEN ist ein solcher Name, in dem sich gestützt von einer mehr als einem halben Jahrhundert getragenen Tradition die reichen und unschätzbaren Erfahrungen vieler Generationen von Ingenieuren und Konstrukteuren widerspiegeln.

Überall in der Welt schlagen TELEFUNKEN Kurzwellensender Brücken von Kontinent zu Kontinent.

Musik wird oft nicht schön empfunden.

Magnetophon 97
Vierspur-Stereo · 19 + 9,5 + 4,75

Magnetophon 98
Halbspur-Stereo · 19 + 9,5 + 4,75

Das Einmaleins des Tonbandes . . .

Magnetophon 85
Halbspur · 19 + 9,5

Keiner spielt wie Michael . . .

Ein Fußball-Fan verhindert?

Goethe kam um Mitternacht

Schreie in der Nacht

Magnetophon 75
Halbspur · 9,5 + 4,75

Magnetophon 76
Vierspur · 9,5 + 4,75

„Achtung Aufnahme . . .
das Tonband läuft!"

Sie erklingt aus einem Lautsprecher die Ströme des Tonmeisters — sachlich, nüchtern, ohne etwas von der erregenden Stimmung zu vermitteln, die immer wieder alle Beteiligten bis vor einer Aufnahme im Rundfunk- oder Schallplatten-Studio ergreift.

Der Kapellmeister am Dirigentenpult hebt den Taktstock. Die Musiker hören auf, ihre Instrumente zu stimmen, und die Solisten werfen noch einen kurzen Blick auf ihre Noten. Alles verstummt und verharrt in gespannter Konzentration.

Plötzlich löst ein brausender Akkord die Spannung und erfüllt den Raum. Gemächlich, wie von Geisterhand geführt, streichen unsichtbare Geigenbogen über die Saiten, läuten die Finger der Bläser wie spielend über die Ventile.

Mit geschulten Ohren verfolgt dabei der Tonmeister das Geschehen im Senderaal. Er beobachtet das erregende Vibrieren des Zeigers am Aussteuerungsmesser, regelt und mischt die feiner elektrischen Ströme, die von den Mikrofonen von dem Orchester kommen und führt sie schließlich zu einem Tonband gerät, das den ganzen Wohlklang des Orchesters vom tiefsten Baß bis zu den höchsten Tönen, vom Paukufo-Flöte auf einem schmalen braunen Band festhält.

Eigener Tonmeister sein, selbst Regie führen — wäre das nichts für Sie? Vielleicht steht auch Ihnen ein Orchester zur Verfügung, oder selbst ein Lied zur Guitarre oder ein „selbstgezimmertes" Hörspiel auf Tonband aufgenommen, bereitet genau soviel Freude. Versuchen Sie's mal! Das Studio-Tonbandgerät Magnetophon 24 mit seiner ausgereiften Technik wird Ihnen dabei helfen.

Ein Tastendruck genügt –

die Sendung ist auf dem Band. So einfach ist die Aufnahmen mit dem Magnetophon automatic. Betraut von der Technik kann jeder die Freuden des Tonbandkino erleben. Ein Tastendruck genügt, und alles andere nimmt Ihnen das Magnetophon automatic ab — viel genauer, als Sie es je von Hand für tun könnten. Ganz gleich, ob Sie eine Mikrofonaufnahme machen, von der Platte oder vom Rundfunk überspielen — die Aufnahme „sitzt".

Letztes Jahr in Bad Neuenahr . . .

Sonnige Tage voller Fröhlichkeit, Winzerfeste und Kurkonzerte — all das zeigt das Bild. Doch wo bleibt der Ton, wo das echte Geschehen? Erst ein Tonbandgerät Magnetophon erweckt die stummen Aufnahmen zum Leben. Sprache, Musikuntermalung und Geräusche vermitteln immer wieder die ganze Urlaubsstimmung.

Wenn dann noch das Bild synchron zum jeweiligen Sprechtext und Geräusch wechselt, ist die Wiedergabe lebenssecht. Das Steuergerät — der Diachron — und der automatische Bildwerfer sorgen für den genauen Bildwechsel. Jede Vorführung im Familien- oder Freundeskreis begeistert alle Zuschauer.

Biene is danz leise . . .

und Vati hebt das Mikrofon ganz nah an Sabines Mund.

Stammbuch und Familienchronik werden heute sinnvoll durch das Tonband ergänzt. Die moderne Familie birgt die Erinnerungen nicht mehr in einem Fotoalbum, sondern läßt farbige Dias sprechen. Der erste Schrei, das erste Wort, von einem Tonbandgerät Magnetophon festgehalten, bleibt für immer erhalten.

Caterina und Wolfgang Amadeus . . .

beide sind Nachbarn in Ihrem Tonbandarchiv. Ob sie es wohl auch im richtigen Leben gewesen wären? Auf jeden Fall verträgt sich die mehrfache Schallplatten-Millionärin Caterina Valente gut mit dem armen Salzburger Hofkapellmeister Mozart, dem sie an Aufführungsfolgen in nichts nachstent. Auf TELEFUNKEN Tonbändern festgehalten, feiern sie beide mit ihren Melodien auf Wunsch jeden Tag Premiere.

Auch nach Jahren noch erfreut Sie immer wieder die Qualität der Wiedergabe — nicht ohne Grund zu TELEFUNKEN Tonbändern gehören immer die praktischen Schwenk-Kassetten, die das Tonband gegen Staub schützen und die die Aufbewahrung mitgeliefert werden. Wenn Sie die Kassetten mit Stecktüteln sicher verbinden, können Sie aus ihnen leicht ein übersichtliches Tonband-Archiv zusammenstellen.

Bandarten	Spulendurchmesser in cm	Bandlänge in m	Laufzeit	Spurkammern in Stunden		Preis DM inkl.
Normalband	11	185	15 M.	2 x 1		.4,60
Normalband	13	270	15 M.	2 x 1½	2 x 1½	12,80
Normalband	15	360	18 M.	2 x 3	2 x 3	13,95
Langspielband	13	270	11½	2 x 1½	2 x 1½	12,50
Langspielband	15	540	1½ h.	2 x 2½	2 x 2½	19,90
Langspielband	18	585	1¾ h.	2 x 3	2 x 3	21,80
Doppelspielband	11	540	1½ h.	2 x 2	2 x 2	13,50
Doppelspielband	13	540	1½ h.	2 x 2	2 x 2	24,80
Doppelspielband	15	720	1½ h.	2 x 3	2 x 3	34,50
Uerspelband	15	720	1¾ h.	2 x 2	2 x 2	32,50

Alles spricht für
TELEFUNKEN

Wünschen Sie weiteres Informationsmaterial, rufen Sie bitte TELEFUNKEN Hannover 00 11/17 40 74 an.

Wir beraten Sie gern und laden zu einer unverbindlichen Vorführung ein.

AEG-TELEFUNKEN

Das auto-mobile Studio-
Magnettongerät

magnetophon 12A

opposite

THE STUDIO MUSICIAN

As the 1960s drew to a close,
musicians began to gain a greater
understanding of the recording
process. Some, like former Beatle
Paul McCartney (seen here in
around 1965), were sufficiently
confident, and wealthy, to set
up small studios in their own
homes. Much of his 1970 debut,
McCartney, was created on a
Studer four-track tape recorder
on his farm in Scotland.

left

TELEFUNKEN MAGNETOPHONS

The Magnetophon 12A was a
popular studio model that
launched in 1978. The Magnetophon
3000 debuted in 1973 and was aimed
at the domestic hi-fi market.

RAY DOLBY

<u>INVENTOR OF NOISE-
REDUCTION TECHNOLOGY</u>

<u>1</u>

A prodigiously talented engineer, by the time Ray Milton Dolby left high school he had already spent several years working part-time for the Ampex Corporation on their first tape recorders. He filed the first of his fifty patents at the age of nineteen, and even before graduating from Stanford University in 1957 he'd played a key role in the development of the Ampex quadruplex video recorder.

Winning a prestigious Marshall Scholarship, Dolby moved to the UK where, in 1961, his research earned him a PhD in physics from the University of Cambridge. In 1965, he founded Dolby Laboratories in London, relocating two years later to California. The first product he developed was the noise-reduction system that would become synonymous with his name.

Background noise is an inherent problem when making analogue audio recordings on magnetic tape. During quiet passages of music or spoken-word recordings, it results in clearly audible high-frequency 'hiss'. When recording audio onto magnetic tape, the embedded oxide particles are subjected to a fluctuating magnetic field at the recording head in proportion to the fluctuations in air pressure of the audio signal. Some of these oxide particles, however, are thicker than others and take longer to become magnetized; with quieter sounds, the magnetic field also becomes weaker and so these oxide particles never become fully magnetized. When 'unmagnetized' particles pass the playback head, it results in tiny distortions to the sound, audible in the higher frequencies as 'tape hiss'.

Dolby designed circuitry that used dynamic 'pre-emphasis' during the recording stage and 'de-emphasis' in the playback, thus improving the signal-to-noise ratio. In practice, this meant boosting the level of the quieter high frequencies so that they became louder in relation to the background noise during the recording process ('encoding'), and mirroring this in the playback

<u>1</u>
DOLBY ON DOLBY
'I was so far ahead in my credits that I didn't have to worry about getting into college,' he recalled in 1988, 'so I went to school three hours a day and worked five at Ampex.'

('decoding'), so that those high-frequency sounds are lowered to the correct volume, while also making the background hiss lower than it otherwise would have been.

His first noise-reduction system was unveiled in 1965 and was launched as Dolby A. For the system to work, both the decoding and encoding had to be correctly calibrated, meaning that recordings made using a Dolby A encoder were useless unless played back through a matching Dolby A decoder. Nevertheless, designed with professional studios in mind, Dolby A was very quickly adopted as an industry standard.

The timing of Dolby's invention coincided with the rise of the compact cassette. Devised as a more convenient alternative to bulky quarter-inch (0.5-cm) reel-to-reel tape, cassette tape was only ⅛-inch (0.3 cm) wide and ran at 1⅞ inches (4.75 cm) per second – an eighth of the speed of a professional tape recorder. This made background hiss a serious problem. The simpler Dolby B system was created in 1968 with domestic cassette tapes in mind. Although not as powerful as its professional counterpart, Dolby B was designed so that an encoded tape could still be played back on a cassette deck without a matching decoder. The effect would be a brighter sound with the high frequencies emphasized. From the mid-1970s until the demise of the compact cassette format in the early 21st century, almost all pre-recorded tapes produced globally were encoded with Dolby B, and cassette decks were

2 universally equipped with a Dolby B decode button.

Ray Dolby died from leukemia in 2013, aged eighty. His inventions and business acumen made him a billionaire, and in his will he bequeathed some $52 million to his old alma mater, Pembroke College, Cambridge. Noise-reduction technology has largely gone the way of analogue magnetic tape recording, but Dolby's pioneering work in cinema sound has ensured that his

3 name remains prominent in the world of audio technology.

RAY DOLBY
Born: 18 January 1933, Portland, Oregon, USA
Died: 12 September 2013, San Francisco, California, USA

2
SURROUND SOUND
Although Ray Dolby went on to develop the less widely used C, SR and S noise-reduction systems, with the emergence of digital recording and the compact disc during the 1980s, the need for such technology declined. By this time, however, Dolby Laboratories was focused mainly on cinema sound technology, developing the surround systems used in movie theatres and homes across the globe.

3
DOLBY AND CINEMA
The significance of his work in this field was marked in 2015 when he was posthumously awarded a star on the Hollywood Walk of Fame.

below
PORTABLE MUSIC (1967)

The compact cassette
revolutionized the way music was
consumed. Small, battery-operated
portable units such as the
Telefunken Magnetophone CC Alpha
(below), enabled people to take
their favourite music with them
wherever they went - something
only previously possible by means
of small transistor radios.

opposite
PEAK POPULARITY

By the early 1970s, every major
release was available on LP and
compact cassette. At the start
of the 1980s, blank cassette
sales were so high that Britain's
music industry launched the
'Home Taping is Killing Music'
campaign. Between 1985 and 1992,
the compact cassette was the most
popular music format in the UK.

PYE Bob Leaper Big Band / Try This On For Size — ZCP 18339

Tony Macaulay presents The London Pops Orchestra — ZCP 18241

Tony Hatch Orchestra— Brasilia Mission — ZCP 18303

Stephane Grappelli 1971 — ZCP 18360

Various Artists / Chartbusters Vol. 2 — ZCPCB 15001

Rogeros Brazilian Brass — ZCP 18320

BACK SEAT DRIVING with TONY HATCH — ZCP 11057

BACK SEAT DRIVING with VICTOR SILVESTER — ZCP 11056

MAX COLLIE RHYTHM ACES / world champions of jazz — ZCBD 12137

CARL PERKINS / Guitar Pickin', Rock Singin', Country Boy — ZCSUN 18056

HUMPHREY LYTTELTON / hazy crazy & blue — ZCBLP 12160

DUDLEY MOORE / AT THE WAVENDON FESTIVAL — ZCBLP 12151

SALUTE TO SATCHMO / A Tribute to LOUIS ARMSTRONG with ALEX WELSH & his BAND · GEORGE CHISHOLM HUMPHREY LYTTELTON · BRUCE TURNER — ZCBLP 12161

ALEX WELSH / if i had a talking picture of you — ZC BLP 12109

ISLAND JOHN MARTYN / GRACE AND DANGER — ZCI 9560

IN CROWD / MAN FROM NEW GUINEA — ZCI 9577

Tequila Mockingbird / Chamber Ensemble Opus 1 — ZCI 9529

SERGE GAINSBOURG / AUX ARMES ET CAETERA — ZCI 9581

J. J. CALE / 5 — ZCSA 5018

THRILLER — EDDIE + HOT RODS — ZCI 9563

HI TENSION — ZCI 9564

Cat Stevens / Back To Earth — ZCI 9565

LINTON KWESI JOHNSON / Forces of Victory — ZCI 9566

Cat Stevens / Mona Bone Jakon — ZCIR 15021

INNER CIRCLE / Everything Is Great — ZCI 9558

Roger McGough / Summer With Monika — ZCI 9551

Zap-pow — ZCI 9547

UTOPIA / DEFACE THE MUSIC — ZCI 9642

292-293

mfp

HOT
HITS
XIII

LIBRARY COPY
do not remove

The Slider
You wear it well
Schools out
Seaside shuffle
Popcorn
10538 Overture
My guy
Automatically sunshine
The locomotion
Samson and Delilah
Silver machine
Where is the love

third wave : MAGNETIC ERA

COVER ALBUMS

Music for Pleasure (MFP) was launched by EMI in 1965 to release budget-priced albums. One of the label's most successful album series was *Hot Hits*, which featured cover versions of contemporary hit records performed by unnamed session musicians. Costing little more than a 7-inch (18-cm) single, these LPs were hugely popular. Cover albums were a useful source of income for session players such as Reg Dwight, who appeared on many such records in 1969 and 1970 before becoming more widely known in his own right - as Elton John.

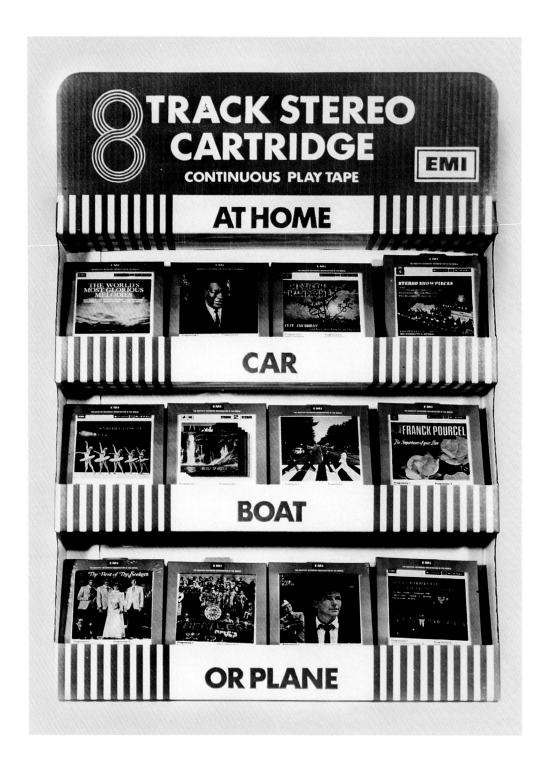

THE CONTINUOUS-PLAY TAPE
The eight-track stereo cartridge was created in 1964. It comprised a long loop of magnetic tape that enabled music to be played continuously. Although intended for in-car use, eight-track decks also found their way into domestic hi-fi systems. By the middle of the 1970s, however, the compact cassette had rendered the eight-track redundant.

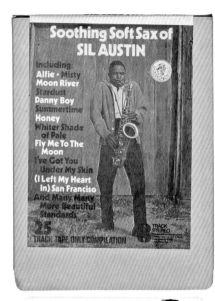

THE GOLDEN AGE OF SLEEVE DESIGN

The first half of the 1970s saw sleeve design for long-playing records evolve into an art form in its own right. London-based studio Hipgnosis - formed by Storm Thorgerson and Aubrey Powell - produced stunning sleeve artwork for many of the leading bands of the era, among them Pink Floyd, Genesis and Led Zeppelin.

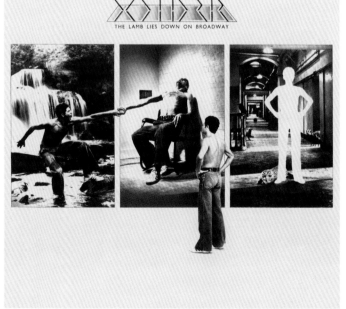

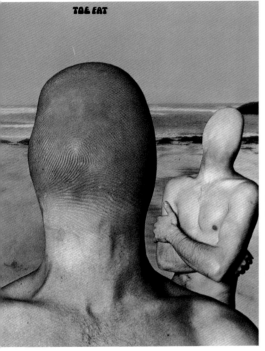

TOE FAT

ELEGY/THE NICE

KITSCH
HEAVY METAL KIDS

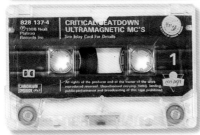

HIP-HOP CASSETTES (1984-94)

The compact cassette was a popular format in the world of hip-hop, with sales of pre-recorded releases generally exceeding those of vinyl.

As a cheap, recordable format, it also played a significant role in the evolution of the genre. In the early days, would-be rappers would perform live over the top of rhythmic backing cassettes - 'beat tapes' -

played on a large portable 'boombox'. Rappers could develop a following as mixtapes of their performances circulated. In the 1980s, some DJs established themselves via 'house tapes' made in their home studios.

below

TEAC PORTASTUDIO 144
(1979)

Before the launch of the
TEAC 144, recording music in
a bedroom studio was a serious
and expensive hobby. The
Portastudio was a portable four-
track recorder that used cheap
cassette tape combined with a
very basic mixing desk. Musicians
were able to save themselves
money by making demonstration
recordings at home rather
than paying for expensive
studio time.

opposite

HOME TAPE RECORDING
(1981-83)

In the 1980s, Japanese brand
Fostex sold budget reel-to-reel
tape recorders and ancillary
equipment for home recording. The
B16 (below) launched in 1983 was
a sixteen-channel tape recorder
that used ½-inch (1-cm) spools
of magnetic tape. The outputs
were plugged into a mixing desk
and stereo 'master' would be
recorded on a separate two-
channel tape recorder, such as
the TEAC X-1000 (1981) seen above.

overleaf

SONY WALKMAN TPS-L2
(1979)

The Sony Walkman made portable
music even easier for the
listener to carry around. More
than 200 million Sony Walkman
cassette players were sold until
the line was retired in 2010.
A further 200 million Walkman CD
and MP3 players have also been
sold to date.

302.303

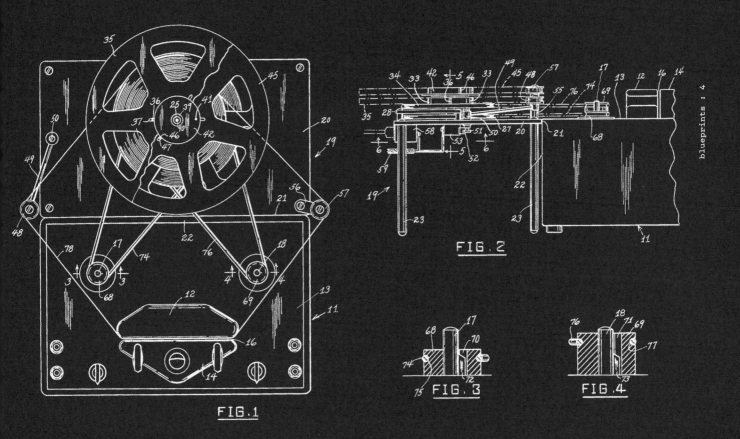

FIG.1

FIG.2

FIG.3

FIG.4

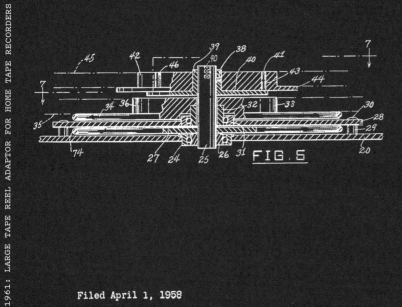

FIG.5

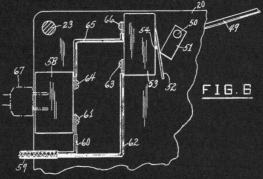

FIG.6

blueprints : 4

1961: LARGE TAPE REEL ADAPTOR FOR HOME TAPE RECORDERS

Filed April 1, 1958

INVENTOR.
ROBERT H. BODHOLDT
BY Herman L. Gordon
ATTORNEY

304.305

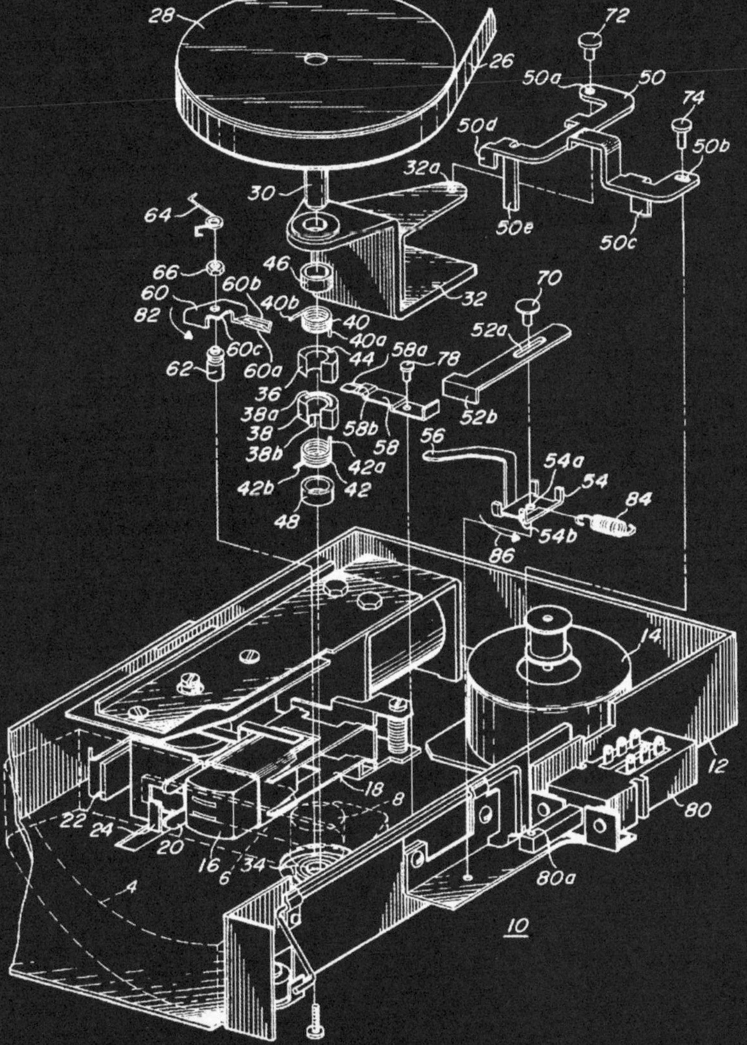

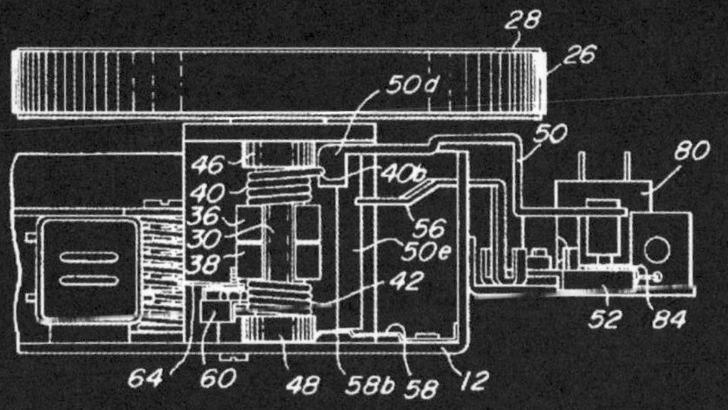

Fig. 2

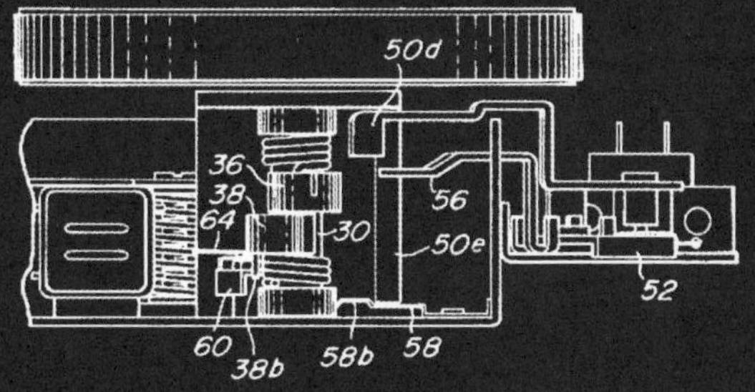

Fig. 3

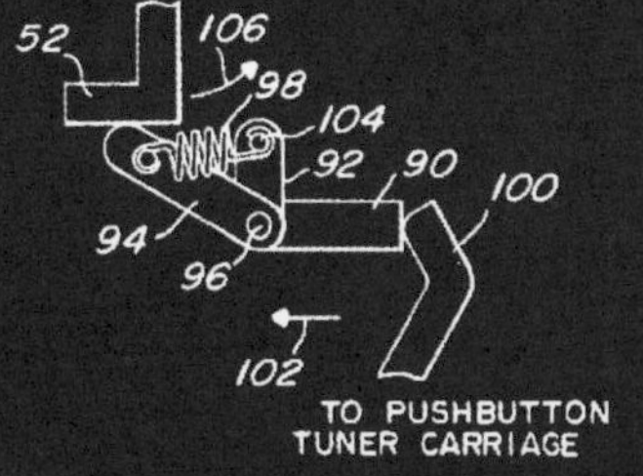
TO PUSHBUTTON
TUNER CARRIAGE

Fig. 4

1977: EIGHT-TRACK RECORDER

F I G. 1

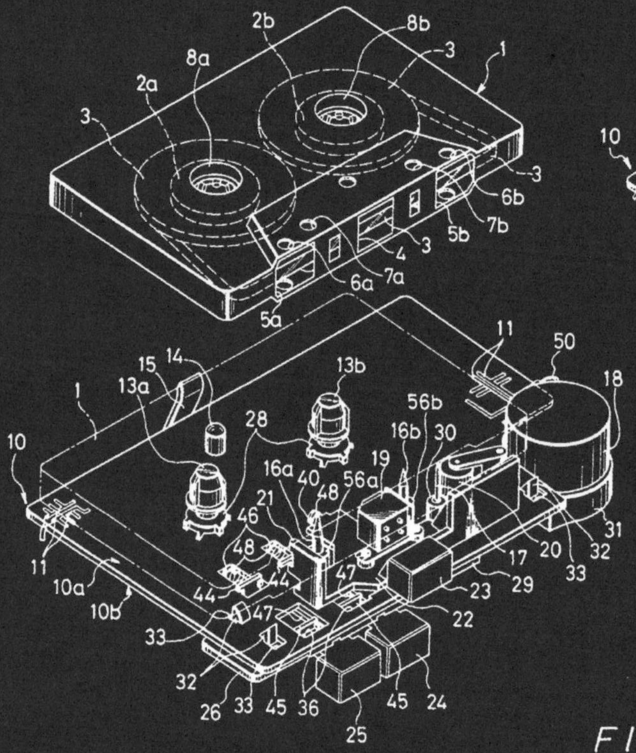

F I G. 2

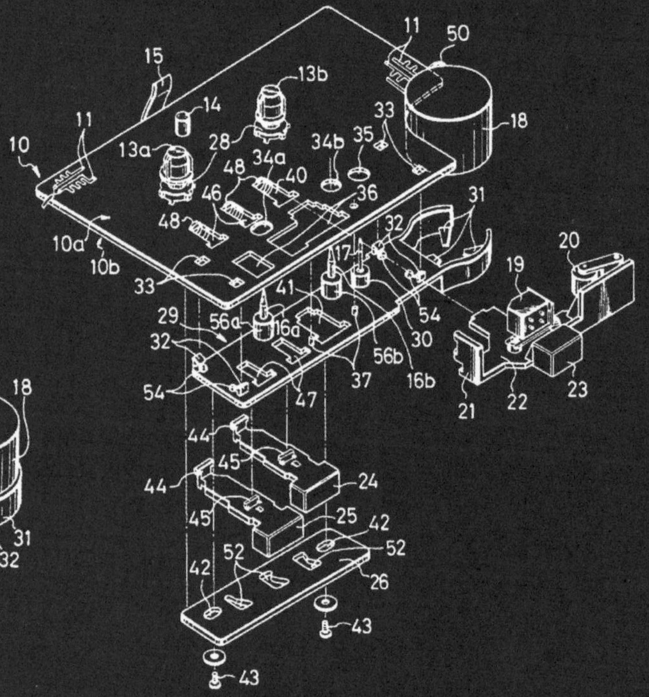

F I G. 3

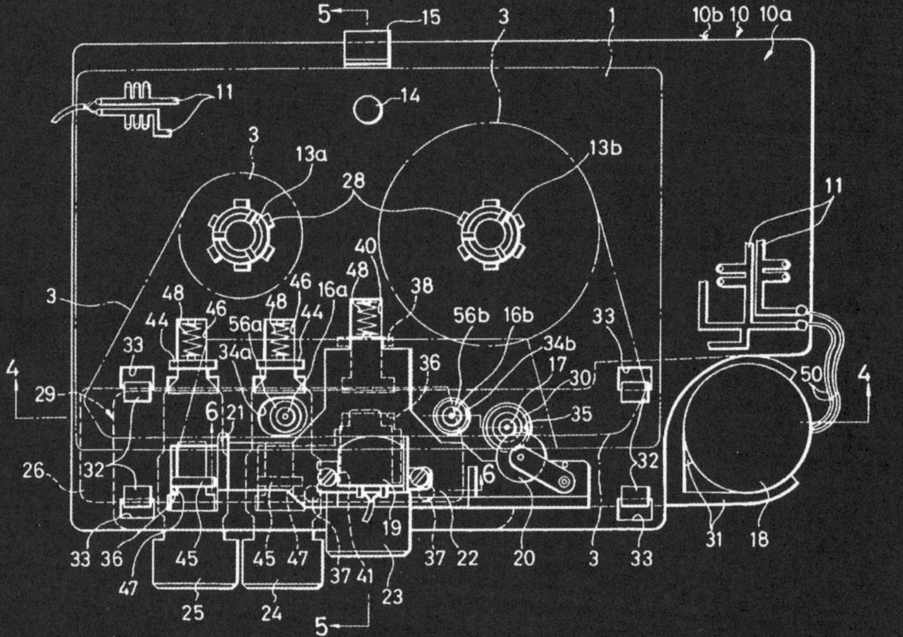

blueprints : 4

306.307

1989: CASSETTE PLAYER

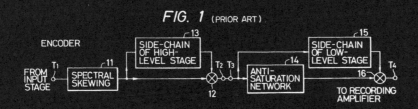

FIG. 1 (PRIOR ART)

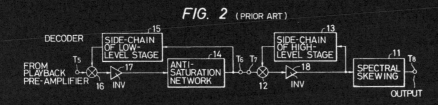

FIG. 2 (PRIOR ART)

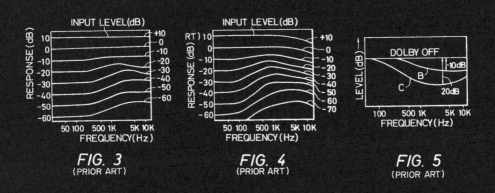

FIG. 3 (PRIOR ART)   *FIG. 4* (PRIOR ART)   *FIG. 5* (PRIOR ART)

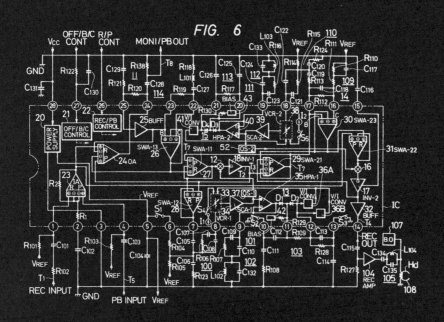

FIG. 6

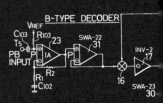

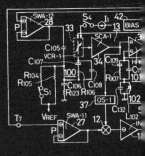

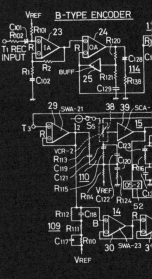

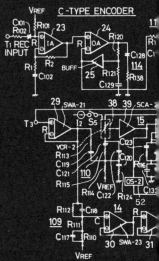

4,476,502

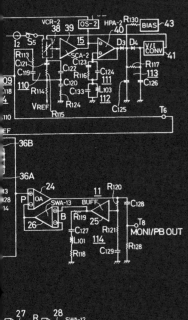

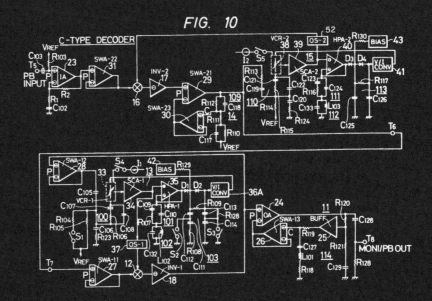

FIG. 10

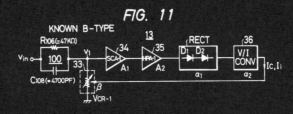

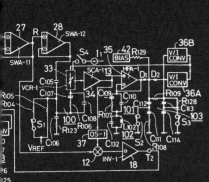

FIG. 11

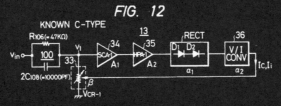

KNOWN B-TYPE

FIG. 12

KNOWN C-TYPE

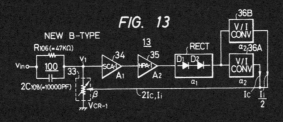

FIG. 13

NEW B-TYPE

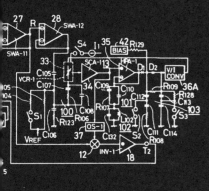

FIG. 14

NEW C-TYPE

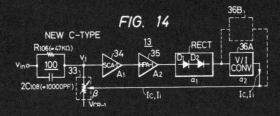

blueprints : 4

308·309

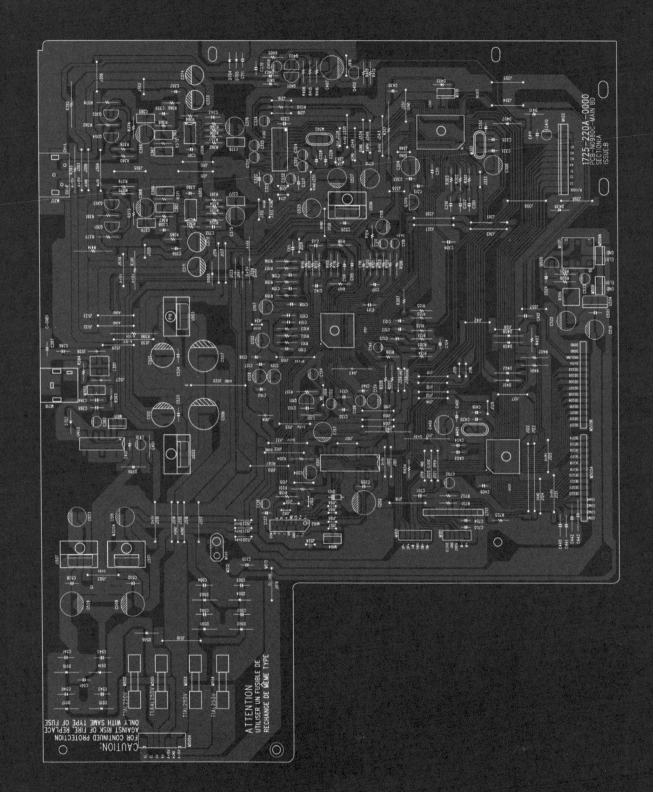

2004: NAD C521 COMPACT DISC PLAYER

2006: SONY MINIDISC RECORDER/PLAYER MXD-D5C

[MAIN BOARD] (COMPONENT SIDE)

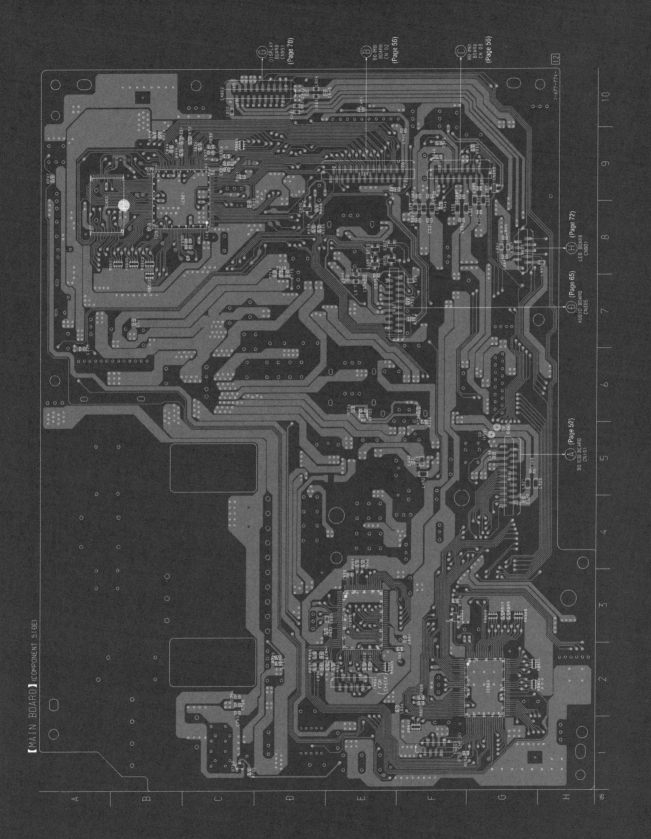

blueprints : 4

310.311

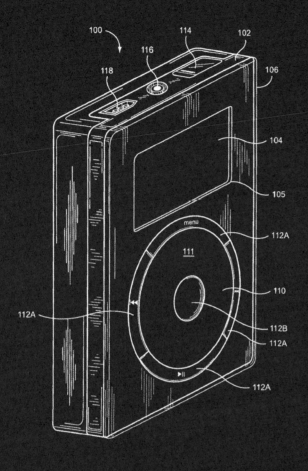

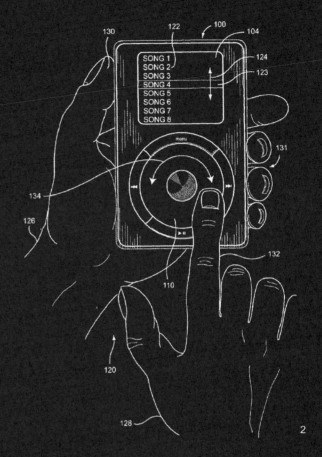

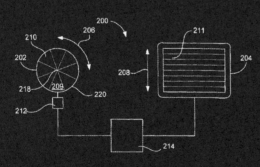

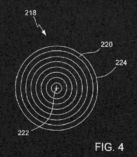

FIG. 4

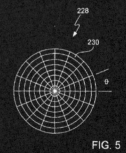

FIG. 5

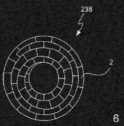

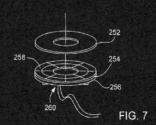

FIG. 7

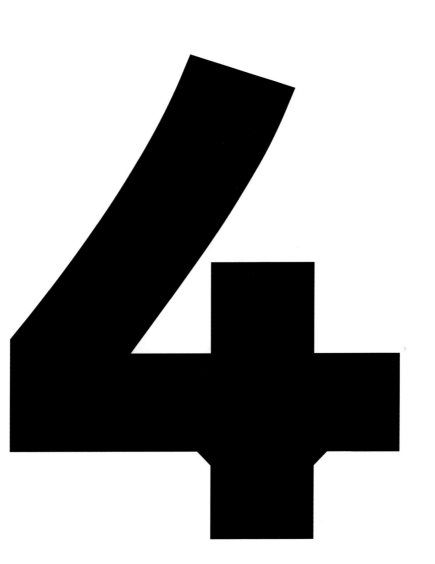

fourth wave
DIGITAL ERA

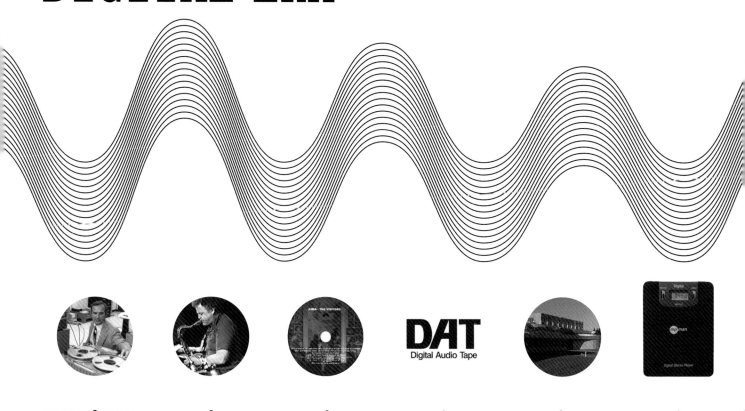

1969	1971	1982	1987	1991	1997

Dr Thomas Stockham carries out initial experiments into digital tape recording.

Something Else, by Steve Marcus, becomes the first commercially released album to be recorded digitally.

On 17 August, the compact disc (CD) makes its commercial debut – a set of Chopin waltzes recorded by Claudio Arrau. The first pop music CD to be commercially released is ABBA's *The Visitors*.

The digital audio tape (DAT) is introduced. Despite its high quality, it fails to reach a mainstream market, although it is adopted by the recording industry.

The MP3 file format, developed at the Fraunhofer Institute in Germany, is accepted by the MPEG working group. Its use gradually proliferates with the spread of the internet.

Korea's Saehan Information Systems produces MPMan, the first portable MP3 player.

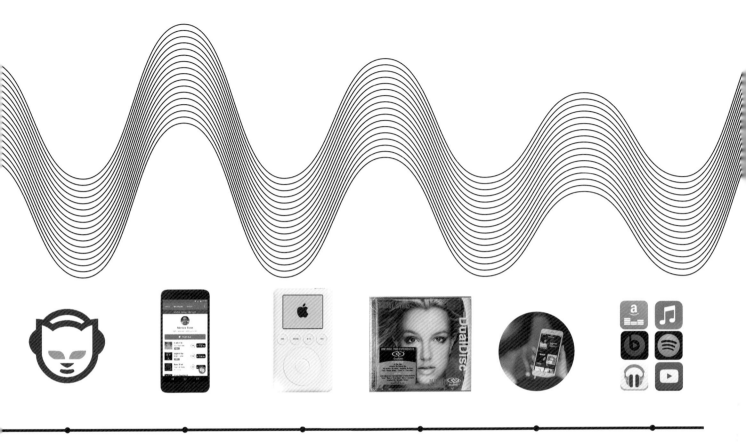

1999

Napster – a peer-to-peer digital file-sharing service – goes live in June. Concerns over music piracy and copyright infringement prompt protests – and lawsuits – from Metallica and Dr Dre among others. It is forced to shut down in July 2001.

2002

The launch of Shazam, the portable music-recognition service.

2003

Two years after introducing the iPod music player, Apple debuts the iTunes online digital music store. Within a year, it has sold 70 million songs, at a cost of $0.99 each. By 2005, Apple is selling 500 million tracks worldwide annually.

2005

The DualDisc (DD) receives its general release in the USA. It combines a CD layer with a DVD layer.

2014

Global revenues from digital music downloads and subscriptions overtake sales of physical formats for the first time.

2015

Global revenues from streamed music account for $2.89 billion, a jump of 45.2% from the previous year. In more than forty countries, including the USA, streaming revenues now exceed those of downloads.

Going back to the days of Thomas Edison's etched tin-foil cylinders, analogue recording works by capturing audio and creating electrical representations of the signal's sound wave. Digital recording involves a very different process: taking samples of a sound wave and storing them as binary information – groups of ones and zeros. This method is known as pulse-code modulation (PCM). There are two discrete parts to the digital audio process: the ADC (analogue-to-digital converter) turns the audio signal into binary data; the DAC (digital-to-analogue converter) reverses the process, reading those one and zeros and converting them back into audio.

Digital sound offers plenty of benefits over its analogue counterpart – not least that annoying artefacts of analogue magnetic tape recording such as hiss and background noise can be avoided altogether. And as the sound has been converted into digital data, it can be easily manipulated, edited and stored using computer software.

The process of digital recording might be compared to a movie – i.e. a rapid sequence of still frames. In a similar way, the ADC samples the sound wave many times each second, giving each one a numerical value. To achieve 'CD-quality' audio, 44,100 samples must be taken every second; this figure is known as the 'sample rate' and is denoted in kHz – thus 44.1 kHz. The other key measure for digital sound quality is 'bit depth', which describes the number of 'bits' (binary digits) of information in each sample, and governs the resolution and signal-to-noise ratio. CD sound is 16-bit, meaning that each sample is made up of a combination of 16 ones or zeros; modern digital studio recording uses 24-bit depth, increasing the dynamic range of the audio.

The principles of pulse-code modulation go back as far as 1937, when English electrical engineer Alec Reeves considered the idea of using a binary representation of sound as a solution

1

1
DIGITAL TERMINOLOGY
The related term 'bit rate' describes how many bits of data are processed each second. 'Bit rate' is measured in kilobits per second (Kbps).

to the problem of additive noise on long-distance telephone lines. This was developed during World War II when Bell Labs created SIGSALY, a secure system for voice communication, and also the first functional PCM technology. In the pre-transistor era, however, with valves both expensive and bulky, Bell Labs envisaged few practical commercial uses for PCM; as late as 1965, Reeves maintained that this was an idea yet to come of age.

From the end of the 1950s, a number of scientists worked on the idea of using PCM techniques with audio, among them Massachusetts Institute of Technology's (MIT) Thomas Stockham, who experimented with capturing speech on a computer. The first true digital audio recorder, however, was produced in Japan, at the research facilities of NHK: in 1967, the first monophonic PCM audio recorder was developed; two years later, NHK's stereo version appeared. Both featuring 13-bit depth and a 32-kHz sample rate. Digital data was stored on a helical-scanning video recorder.

It was one of Japan's leading music technology companies, Nippon Columbia (known for its Denon brand), that saw the potential of digital sound in the recording, storage and playback of music. Denon had long sought a way of improving the quality of vinyl LPs, and had pioneered a return to the idea of direct-to-disc recording, thus bypassing the analogue magnetic tape process altogether. Denon leased the NHK stereo recorder and in 1971 began a series of comparative tests between the two systems. That year saw the release of *Something* by jazz-fusion artist Steve Marcus, the first commercial album to be recorded digitally. Denon continued to refine the system, even producing an experimental multi-track recorder in 1972. During the decade the company recorded more than 400 albums digitally, including releases by many leading American jazz musicians of the period.

2
STAMP OF APPROVAL
Reeves's achievement was marked in Britain in 1969 with the issue of a one-shilling (5 pence/a nickel) stamp depicting pulse-code modulation on a sound wave.

3
FOR THE RECORD
Although recorded digitally, *Something* was released as a vinyl LP. Before 1982, all commercially released music appeared on an analogue format, such as vinyl record or compact cassette tape.

Meanwhile, in 1976 Thomas Stockham produced his own successful digital recording system in the United States. The Soundstream Digital Tape Recorder was 16-bit/37.5 kHz and used a Honeywell computer tape drive for storage. Unlike the Denon system, which was used in studios and broadcasting, Stockham's first audio experiments concentrated on capturing live, on-location performances. The Soundstream captured the interest of many classical music record labels, some of whom hired it – or even paid the $160,000 asking price to have the system installed in their own facilities.

Yet even at this time, some still viewed digital recording as an expensive insurance scheme. In the late 1970s, direct-to-disc analogue recording was still seen as the 'purest' system for recording classical music. It bypassed the inherent faults of magnetic tape recording, eliminating background noise, 'wow and flutter', and multiple generations of master-tape copying. It also placed limitations on producers and musicians. Recordings had to be recorded live with a final stereo mix being cut; musical spontaneity may have been captured, but it also required flawless performances from the players and precision work from engineers and producers. Furthermore, the cutting system itself was prone to occasional failure and so some direct-to-disc recordings were simultaneously captured digitally as a backup in the event of a breakdown.

The American technology giant 3M was working along the same lines during this time, but focused on professional multi-track recording. A prototype – containing thirty-two linear digital tracks stored on a 1-inch (2.5-cm) magnetic tape, and which allowed for overdubbing and digital editing – was built in 1977 and two years later went on the market. The first album to be released using a digital multi-track system was Ry Cooder's award-winning *Bop Till You Drop* album in 1979, recorded on

4

4
DIGITAL CLASSICAL
In 1976, Stockham used the Soundstream Digital Tape Recorder to make the first live digital recording, capturing the Santa Fe Opera's performance of Virgil Thomson's *A Mother of Us All*.

this 3M model at Warner Brothers' North Hollywood studio in California. Ironically, given the state-of-the-art recording system, the album largely comprised cover versions of rhythm and blues standards from the 1950s.

Digital audio multi-tracks gradually came to dominate the professional recording and broadcasting worlds. In 1991, the Alesis Digital Audio Tape (ADAT) was introduced as an affordable option for small studios, capable of recording and overdubbing eight channels of CD-standard audio (16-bit stored on Super VHS videotape cartridges). The initial 'Blackface ADAT' model could only record at a sample rate of 48 kHz; later versions could also facilitate a rate of 44.1 kHz.

In spite of these developments, at the start of the 1980s analogue still ruled the roost as far as the consumer was concerned, largely in the form of vinyl LPs and singles and, to a lesser degree, pre-recorded compact cassettes. Both formats have inherent faults, though. Vinyl can be damaged, suffer from surface-noise crackles and pops and has one insurmountable problem – the speed at which the vinyl passes under the stylus will alter during the course of the album, causing a greater likelihood of distortion the closer the stylus gets to the centre of the record. And cassette tape has the worst problems of all analogue magnetic tape-recording media, since the tape is narrow and slow, making it more prone to hiss and other mechanical issues. A radical solution was around the corner, however.

Two figures played important conceptual roles in the birth of optical digital storage and playback. David Gregg of Westrex filed a patent for a 'videodisk' in 1962, and inventor James T. Russell pioneered recording digital information on an optical transparent foil, lit from behind by a beam from a high-powered halogen lamp. Both patents were later licensed and in 1978 the LaserDisc was launched on the market. Evolving directly from

5

5
FROM TAPE TO HARD DRIVE
The ADAT and Tascam DTRS models were the last significant dedicated multi-track systems to use magnetic tape for storage. Since then, digital storage functions have largely been performed by optical hard drives - whether based around a computer software digital audio workstation (DAW) or a dedicated hard-drive recorder.

6
FLAWED FORMAT
As a home-video medium, the LaserDisc was superior to the VHS and Betamax systems that had recently debuted in the USA. But as it couldn't be used to video-record television shows, the system fell by the wayside.

6

this technology, Sony and Philips set up a joint task force to agree on a format for audio-only optical medium. What emerged was the compact disc (CD). The first digital CDs appeared, to much fanfare, in 1982. An optical digital storage medium, they were not only hailed as a superior-sounding format but were also more robust, smaller, thinner and easier to store.

Manufactured mainly from polycarbonate plastic, the $4^3/_4$-inch (12-cm) disc was backed with a thin layer of aluminium covered with a protective layer of lacquer. With the sound source converted digitally using an ADC process, the CD is made by etching ('burning') the digital data onto the surface of the disc, creating bumps called 'pits'; this creates a two-tiered surface, where a pit represents a zero and no pit (the 'land') represents a one. When the disc is played it rotates at high speed; a laser fires at the surface of the CD and is able to read the zeros and ones, which are then converted by the DAC process in the CD player into electrical current that can be amplified and heard.

The first commercial CD release appeared on 17 August 1982, and was a Philips recording of pianist Claudio Arrau performing a series of Chopin waltzes. Music consumers were very quickly persuaded: by 1988, global CD production was 400 million, and by the end of the decade, sales had usurped those of vinyl.

Several consumer digital recording formats appeared from the end of the 1980s. Sony developed the Digital Audio Tape (DAT) in 1987, intended as a replacement for the compact cassette. DAT faced opposition from the US music industry, which feared that illegal digital versions of copyrighted music would become rife, and lengthy legal processes contributed to its failure as a consumer format. DAT established itself in professional recording studios, however, later often replacing the two-channel reel-to-reel tape recorder as a high-end final mix medium, as well as in computer storage.

7

7
TAPES STAY IN THE MIX
Sales of pre-recorded compact cassette sales also dropped rapidly. There remained a robust market for blank tapes, however - primarily because there was still no viable digital consumer alternative, but also because of the continuing popularity of personal stereos such as the Sony Walkman on which self-compiled 'mix tapes' could be played.

Two other formats followed, once again with the aim of finally putting to the sword the compact cassette. In 1992, Philips and Japanese technology giant Matsushita launched the Digital Compact Cassette (DCC); the same year, Sony launched the MiniDisc (MD). Both formats were in every way superior to the analogue compact cassette and yet neither made much of an impact. Perhaps after the format wars of the 1980s (vinyl/CD; VHS/Betamax/Video2000) the public was wary of choosing a new technology that might quickly become redundant.

As with many other aspects of modern life, the way in which we consume music has been metamorphosed by the internet. From the earliest days, tech-savvy consumers began digitizing music collections, using software to 'rip' CDs to their computer hard drives. And when the MP3 format began to make its mark, compressing file sizes to a fraction of their original size, swapping them across the internet became a popular pursuit. Others, on the other hand, adopted the MP3 format along with the emergence of portable media players such as the Apple iPod. The music industry began to feel the direct impact of this new technology when the use of peer-to-peer (P2P) file-sharing services – such as Napster, which launched in 1999 – became widespread. Sales of CDs rapidly began to drop. For a brief period, attempts were made to prosecute illegal file sharers, but the problem became too vast and the music industry was forced to embrace new ways of making money from the internet.

Today, a growing number of consumers download audio (legally or otherwise) or use subscription online streaming services, such as Spotify, Deezer or Apple Music. And increasingly, fewer desire to collect physical copies of their music. It's clear that 'audiophile' sound quality matters only to a relatively small population of listeners. The message seems to be that for most people, something that sounds OK is perfectly good enough.

8

SHORT SHELF LIFE
DCC was among the least commercially successful of all audio formats, and within four years had been withdrawn altogether. Buoyed by a stronger uptake in Japan, where music labels had offered pre-recorded MiniDiscs, Sony maintained production in a small way, the final models being produced in 2013.

9

SACD AND MP3
In the late 1990s, research laboratories were trying to improve even on CD quality. The Super Audio CD (SACD), with a technical specification bordering on the absurd (a 50-kHz upper frequency limit) made its debut in 1999 - at precisely the same time that use of the comparatively crude MP3 proliferated.

EMI DIGITAL MIXING DESK
(1979)

Considered the first of its
kind, this mixing desk was
developed at EMI's Abbey Road
Studios in London and used
on a number of sessions there.
Very basic by modern standards,
it could nevertheless perform
real-time mixing functions
such as volume fader control
and equalization settings.

SONY AUDIO CATALOGUES
(1981-84)

At the start of the 1980s, Sony
was enjoying unprecedented global
success with its Walkman range.
However, it was the launch of
the CD, which had been devised
jointly by Sony and Philips, that
heralded a revolution in the way
music was consumed, bringing an
end to more than eight decades
of dominance by the gramophone.

DISPLAY OF COMPACT DISCS
(1991-2013)

Although CDs were expensive, the
new format was quick to take off
globally. Music fans re-bought
many of the albums they already
owned on vinyl, attracted to the
idea of a format that promised
to be more robust than a vinyl
record - which could be scratched
or warped - or the cassette,
with its chewed and worn-out tape.

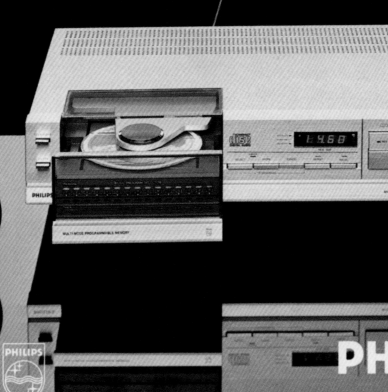

opposite

PHILIPS CD303 (1983)

Philips launched Europe's first
CD player, the CD100, in March
1983. The CD303 was the company's
flagship model and notable
for its unusual exposed
playing mechanism.

right

SONY DISCMAN D-50 (1984)

The first portable CD unit,
the D-50 (also known as the
D-5) played a significant role
in introducing the compact disc
to a non-audiophile market. The
designers were asked to create a
unit that was the equivalent size
of four stacked CD jewel cases.

below

PHILIPS DCC170 (1992)

Devised by Philips and Matsushita
as a replacement for the compact
cassette, the Digital Compact
Cassette (DCC) rivalled DAT
for digital audio quality and
machines could also play analogue
tapes. However, the format was
not successful and production
ended after four years.

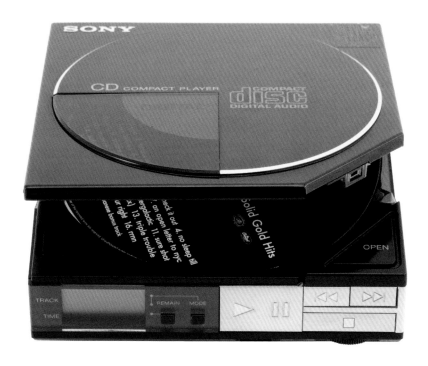

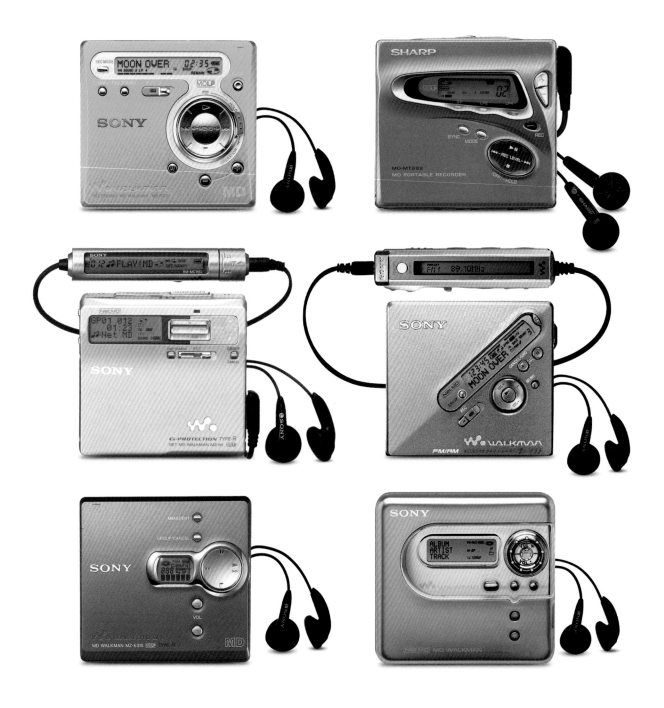

opposite

SONY MINIDISC WALKMAN
(1992-2013)
Sony launched the MiniDisc in
1992, intending to end the reign
of the compact cassette. Sound
was digitally on a small floppy-
disk-style cartridge.

above

PRE-RECORDED MINIDISCS
(1992-2013)
Take-up of the MiniDisc was
initially hampered by a lack of
commercial releases, although by
the end of the 1990s availability
was widespread, particularly in

Japan. Although the MiniDisc
is viewed as a failed format,
Sony alone sold 22 million
units, and the technology
was also licensed to other
major manufacturers.

THOMAS STOCKHAM

<u>THE 'FATHER OF
DIGITAL SOUND'</u>

Music over the past three decades has largely been presented in a digital medium – be it DAT, MiniDisc, compact disc, downloaded computer file or data streamed from the internet. Although many different individuals and research institutions played active roles in pioneering the digital audio revolution, the most significant figure is arguably Professor Thomas Stockham.

After earning his doctorate in electrical engineering at Massachusetts Institute of Technology in 1959, Stockham was offered an associate professorship. During his early days as an academic he worked with fellow faculty member Amar Bose, using MIT's considerable computing capabilities to measure and simulate room acoustics. Bose later founded his own company, creating a stream of innovative domestic audio products.

Stockham's pioneering work began in the early 1960s, when he created digital audio tape recordings of speech using a combination of newly developed analogue-to-digital (ADC) conversion technology and the MIT Lincoln Laboratory's TX-0 mainframe computer.

Digitized audio represented a radical departure. Going back as far as Edison's tin-foil etchings, conventional analogue recording attempted to replicate the original sound wave of the source signal. Digital audio uses an ADC to take samples of the original sound wave and store that information as a string of binary numbers. Each string, in effect, represents the displacement of air pressure that creates the sound at a single moment in time. The higher the number of samples taken each second (i.e. the 'sample rate'), the more detailed information will be held, making the digital conversion more accurate. For playback, that data is converted back into sound by a mirror process called a digital-to-analogue converter (DAC).

Stockham rapidly realized that digitization of sound offered the elimination of hiss, background noise and 'wow and flutter'.

<u>1</u>
WORDS AND MUSIC
Although Stockham's research at this time focused on the potential uses of digitizing speech in the communications industry, in 1980 he recalled: 'It became immediately apparent that if speech could be digitized, so could music.'

Furthermore, after the sound had been converted into digital data it could be manipulated, edited and stored in a way that was simply impossible using analogue means.

In 1968, Stockham left MIT for the University of Utah, where he was allowed to combine institutional research with his own personal interests. While maintaining his academic career, in 1975 Stockham founded his own recording company, Soundstream, to capitalize on the commercial possibilities of digital sound. Japanese electronics company Denon had already been pursuing similar experiments, but it was Soundstream that developed the first viable 16-bit digital audio recording system. The machine comprised a modified eighteen-track Honeywell 5600e computer tape drive for the transport mechanism, and digital recording and playback hardware designed by Stockham himself. The machine stored its data on 1-inch (2.5-cm) Ampex 460 magnetic tape running at the high speed of 35 IPS (inches per second).

At $160,000, the system was hugely expensive – well over $700,000 million dollars when forty years of inflation is taken into account. Nonetheless, eighteen units were sold or leased – mostly to classical music record labels – before the business was taken over by the Digital Recording Company (DRC) in 1980. The new owners invested heavily in the design of a domestic digital audio player using an optical card, but their efforts were overshadowed by the emergence of the compact disc and by 1985 DRC had ceased business.

Thomas Stockham remained a member of the University of Utah's computer science faculty until, at the age of only sixty-one, he was diagnosed with Alzheimer's disease – the illness that would claim his life nine years later. While he could hardly be described as the 'inventor' of digital recording, his role was critical in its evolution and acceptance.

THOMAS STOCKHAM
Born: 22 December 1933,
Passaic, New Jersey, USA
Died: 6 January 2004,
Salt Lake City, Utah, USA

2
HISTORIC RESTORATION
In 1976, Stockham digitally remastered early 20th-century recordings of the noted opera tenor Enrico Caruso. The results were released to considerable acclaim.

3
THE LEGACY
The ideas Stockham pioneered in the area of digital sound editing are now standard practice in every studio in the world – from the grandest of professional recording suites to the home musician running GarageBand on an iPad.

below

3M 479 OPEN-REEL VIDEO TAPE (1978-1990)

During the 1980s pop-video explosion, open-reel magnetic tape such as 3M's 479 was used to record and store audio/visual data. Although superficially it resembled 1-inch (2.5-cm) audio tape, the tape types were not interchangeable.

opposite

MAGNETIC TAPE IN THE DIGITAL AGE (1986-c. 1994)

Until the late 1990s, open-reel magnetic tape recording thrived alongside newly emerging digital formats. They crossed over, in fact, as some broadcast audio manufacturers, such as Nagra, produced digital open-reel tape recorders. To serve these machines, Ampex created its 467 tape, specially formulated for digital machines.

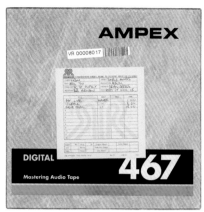

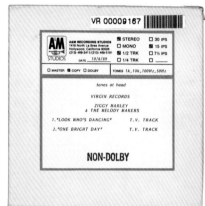

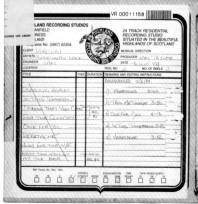
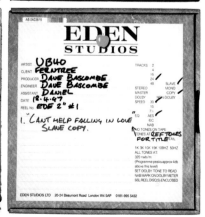

DAT · Digital Audio Tape

DAT 12850 R-64

GERRY MULLIGAN - JAZZ MASTERS
7243 520872 28

BASF

JIMMY SMITH: JAZZ MASTERS

DAT 13099 64

Digital Audio Tape

DAT · Digital Audio Tape

DAT 12850 R-64

GERRY MULLIGAN - JAZZ MASTERS
7243 520872 28

DAT · Digital Audio Tape

DAT 12879 R-94

CLIENT INTERNATIONAL   DATE April 30, 1999
ARTIST BLONDIE
TITLE PICTURE THIS! LIVE
LIVE PHILADELPHIA   5212 5322

AMPEX

DAT · Digital Audio Tape

467 R-64

DAT 8889

AMPEX

CRYSTAL GAYLE: COUNTRY CLASSICS

BASF   N°

PEGGY LEE "THE BEST OF"

DAT 9126

DAT · Digital Audio Tape   DAT MASTER 94

BASF   N°

DAT 2 Jay Hawkins   10.4.97.

DAT 9155 64

Digital Audio Tape

BASF

WAYNE SHORTER: JAZZ MASTERS

DAT 13106 64

Digital Audio Tape

BASF   N°

DAT 1A Jay Hawkins   10.4.97.

DAT · Digital Audio Tape   DAT MASTER 64

AMPEX

DAT 11008

467 R-94

CERTIFIED MASTERING AUDIO CASSETTE

AMPEX

MERLE HAGGARD: COUNTRY CLASSICS

BASF

DAT 13084

abbey road   Julie London

7243522241 28 "HMV Easy"

DAT65   HHb

DAT 9166

PRODUCTION MASTER

DAT · Digital Audio Tape   Professional Audio Applic...

HHb CAPITOL RECORDS   25 MAR 97
8558324
FOO FIGHTERS DAT-CASS MSTR INT'L LP

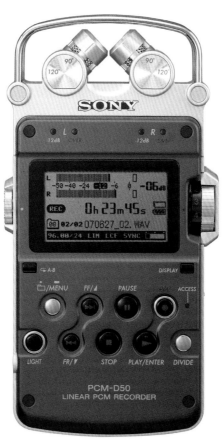

opposite

DAT MASTER TAPES (1996-97)

During the 1990s, the stereo Digital Audio Tape (DAT) largely replaced the open-reel tape recorder for creating final mixes. The DAT had once been considered a viable replacement for the compact cassette as a consumer medium, but record-industry resistance ensured that the price of blank tapes was kept sufficiently high to prevent them becoming a viable alternative.

left

PORTABLE HARD-DISK RECORDERS (2010-15)

Half a century on from portable tape recorders such as the EMI L2, solid-state units are pocket-sized, battery-operated and can record dozens of hours of higher-than-CD-quality audio directly onto a tiny flash card. Some models such as the Olympus LS-100 are also capable of multi-track recording.

overleaf, left

FLOPPY DISK MASTER RECORDING (1987)

Early digital recording was stored on a magnetic tape medium, be it open-reel or video cartridge. Before optical hard-drive storage became the norm in the 1990s, some short-lived systems recorded directly onto standard computer 'floppy disk'.

overleaf, right

CUBASE/PRO TOOLS MUSIC SOFTWARE (1989-PRESENT)

Dedicated multi-track recording systems have now largely given way to computer-based audio and MIDI recording. With a digital audio workstation such as ProTools, the volume of tracks is only limited by the power of the computer, and audio can be endlessly edited.

SS,SD
single side
single density
26 soft sectors
128 bytes

740-0

3M

Id. E62. FR   Format   Date JULY '87 Vol.

PIL

"FAT CHANCE HOTEL"   Mix Disc #1

AB 04571715

KARLHEINZ BRANDENBURG

PIONEER IN
THE DEVELOPMENT
OF MP3 FILES

On Friday 14 July 1995 an email was circulated among a small, elite group of audio engineers and researchers at the Fraunhofer Institute, one of Germany's leading scientific research facilities: 'This is the overwhelming result of our poll: everyone voted for .mp3 as extension for ISO MPEG Audio Layer 3!' No one reading that statement would have predicted the effect it would have on the way audio was to be delivered, stored and consumed.

While no single individual could claim responsibility for the MP3 file format, the most significant figure in its development was Karlheinz Brandenburg. Born and bred in Bavaria, in the south of Germany, Brandenburg studied mathematics and electrical engineering at the Friedrich-Alexander University of Erlangen-Nuremberg. His groundbreaking work into digital audio coding began when he was a doctoral student at the university. In the early 1980s, digital audio research focused on capturing the full frequency range of any recording, even if some of that data fell outside of the human auditory system.

Having conceived the idea of a music-streaming system more than two decades before the likes of Spotify appeared, Brandenburg's supervisor, Professor Dieter Seitzer, sought a PhD student who could conceive a way in which digital audio could be reduced in size without compromising quality. Brandenburg's task was to develop a process that could compress sound files, removing digital information in a way that would be missed as little as possible by the ear. His approach was to filter the signal into multi-frequency layers and use his own algorithms to decide

1   what data could be discarded. While still a research student, Brandenburg received his first patent for this compression process. His algorithm became known as optimum coding in the frequency domain (OCF).

After completing his PhD, Brandenburg moved to the Fraunhofer Institute for Integrated Circuits, a government-

---

1
A QUESTION OF SIZE
Earlier attempts at file compression were rather less streamlined. At one point, engineers had managed to reduce a sound file to just 8 per cent of its original size, but the machine they used to do so was the size of a refrigerator.

funded research organization. His initial task was to improve the OCF process, which worked well for most musical instruments but less so for the human voice. His test subject was Suzanne Vega's a cappella version of her song 'Tom's Diner', which was subjected to hundreds of tiny refinements in the algorithm before Brandenburg was happy with the result.

In 1991, the Fraunhofer Institute submitted the OCF process to the Moving Picture Experts Group (MPEG), an organization that agreed global encoding standards to be used with new technologies that were about to launch. The commercial stakes were high, as those selected stood to gain a fortune in licensing fees. Of the fourteen applicants, it was MUSICAM, a body linked to the Dutch corporation Philips (which held patents on the compact disc), that took the main prize; its process was given the name MPEG Audio Layer 2, and would be used on all audio on DVDs and CD-ROMs. Brandenburg's system was not chosen for any specific technology, but was accepted as an official standard and named MPEG Audio Layer 3.

In the mid-1990s, as the idea of listening to audio files on a computer and distributing them via the internet began to take off, Brandenburg and his colleagues released MP3 players as free-to-use shareware and gave developers a free hand in using the format. The gamble paid off and by the end of the decade, MP3 had swept all other internet audio file formats aside. The Fraunhofer Institute would eventually claim a licensing fee for every copy of iTunes or any other MP3 player downloaded, or any hardware that could play MP3 files – including every iPod, iPad or smartphone.

Brandenburg's research in the field of audio coding has earned him many awards and honorary doctorates, although he is modest about his own role in the story: 'Everybody looks at me when talking about the birth of MP3, but they don't know who else was involved...being [lauded as] the only one is completely incorrect.'

KARLHEINZ BRANDENBURG
Born: 20 June 1954,
Erlangen, Germany

fourth wave : DIGITAL ERA

338.339

2
WHY 'TOM'S DINER'?
In 2000, Brandenburg told
Business 2.0 magazine 'I was
ready to fine-tune my compression
algorithm….Somewhere down the
corridor a radio was playing
"Tom's Diner". I was electrified.
I knew it would be nearly
impossible to compress this
warm a cappella voice.'

above

APPLE IPOD CLASSIC: SIX
GENERATIONS (2001-14)
The Apple iPod was a major
influence on the acceptance and
uptake of the MP3 format. The
original iPod Classic, launched
in 2001, could hold up to 10
GB of storage - perhaps 2,500
tracks. By the time the sixth
generation of the iPod Classic

appeared in 2007 it was possible
to store and carry around up to
40,000 tracks!

opposite

DIGITAL/ANALOGUE CONVERSION
(c. 2000)
Using breakout boxes connected
to a computer system, like
the rack shown here, analogue
audio signals can be captured
and converted and stored in
the digital domain; they are
converted back to analogue
so that they can be heard.

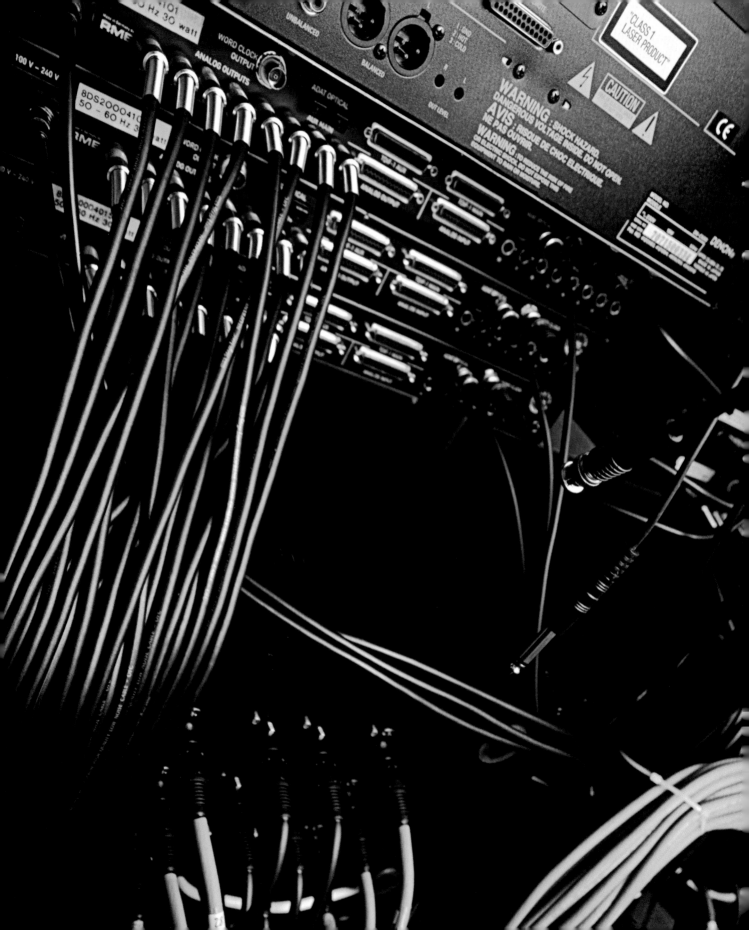

SHAWN
FANNING

<u>MASTERMIND
BEHIND NAPSTER</u>

<u>1</u>

At the end of the 20th century, the internet had not yet evolved a satisfactory means for distributing music; with slow, pre-broadband domestic dial-up connections, downloading a CD could take hours. This changed with the advent of the MP3 compressed file format, which could shrink the size of a computer audio file by more than 90 per cent of its original size. And in 1999, a new era was heralded with the launch of Napster, a peer-to-peer (P2P) program that enabled a network of connected users to share their audio files quickly and simply.

Behind this software was teenager Shawn Fanning, then in the second year of a computer studies degree at Northeastern University in Massachusetts. Frustrated by the difficulties he'd had in downloading or exchanging music files with his friends online, he wrote a small C++ program that attempted to make the process less arduous – and circumvent the inconvenience of existing music on the internet often being unavailable through broken hyperlinks or disappearing web pages. When connected to the internet, anyone running Fanning's program would form part of a network of 'clients' linked by a central server, each individual creating a directory containing the audio files they were prepared to share. The software featured a simple search function allowing users to key in the names of bands or songs; the search listed only results that were online and available at that moment. With a click on an entry from the list, the audio file would copy across from the hard drive of the sharer's computer.

On 1 June 1999, Fanning announced the existence of his software on w00w00 ('Woowoo'), an elite online hacker's forum. Offering the code to a small number of his colleagues, he named the software after the handle he used on the forum – 'Napster'. Within days, some 15,000 copies of the program had been circulated globally. Fanning turned to his uncle, John Fanning – an online chess software entrepreneur – and another of his

<u>1</u>
PRE-INTERNET SHARING
In the 1980s, most file sharing was carried out by means of a modem connected to a telephone landline. This set-up allowed for a maximum download speed of around 9,600 bits per second.

forum colleagues, Sean Parker, to develop Napster into a viable business. Its brief success was spectacular: at peak usage, early in 2001, there were said to be 60–80 million registered Napster users across the globe.

On 13 March 2000, the band Metallica, having discovered a private demo version of their song 'I Disappear' being shared on Napster, filed a lawsuit against the company. Eventually, a joint action by A&M Records and other labels via the Recording Industry Association of America (RIAA) won a landmark case: Napster was judged to be responsible for the copyright violations of its users. The company was told that it must keep track of the activities of its network and prevent access to infringing material. Unable to police their users, in July 2001 Napster shut down, filing for bankruptcy a year later. The name was sold to several third parties, and now exists as a successful (and fully legal) music subscription streaming service.

The impact of Napster on the global music business was shattering, as numerous other P2P networks – such as Gnutella, Kazaa, Scour, LimeWire and Grokster – rose up. Gradually, the music industry responded by focusing less on prosecution and more on supporting convenient ways of delivering online music that would also earn money – giving rise to download sites such as Apple's iTunes and streaming services such as Spotify.

Perhaps Fanning and Napster's most significant legacy is that it made the compressed MP3 format – which by its very definition is lower in quality than a CD – the *de facto* norm for a generation more likely to listen to its music on a smartphone, tablet or laptop than a traditional hi-fi. It could also be argued that the pick-and-choose/shuffle approaches to listening adopted by many younger downloaders have triggered a cultural shift away from the album format favoured by artists themselves, to place greater emphasis on an individual track.

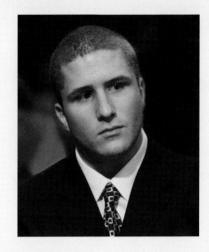

SHAWN FANNING
Born: 22 November 1980,
Brockton, Massachusetts, USA

fourth wave : DIGITAL ERA

342.343

STREAMING, TORRENTS AND
PEER-TO-PEER (1999-PRESENT)
The 21st century has seen music
consumers less interested in
owning traditional physical
copies of their music than either
downloading and storing albums
as computer files or 'streaming'
the music from sources on
the internet. Shown here are
the logos for software brands:
Napster; LimeWire; eMule;
Pirate Bay; iTunes; YouTube;
MySpace; Soundcloud; Bandcamp;
Google Play Music; Spotify;
and BBC iPlayer.

above

DIGITAL PLAYBACK MEDIA
(2004-PRESENT)
Launched in 2004, the Bose
SoundDock (top) is an amplifier
and speaker system with an in-
built dock for Apple products
such as the iPod or iPhone -

as is the Bowers and
Wilkins Zeppelin (centre).
The Sonos Play:1 (above)
connects wirelessly to the
internet and can stream high-
quality music from subscribed
online sources.

overleaf

OCEAN SOUND RECORDINGS
STUDIO, NORWAY (2016)
Norway's Ocean Sound
Recordings combines the
sound and feel of classic
analogue recording with
digital flexibility.